INDEPENDENCE FROM AMERICA

For Helen and Lena

Independence from America
Global Integration and Inequality

JON V. KOFAS

ASHGATE

Published by
Ashgate Publishing Limited
Gower House
Croft Road
Aldershot
Hants GU11 3HR
England

Ashgate Publishing Company
Suite 420
101 Cherry Street
Burlington, VT 05401-4405
USA

Ashgate website: http://www.ashgate.com

British Library Cataloguing in Publication Data
Kofas, Jon V.
    Independence from America : global integration and
    inequality
    1. International economic integration 2. United States -
    Foreign economic relations 3. European Union countries -
    Foreign economic relations 4. Developing countries - Foreign
    economic relations
    I. Title
    337.1

Library of Congress Cataloging-in-Publication Data
Kofas, Jon V.
    Independence from America : global integration and inequality / by Jon V. Kofas
        p. cm.
    Includes bibliographical references and index.
    ISBN 0-7546-4508-8
    1. International economic integration. 2. United States--Foreign economic relations. 3.
European Union countries--Foreign economic relations. 4. Developing countries--Foreign
economic relations. I. Title.

    HF1418.5.K65 2005
    337.1--dc22

2004030879

ISBN 0 7546 4508 8

Printed and bound in Great Britain by MPG Books Ltd, Bodmin, Cornwall

Contents

Acknowledgement

This book would not have been possible without the kind and generous assistance of a major research grant from Indiana University Graduate School, Indiana University, Office of International Programs, and Indiana University-Kokomo, Summer Research Grants. I am very grateful to all of them. I am also grateful for having access to the Greek Foreign Ministry Archives, Karamanlis Foundation, Public Record Office in the UK, the National Archives in College Park, MD, World Bank Archives, IMF Archives, and the Libraries of presidents Ford, Carter, and Reagan.

Introduction

Synopsis of Postwar U.S. Transformation Policy

Divergent Models under One World System

Five hundred years after capitalism's nascent stage in northwest Europe, the manner by which the system creates poverty as it concentrates wealth, social inequality, unequal exchange, and uneven world development have remained the most compelling political issues in the postwar era. Since the 1950s, United Nations Economic and Social Council studies, and scholars like Raul Prebisch, Celso Furtado, Immanuel Wallerstein, Andre Gunder Frank, Samir Amin, Nicos Poulantzas, and many others have argued that the advanced capitalist countries have historically exercised a far reaching influence on shaping the international division of labor, national institutions, and the status of underdeveloped areas (periphery) in relationship to the economically advanced countries (core).[1]

At the dawn of the 21st century, the international political economic structure remains unaltered, and it appears much stronger after the collapse of Communist regimes in the early 1990s. While integration advocates emphasize the benefits of increased trade and the futility of autarky in the age of globalization, critics question whether national sovereignty is sacrificed in the process along with social justice. Besides social polarization inherent in the market economy, uneven development and asymmetrical trade relationships between the advanced and underdeveloped countries, capital concentration and chronic balance-of-payments deficits leading to cyclical Third World debt crises are realities of macroeconomics that impact billions of people at the microeconomic level from Jakarta to Santiago de Chile, from Manila to Cairo. The inexorable link between increased global integration and inequality is too overwhelming to be glossed over by econometric models or analytical studies trying to find the exception to the rule, or to apportion blame on indigenous cultural elements.

It would be easy dismiss as captive to Hegelian-Marxist historicist ideology the nexus between capital concentration in the metropolis and poverty in the periphery, or to engage in post-modernist intellectual exercises where process obfuscates substance and evades the complex sources of polarization. World Bank and the United Nations (UN) studies concur that poverty has been growing along with social and geographic inequality on a world scale in the past forty years just as asymmetrical integration has been increasing. Without diminishing the multifaceted causes of inequality rooted in each country's social structure, political economy, and culture, global integration has contributed rather than alleviated inequality, and it has exacerbate social and political instability.[2]

During the tumultuous decade of the 1970s amid sharp rise in political violence and revolutions from Managua to Tehran, Third World scholars and political observers cried out that America's pets enjoyed a better diet and medical care than half the world's people who barely subsist on a couple of dollars a day. In 1995 the U.S. had about 4 percent of the world's population, but owned 26 percent of the world's GNP share, while Japan accounted for 18 percent, and Germany, France, UK, and Italy for another 21 percent, leaving 35 percent GNP share for the rest of the world which makes up about 80 percent of the people. The average per capita income discrepancy between the G-7 and the Third World rose from 10 to 1 in 1960 and 14 to 1 in 1970. By the end of the 20th century more than 1.2 billion of the 6 billion people in the world lived on less than $1 per day.[3]

With the triumph of markets over states at the dawn of the 21st century, poverty has doubled, malnutrition and epidemics are ravaging millions around the world, sex-worker global traffic is third in the world behind illegal drugs and weapons, the environment is devastated in the name of progress that is synonymous with globalization, and all because of a narcist and pathological quest for quick high profits rooted in a political economy that has capital accumulation as a core value. A tragic reality that is at the root of political violence and instability, lack of social justice has immense costs for the political and social elites and the masses alike. Decades after Franz Fanon published his illuminating study *Wretched of the Earth* there has been no structural change in the cycle of endemic poverty, the cycle of debt, and foreign dependence and decapitalization of the wretched of the Third World.[4]

More than just World Bank and UN statistics, global inequality, poverty, disease, and environmental devastation are tragic realities of every day life that one sees on the faces of women and children in the slums of Jakarta, Lagos, Lima, in any Third World city where opulence for the local and foreign elites coexists within a few kilometers of where the masses struggle to live another day. From the mining workers of Peru to the oil workers in Nigeria and Indonesia, ubiquitous inequality and social injustice are contributing causes of social, ethnic, racial, and political violence.

Concerned that rising poverty poses a threat to long-term global economic and political harmony, former National Security Advisor Zbigniew Brzezinski recently questioned whether democracy is facing an uncertain future amid growing socioeconomic and geographic gap of an integrated world system.[5] Malthusian and traditionalism theories have some merit in explaining the root causes of systemic social and geographical inequality. However, capital accumulation on a world scale, grossly uneven income distribution, and asymmetrical trade relationships have always been at the heart of the system for the past five hundred years.[6]

As World War I changed the global balance of power, the great powers and the League of Nations laid the foundations for expanding global trade and investment, and providing development loans. The continuity of colonialism, the absence of international institutions like the IMF and World Bank, and the absence of financial and political leadership combined with the chaos of the Great Depression precluded the successful implementation of a global integration model.[7]

Although various integration models were possible at the end of the Second World War, the U.S. superimposed its own brand of transformation policy on the rest of the world. Having formulated plans for global integration during World War II, the U.S. under the Truman administration reintegrated northwest Europe and Japan on a model of inter-dependence designed to foster greater trade symmetry and to raise living standards as a means of keeping the U.S. economy hegemonic for the duration. As an additional consideration in strengthening western Europe, the U.S. was eager to prevent workers and lower middle classes from voting for the Communist parties, especially strong in France and Italy.[8]

At the same time, the U.S. planned the regional integration of South Korea and Taiwan as the semi-periphery with Japan as the center of the regional Asian capitalist economic system under the global aegis of the U.S. which had overriding geopolitical and economic interests against the background of the successful Chinese Communist revolution, and the strengths of North Korea's Kim Il-sung and Vietnam's Ho Chi Minh. In 1951 World Bank president Eugene Black concurred with containment policy author George F. Kennan that economic containment was more essential than military containment. From the early Cold War to the present, development loans serve not just narrow U.S. economic interests, but broader political and strategic goals which are inexorably linked. While this does not mean that global integration and the Cold War are or should be equated, expanding world trade, moving capital across national borders, and global integration have occurred against the background of U.S. global military expansion.[9]

To prevent spheres of influence and trading blocks like the Sterling zone, and to help manage the world political economy under its aegis, especially against the background of the Soviet competition for global political, strategic, and economic influence, the U.S. needed strong junior partners. As colonial powers with roots in the Third World, western Europe and Japan were a practical political and strategic option for Washington during the Cold War that provided a convenient pretext for U.S. hegemony in the name of freedom and democracy. Equating it with U.S.-style market economy and the bourgeois social order, freedom and democracy would become America's Trojan Horse during and after the Cold War.[10]

Helping to forge pro-U.S. institutions abroad and allowing sovereignty as long as it furthered Pax Americana, Washington's postwar partnership with western Europe,

Japan, Australia, and Canada was necessary to manage the non-Communist world and ultimately to defeat Communism. Whereas the U.S. injected massive capital into western Europe and Japan while providing for their security, capital flowed out from the Third World, especially from Latin America which had accumulated a substantial surplus during the war, to the U.S. and its junior partners. Presented as part of the postwar "transformation" policy, the U.S. projected its political economy as the most significant export. Transformation policy carried all the Americentric assumptions from value system and institutions to concepts about progress and success.

The question is whether the superimposed U.S. transformation policy benefited all countries and social classes as modernization theorists promised would be the case, or whether it was just a new kind of imperialism operating under the cloak of fighting Communism and making the world safe for Democracy? Was the transformation policy from the Truman Doctrine (Greece and Turkey) to the Bush Doctrine (Iraq and Afghanistan) under the guise of managing the world economy toward modernization equated with Democracy or Americanization of the world? Beyond the cost-benefit ratio issue, the inherent contradiction in transformation policy is that historically the U.S. was interested in preserving its domestic status quo by superimposing its values, its institutions, its system on other countries without regard to the hypocrisy inherent in such Wilsonian missionary diplomacy that compromised other nations' autonomy and sovereignty.[11]

The success of the interdependent U.S.-west-European-Japan integration model was necessarily predicated on an unequal political, military, economic, financial, trade, and social relationship between the developed and the underdeveloped countries. This is not to suggest that there was or is equality between the U.S. and its junior partners, any more than equality between the junior partners. Only that the inter-dependent U.S.-west Europe-Japan-Canada-Australia relationship was based on much greater equality when compared with the U.S.-Third World and western Europe-Third World relationships. Based on the patron-client relationship of the Great Powers with their colonies and dependencies, the neoclassical (patron-client) integration model is patterned after a political relationship between advanced countries and their satellites for the past half century.

Though the patron-client model operates under an asymmetrical relationship, the inter-dependent model since Bretton Woods has been more symmetrical between the U.S. and its junior partners. While there is a case to be made regarding race and ethnicity as salient factors in the interdependent model, political, economic, and strategic considerations have always been overriding. Despite intense intra-bloc economic-technological competition and political rivalries, western Europe, Japan, Canada, and Australia accepted U.S. tutelage in the past half century because they derive multiple benefits from the U.S.-dominated world system.

By the same token, so have South Korea and Taiwan whose special geopolitical significance accounted for their unique development during the Cold War and their gradual postwar transformation from client states to establishing a junior partnership with Japan and symmetrical relationship with the G-7. Like southern Europe and many Third World countries, Taiwan and South Korea operated under authoritarian regimes that violated human rights like banning labor strikes and trade unions. Israel also falls into a category somewhat similar to Taiwan and South Korea. Emulating Taiwan which became a platform for Japanese industries and enjoyed a special trade relationship with the U.S. and Japan, Singapore and Hong Kong transformed themselves as conduits for international capital and intermediaries between core and periphery. Underdeveloped and semi-developed countries, however, recognize that U.S. hegemony necessarily entails compromising not just their independence, sovereignty, institutions, autonomy, and living standards, but above all, their perpetual status in the unequal world system.[12]

Having its foundations in the Marshall Plan, European integration evolved into a strong trading bloc competing with the U.S. Though as Michael J. Hogan argues, Washington's intention was to refashion Western Europe after America's image as part of the transformation policy, the European integration model was designed so that all full members are institutionally closer to the level of the strongest ones under a fairly common set of rules and regulations on trade, monetary, fiscal, labor, and social policies. Whereas the European interdependent model aims to close the per capita GNP gap between full members, the patron-client model perpetuates and exacerbates GNP gaps. From the early Cold War to the consolidation of the European Union (EU) in the 1990s, regional integration results in a relatively stronger state structure under strong legislative and judicial branches with multiparty systems. Unlike underdeveloped countries, strong government intervention in strengthening the economy was the norm during the critical two decades after the war.[13]

Unlike their policy toward western Europe and Japan, the U.S. and the multilateral banks encouraged Third World governments not to intervene in the economy and to allow the free market forces to prevail. A weak state structure under strong executive and weak legislative branch that characterizes the Third World, invariably under an authoritarian or semi-authoritarian regime, entailed a strong foreign-dominated private sector. Such conditions made the patron-client integration model possible. In the past half century the "special providence" ideology and the doctrine of exceptionalism as integral parts of Pax Americana have been inculcated into the political culture that accepts the patron-client integration model with the Third World as "natural" or "organic". And while the U.S. has been preaching freedom and democracy to the rest of the world, it has done so at the expense of demanding that national autonomy and sovereignty be subordinated to "globalism," a foreign policy imperative since the Truman Doctrine.[14]

All postwar integration models operate under the umbrella of a common evolving world system that has survived for 500 years on the basis of social and geographic inequality, as Immanuel Wallerstein and others have observed in numerous studies. This is not to suggest that the west has monopoly on global integration models, or that historically a single model has existed. There are indeed some wrong assumptions that globalization narrowly defined is a post-Cold War phenomenon, that it is another way of articulating and celebrating the preeminence of the west and particularly of the U.S. over the world, and that there is a single model superimposed by the U.S. and the International Financial Institutions (IFIs) on which the world can only operate successfully.

History has demonstrated that a variety of models are possible, though the Americentric patron-client model has prevailed since the 1940s. Though Communism served as a pretext for the patron-client model during the Cold War, the U.S. and its junior partners have demonstrated that the driving force has been the desire of the political and economic in the core to carry on the legacy of imperialism which preserves their privileges. Similarly, the political and social elites in the semi-periphery and periphery historically have preserved their privileges by accepting cooptation into the world system. At the center of the patron-client model is not just a polarizing socioeconomic system, but invariably an undemocratic political system on which the former rest.[15]

Unlike the patron-client model, the EU interdependent model within its own membership promotes uniform legal structures and human rights, it provides minimum protections for the environment, labor, minorities, and women, thereby fostering a more symmetrical and less exploitative system, at least more in theory than in practice. This does not mean that western Europe has been free of a class struggle, that the "embourgeoisment" theory is a reality, that there is no permanent proletariat, or that per capita GNP is the same in Germany as in Portugal and Greece. Even within southern Europe whether under the patron-client or inter-dependent models, Portugal was always concerned about Spain compromising its sovereignty by having a dominant political and economic influence.

In general, the interdependent model entails that Europe has fostered the growth of a lower middle class, provided greater social mobility, and built a strong welfare state and institutional structures that are simply absent in underdeveloped countries. Despite critics from British conservatives to southern European Socialists, and notwithstanding the valid concern about the diffusion of Eurocultural humanism as another form of imperialism, the EU integration model, especially after the Maastritch Treaty of 1992, has demonstrated that it protects and enhances national sovereignty in a world dominated by Pax Americana.[16]

While more egalitarian toward its full members because of the multi-polar political dynamics at work, the European Economic Community (EEC) has historically preserved privileges for itself, while it operates under the same rules of uneven social and geographic development as the U.S.-led patron-client model outside the regional bloc. In short, the EEC has not changed the world system from which it benefits. Third World governments and people are not blind to the hypocrisy of the privileges that the advanced capitalist countries reserve for themselves, while imposing a different set of rules on the rest of the world. As instruments of international finance capital, the World Bank, International Monetary Fund (IMF), European Investment Bank (EIB), Paris Club, the World Trade Organization (WTO), the African, Asian, and Inter-American Development Banks, and Export-Import banks of the G-7 (U.S., Canada, Germany, Japan, France, Italy, and Great Britain) collaborate with the central banks to manage the world economy, thus shaping the contemporary world political economy and division of labor.

Because the IMF and World Bank since Bretton Woods have been coordinating their policies with the U.S. Federal Reserve Bank, and with the departments of Treasury, Commerce, and State, their decisions have been largely political and not merely based on financial and economic criteria as they claim. Historically IFI and U.S. bilateral loans have served the political goal of legitimizing regimes, many of which were among the tyrannical dictatorships with egregious human rights records. Operating under a broad range of political regimes from military dictatorships to Socialism, IFI-U.S. policies have historically promoted capital accumulation and concentration while undermining democratic institutions. Promising universal prosperity, exporting the "American Dream" to the world, such policies safeguard and foster corporate welfare. Meanwhile, labor's living standards remain low, and are much lower as we move down the pyramid from the advanced to the underdeveloped countries.[17]

Structural Characteristics of Southern Europe and Third World

Regardless of integration models, common characteristics of semi-developed and underdeveloped countries include high defense budgets, chronic balance-of-payments deficits arising primarily from lack of economic diversification and unfavorable terms of trade, high percentage of debt-to-GDP ratio, and lower private consumption in comparison with the advanced capitalist countries. Besides high levels of structural unemployment and underemployment, semi-developed and underdeveloped countries historically have had relied on indirect taxes, and have difficulty with collection and controlling the subterranean or informal economy that includes everything from street vendors to narcotics trade.

Collaborating with the IFIs, the state plays a catalytic role in transferring capital from labor to strengthen domestic and foreign capital, thereby precluding greater self-sufficiency. Operating within a world system whose inherent polarizing conditions are difficult to overcome, geographic and social inequality, whether in Indonesia or

Portugal before EEC membership, is symptomatic of the combination of local elites whose fortunes are linked to the metropolis, and the determining role of the world system on the division of labor and domestic institutions.[18]

Unlike advanced capitalist countries, the fiscal structure of a dependent society is weak, unstable, and inordinately dependent on consumption taxes. This was the case in southern Europe before EEC membership, and it has been the case in the Third World. Wages, labor laws, and trade unions are much stronger in the advanced countries than in Indonesia, Peru, and Nigeria, or southern Europe before EEC. Once they became full members of the EEC, Spain, Greece, and Portugal strengthened the social welfare system, they enjoyed more leverage in foreign policy, the state was stronger, as was the legislative branch. By contrast, underdeveloped countries have weak and docile trade unions which in many cases are appendages of the ruling party. Moreover, underdeveloped countries are subjected to a strong executive invariably backed by the armed forces that frequently intervened or exerted inordinate influence in the political arena, as the cases of Indonesia, Nigeria, and Peru demonstrate in the past half century.

Somewhat more secular and less traditional than underdeveloped countries until the mid-1970s, southern Europe succumbed to the western materialistic-hedonistic value system, thereby compromising its prewar communitarian way of life. However, religion and traditions remain a strong cultural force both among Greek Orthodox and Catholic Iberians, just as it does throughout the Third World. Contrary to Modernization theory scholars who claim that traditionalism is incongruent with socioeconomic development and the root cause for backwardness, southern Europe, Japan, Taiwan, and South Korea retained their traditions but managed to make material progress under heavy U.S. subsidies and strong state. During the Truman and Eisenhower administrations Taiwan and South Korea forged a strong state structure under a neo-corporativist system that enabled both countries to move ahead of the Third World. Hence, the integration model is far more significant in the type of development that takes place than adherence to tradition which is the salient factor that modernization theory advocates have stressed to explain "backwardness."[19]

Income inequality is by far the most obvious difference between developed and underdeveloped societies. The ratio between the income earned in the G-7 and the underdeveloped countries during the mid-1960s was ten-to-one and it has not changed much since then. The result was large-scale emigration from southern Europe as well as underdeveloped countries to the G-7. Elitism and clientism are more obvious in the Third World and in the advanced capitalist countries. A few thousand politically-entrenched families owned most of the wealth in all three southern European countries, just as they do in Peru, Nigeria, and Indonesia, though conditions for Third World workers and peasants lagged behind southern Europe after the mid-1970s.

The human rights records of southern Europe and most Third World countries until the mid-1970s were comparable, a record that did not improve until after the end of dictatorships in the mid-1970s. Like Third World countries, Spain, Greece, and Portugal operated under patronage systems that extended from top government jobs to low-level bureaucrats. The structure of paternalistic capitalism invariably relied heavily on reciprocal obligations between the oligarchy and the authoritarian state, more or less about the same in Suharto's Indonesia as in southern Europe before EEC accession in the 1980s. Southern Europe like the Third World suffered from grossly uneven geographical and social development, as there was high concentration of income in a few major cities and a social oligarchy.

More egregious in Portugal and Greece, as in the Third World, uneven geographic development was a problem for Spain which tried to address it earlier than other countries. In 1962 Spain's commerce minister noted that the country could not proceed with industrial development given that the average income in the province of Vizcaya was 30,000 pesetas while in Granada it was 8,000 pesetas. Income concentration and economic centralization was much worse in Portugal where Oporto and Lisbon were the centers of economic activity, and in Greece where there was not much capital or development outside of Athens-Piraeus and Thessalonike, not very different than Latin America and most Asian countries where the capital city and one or two others were developed while the rest of the areas were poor.[20]

Well aware that endemic poverty and uneven geographic development were root causes of radical political activity, the Organization for Economic Cooperation and Development (OECD), IFIs, and U.S. proposed after John F. Kennedy took office that the solution rested with more thorough commercial integration of all areas in a country. But the problem whether in southern Europe, Latin America, Africa, or Asia was that authoritarian regimes catering to a domestic oligarchy objected even to modest reform measures designed to foster rural integration and create small capitalist farmers out of peasants whether in Peru, Greece, or any other underdeveloped country. Promoting socioeconomic reform measures within the patron-client model often clashed with the political elites that the U.S. needed for diplomatic and defense considerations.[21]

Much like Indonesia, Peru, and Nigeria, crony capitalism was more characteristic of Spain, Portugal, and Greece than western Europe, U.S., Canada, or Australia where official corruption was not necessarily linked to any political party. Because public sector jobs, contracts, and licenses were granted based on loyalty to the regime, the survival instinct compelled many people to remain docile and support the regime. While the politically-entrenched wealthy benefiting from crony capitalism paid a small percentage of taxes, the majority of revenue emanated from indirect taxes in southern Europe and in the Third World. Unlike developed countries, the state in southern Europe and Third World allocated a small percentage on education, health, and social services. Far from serving the needs of society, Third World politicians and military officers historically used the bureaucracy and public enterprises as part of their patronage systems even more than in southern Europe.[22]

Regional and Global Dynamics of Integration: Southern Europe and Third World

In this book there are a number of themes linking the Third World and southern Europe, before and after Spain, Greece, and Portugal became full members of the EEC in the 1980s. The Third World had many common characteristics with Southern Europe until the end of authoritarianism in the mid-1970s. Most notably, Spain, Greece, and Portugal, like the Third World, were integrated under the patron-client model after Bretton Woods. Chosen for this study to represent the Third World from an overview perspective, Indonesia, Nigeria, and Peru share with southern Europe some common institutional experiences and a common relationship with IFIs and the advanced capitalist countries.

Unlike southern Europe which achieved junior partner status within the EU and serves a semi-periphery role, the patron-client integration model has not changed between the G-7 and the Third World. Without minimizing the obvious significance that each country's unique history, culture, traditions, institutions, elites, and internal dynamics, the book analyzes external political-economic dynamics with special focus on the IFIs and U.S. foreign policy as salient factors. This holistic approach naturally assumes that IFIs and the U.S. historically enjoyed preponderate influence in shaping the institutions of underdeveloped and semi-developed countries.

Realizing their distinct identity as Third World, especially after the Afro-Asian Bandung Conference of 1955 and Latin America's close affinity with Asia and Africa, underdeveloped nations have common social and economic development problems, common domestic and external obstacles to material and human progress, and the burden of a common colonial legacy. Equally significant, the IFIs and the U.S. have treated Third World political economy as a monolith under the asymmetrical patron-client model, though the East-West and China-Russia rivalry, regional conflicts like India-Pakistan, Greece-Turkey, Israel-Egypt, etc, and competition among the G-7 for control of raw materials and energy resources have entailed that the patron-client model has been implemented differently in each country.[23]

A reflection of the social structure and domestic political economy, the patron-client model was an outgrowth of America's historical experience since the Spanish-American War, though the Monroe Doctrine and the war with Mexico established the precedent. Similarly, the EU interdependent model which evolved since the late 1950s is a reflection of western Europe's postwar institutions and domestic policies which some scholars regard as quasi-statist in comparison with the U.S. neoliberal experiment. Finally, just as the U.S. developed a patron client model for its satellites, so did the USSR under the Comecon and Warsaw Pact system which was a reflection of the Soviet Union's domestic and foreign policies.

It is instructive not just for the Third World, but the former Communist countries whose social, economic, and political institutions are comparable to the Third World, to study southern Europe's integration under the EU model. Besides extreme socioeconomic polarization, endemic corruption and contraband trade ranging from narcotics to humans, and the authoritarian nature of some of the former Communist regimes, former Communist regimes are torn between the EU which offers the greatest integration benefits, the U.S. which is the sole superpower, and the Russian Federation which became the eighth member of the G-7.

The process of southern Europe's EEC integration clearly illustrates that external forces matter as much if not more than domestic sociopolitical dynamics, that dependence on the U.S. can be counterpoised or at least used as leverage, and that a client society can experience higher living standards and enjoy greater national autonomy by strengthening the state structure. Becoming integrated into a larger entity like the EU provides tangible benefits to its members far greater than the patron-client model. Even relations between the EEC and Association for South East Asian Nations (ASEAN) established under the Cooperation agreement in 1980 have helped to raise some awareness about fostering "democratic" institutions and respecting human rights. However, because of the asymmetrical relationship between the advanced capitalist countries and regional blocs like ASEAN, combined with multifarious internal institutional obstacles to material progress and upward mobility for workers and peasants, southeast Asia's client role in the world system and its division of labor have remained fundamentally unaltered.[24]

The historical dialectic between regional dynamics versus global integration worked to the advantage of southern Europe. So did the fact that Spain, Greece, and Portugal benefited from an asymmetrical trade relationship with underdeveloped non-European countries. Because they operate under the patron-client model, it is far more difficult for regional blocs like ASEAN, the Latin American Integration Association (LAIA), Southern Africa Development Community (SADC), and others to take advantage of the G-7 intra-bloc competition.

Individual Third World countries and small regional blocs have tried to use G-7 competition as leverage, but without much success. History has demonstrated that geographic inequality does not and it is not likely to diminish in Third World regional blocs as they are currently constituted. Just as the U.S. enjoys undisputed economic hegemony over the western hemisphere, besides its global reach, Japan and to a much lesser extent Australia dominate in Asia, and the EU dominates in Eastern Europe, parts of Eurasia, and most of Africa. In no small measure because of adherence to IFI policies and because the EU itself is an integral part of a larger hierarchical and polarizing world system, even southern Europe's full membership in the EU has entailed perpetual geographic and social inequality.[25]

Another important theme in this book is that IFIs, which are indispensable catalysts in global integration, pursue policies driven by a combination of G-7, especially U.S.

foreign and domestic policies, U.S.-NATO strategic considerations, and global economic interests. The political and socioeconomic elites in client states benefiting from IFI loans exercise some influence. Historically the elites in client states have exploited U.S. concerns about domestic revolutionary or nationalist grass roots movements, Communist bloc threats during the Cold War, rivalry between the advanced capitalist countries, and competition between multinational corporations. While U.S-led globalization cannot blamed for the exorbitant defense spending, including nuclear arms development for some, by client states, historically there has been an inexorable link between defense-aid weapons sales and economic aid and trade between patron and client.

While the Cold War afforded Pax Americana a convenient political camouflage of "western democracy's" struggle to contain "international Communism," a generic label given to all forms of social revolution, it was actually a propitious ideological cloak to preserve the patron-client model. U.S. global hegemony and its role in perpetuating the patron-client model was difficult to conceal during the Cold War and after. Not only did American capital and products dominate world markets, U.S. soldiers were never far from any country protecting capital and markets, and determining the world balance of power. In spite of countless beguiling rationalizations for superimposed patron-client integration, the historical record of U.S. and G-7 support of authoritarian regimes in Latin America, Asia, Africa, and southern Europe exposed the Cold War and post-Cold War veneer of "external threats" as a pretext for hegemony.[26]

Challenging the prevailing perspective of the past half century that the Cold War can be understood solely by examining the political and military dimensions of contemporary history in the absence of analyzing the socioeconomic dynamics on a global scale, this study raises questions about the pivotal role of the IFIs operating under different integration models.[27] Besides the historic and direct correlation between U.S. foreign policy and global geopolitical interests designed to maintain Pax Americana, and the obvious links to the IFIs, the power struggles within the G-7 also help shape the patron-client integration model. Invariably, foreign grants and loans have been linked to military and foreign policy agreements and armaments exports designed to strengthen the advanced capitalist countries' global position.

Hence, the patron-client integration model is really a reflection of the patron-client political model between the G-7, especially the U.S., and dependent societies. Following the long-standing scholarly tradition popularized by Charles Beard, William Appleman Williams, Gabriel Kolko, Noam Chomsky, and others, and combining the theoretical studies of the dependency and modern world-system schools, this book argues that there is remarkable continuity in U.S. foreign economic policy best understood in a historical context of America's domestic political economy. Based on external hegemony and social inequality, the U.S. domestic political economy is projected globally under different integration models designed to sustain a world system.[28]

At the annual meeting of the IMF-World Bank in Bangkok in October 1991, Portugal's finance minister Luis Miguel Couceiro Pizarro Beleza expressed a sense of euphoria shared by many Europeans upon the collapse of the Communist bloc and prospects for global integration. He noted that:

> Jean Monnet (*Memoirs*, 1975) once said on the then infant European Communities 'like our provinces in the past, today our peoples must learn to live together under freely accepted common rules and institutions if they want to attain the necessary dimensions to their progress, and remain masters of their own destinies.' I believe that those prophetic words ought to and hopefully will in the near future be appropriate to the world as a whole, and not just to the European Communities and of course, the Bretton Woods Institutions are at the forefront in this respect.[29]

Despite the optimism and remarkable confidence in Bretton Woods institutions to deal with issues like development, poverty, and the environment, the minister's views reveal his belief that integration under the interdependent (EU model) model could be a universal instrument for engendering global harmony. Clearly, the asymmetrical patron-client model has been the source for global disharmony.

Optimistic that the "American Dream" can be shared with the world under the globalization model, advocates of greater integration between the developed and the underdeveloped countries assume that those who have privileges and power will voluntarily surrender it. Nor do they take into account that if the U.S. does not pursue world hegemony the domestic social order and the uneven world system will inevitably lead toward social discontinuity, that is, systemic change in the mode of production and social order. If it were possible for the U.S. and the IFIs to manage the devolution of Pax Americana and the passing of the torch of hegemony, the fundamental question is whether social discontinuity can be managed when history offers no such evidence. And if indeed the post-Keynesian world economy can be fine tuned to the degree of devolution, another significant issue is whether such a system is worth preserving, given that it has not served humanity or the physical environment thus far.

Critics of the terms of trade, G-7 preponderate power, the IMF's overbearing role in monetary policy, and WTO's rules favoring advanced capitalist countries argue that the solution is a more symmetrical relationship between rich and poor nations that would include everything from debt forgiveness to massive aid. Such thinking assumes altruism on the part of the rich nations. Advocates of systemic societal change argue that the answer is to opt out of the capitalist world system altogether in some form of economic nationalism, Socialism, mixed economy, or regional blocs. In an interdependent world, how likely is a country to survive and thrive is a question that needs realistic appraisal.

IFI critics contend that putting an end to the IMF and World Bank would take care of the problem of global inequality. Such criticism assumes that the IFIs are the source of the problem, instead of the political economy under which they operate. In the long-term the world economy will undergo structural changes owing to inherent contradictions already apparent in the system. For the short to intermediate term, this book argues that southern Europe's integration model can be replicated under various modalities to suit specific national conditions of Third World countries and improve societal conditions in the southern hemisphere. The first step of the transition from the patron-client model to the inter-dependent, as the case studies illustrate, must be a systemic change in the political regime from an authoritarian to a representative government. By itself such a step will not result in an interdependent relationship, unless the regional bloc of which the country is integrated has the disposition to provide fair and equitable terms to its affiliates.

Notes

1. Raul Prebisch, "Commercial Policy in Underdeveloped Countries," *American Economic Review* 49 (1959): 251-61; Samir Amir, *L'echange inegal et la loi de valeur* (Paris, 1988); Celso Furtado, *Les Etats-Unis et les sous developpement de l' Amerique Latine* (Paris, 1970); Jose Moncada Sanchez, *Economia y globalizacion* (Quito, 2001); Ruy Mauro Marini, *Dialectica de la Dependencia* (Buenos Aires, 2000); Celso Furtado, *Accumulation and Development: The Logic of Industrial Civilization* (Oxford, 1983); Nicos Poulantzas, *Political Power and Social Classes* (Atlantic Highlands, NJ, 1975); Andre Gunder Frank, *Dependent Accumulation and Underdevelopment* (London, 1978).
2. Immanuel Wallerstein, "Underdevelopment and its Remedies," in S. C. Chew and R. A. Denemark (eds), *The Underdevelopment of Development* (Beverly Hills: Sage, 1996), pp. 355-61; Samir Amin, "On Development: For Gunder Frank," in Ibid., pp. 59-66; World Bank, *Income Poverty. Trends in Inequality.* 5/28/2004; Ibid. Press Release SG/SM/8935, OBV/384, 10/10/2003.
3. World Bank, *Global Poverty Report.* Okinawa Summit (July 2000); L. S. Stavrianos, *Global Rift: the Third World Comes of Age* (New York, 1981), pp. 25, 38.
4. K. Kempadoo and Jo Doezema, (eds) *Global Sex Workers: Rights, Resistance, and Redefinition* (London,1998); United Nations, *Trafficking in Persons* (New York, 2003); Chinweizu, *The West and the Rest of Us: White Predators, Black Slavers, and African Elite* (New York, 1975); Franz Fanon, *The Wretched of the Earth* (New York, 1976).
5. Zbigniew Brzezinski, "Epilogue: Democracy's Uncertain Triumph," in M. F. Plattner and A. Smolar (eds), *Globalization, Power, and Democracy* (Baltimore, 2000), pp. 152-54.
6. Walden Bello and Bill Rau, *Dark Victory: The United States and Global Poverty* (Oakland, CA, 1995); Lourdes Beneria and Shelley Feldman (eds), *Unequal Burden: Economic Crises, Persistent Poverty, and Women's Work* (Boulder, 1992); Nancy Birdsall,

"Population Growth and Poverty in the Developing World," *Population Bulletin*, 35/5 (1980): 3-45.

7. Akira Iriye, *Cambridge History of American Foreign Relations: The Globalizing of America, 1913-1945* (New York, 1995), III; Tietting Su, "World Trade Networks from 1928 to 1938," *Journal of World Systems Research*, 7/1 (2001): 32-50; Jari Eloranta, "Weak European States in the International Arms Trade of the Interwar Period" (University of Jyvaskylan, 2001): 1-28.

8. Joyce and Gabriel Kolko, *The Limits of Power: The World and United States Foreign Policy, 1945-1954* (New York, 1972), pp. 16-26; Federico Romero, *GLI Stati Uniti e il sindicalismo europeo, 1944-1951* (Rome, 1989), pp. 200-31; Irving Wall, *L'Influence americaine sur la politique francais, 1945-1954* (Paris, 1989), pp. 150-202; Sergio Turone, *Storia del Sindicato in Italia, 1943-1969* (Bari, 1974), pp. 122-43.

9. Dean Acheson, *Present at Creation* (New York, 1969), pp. 345-75; J. V. Kofas, *Foreign Debt and Underdevelopment: U.S.-Peru Economic Relations* (Lanham, MD, 1996), p. 42.

10. Akira Iriye, *Global Community: The Role of International Organizations in the Making of the Contemporary World* (Berkeley, 2002), pp. 104-06; Michael Beaud, et al. eds. *Mondialisation: Les mots et les choses* (Paris, 1999); J. V. Kofas, "America's Trojan Horse: Lessons from the Truman Doctrine and the Greek Civil War," in Bernd Greiner (ed), *Hot Wars During the Cold War* (Hamburg, Germany, 2005); Ursula Lehmkuhl, *Pax Anglo-Americana. Machtstrukturelle Grundlagen anglo-amerikanischer Asien-und Fernostpolitik in den 1950er Jahren* (Muchen, 1999), pp. 50-60.

11. Wolfgang Merkl, *Systemtransformation. Eine Einfuhrung in die Theorie und Empire der Transformationsforschung* (Opladen, 1999); Ali Mazrui, "From Social Darwinism to Current Theories of Modernization: A Tradition of Analysis," *World Politics*, 21 (October 1968): 69-83; E. A. Bret, *The World Economy since the War* (New York, 1985), 60-106; Kolko, *The Limits of Power*, pp. 74-89; Barbara Stallings, *Banker to the Third World* (Berkeley, 1987), pp. 310-20.

12. George Aseniero, "Asia and the World System," *The Underdevelopment of Development*, pp. 179-80; Sylvia Ostry and R. R. Nelson, *Techno-Nationalism and Techno-Globalism: Conflict and Cooperation* (Washington, D.C.,1995); M. Shalid Alam, *Poverty and the Wealth of Nations: Integration and Polarization in the Global Economy since 1760* (New York, 2000); Philip McMichael, *Development and Social Change* (Thousand Oaks, CA, 1996), pp. 175-80.

13. Michael J. Hogan, *The Marshall Plan: America, Britain, and the Reconstruction of Western Europe, 1947-1952* (New York, 1987); Elizabeth Meehan, *Citizenship and the European Community* (Beverly Hills, 1993); M. M. Postan, *An Economic History of Western Europe, 1945-1964* (London, 1967).

14. S. N. Eisenstadt and Rene Lemarchand, *Political Clientism and Patronage in Development* (Beverly Hills, 1981); J. V. Kofas, *Under the Eagle's Claw: Exceptionalism in Postwar U.S.-Greek Relations* (Westport, CT, 2003), pp. 11-12, 243-45; E. C. Luck, "American

Exceptionalism and International Organizations: Lessons from the 1990s," in Rosemary Foot, et al. (eds), *The United States and Multilateral Organizations* (Oxford, 2002); Kofas, *Foreign Debt and Underdevelopment*, pp. 21-2.

15. A. G. Hopkins, *Globalization in World History* (New York, 2003).

16. E. L. Jones, *The European Miracle* (New York, 1981), pp. 118-25; Philippe C. Schmitter, "La Democratie dans l'Europe politique naissaante," in *Repenser l'Europe* edited by Mario Tello and Paul Magnette (Brussels, 1996), pp. 45-68; Carsten Schittek, *Ordnungsstrukuren im Europaischen Intehrationsprozess: ihre Entwicklung bis zum Vertag vo Maastricht* (Stuttgart, Germany, 1999); John McCormick, "Policy Performance in the European Union," in E. E. Zeff and E. B. Pirro (eds), *The European Union and the Member States* (Boulder, 2001), pp. 7-26.

17. International Monetary Fund, *Articles of Agreement of the International Monetary Fund* (Washington, D.C., 1973); Cheryl Payer, *The Debt Trap. The International Monetary Fund and the Third World* (New York, 1974), pp. 23-4, 36.

18. Roberto de Oliveira Campos, *Reflections on Latin American Development* (Austin, TX, 1967), pp. 93-109; Harry Magdoff, *The Age of Imperialism* (New York, 1967), pp. 54-7; Amin, *Accumulation*, II, pp. 449-52.

19. W. W. Rostow, *The Stages of Economic Growth: A Non-Communist Manifesto* (Cambridge, 1960); David Apter, *Rethinking Development: Modernization, Dependency, and Post-Modern Politics* (Beverly Hills, 1987); T. J. Biersteker, Reducing the Role of the State in the Economy: A Conceptual Exploration of IMF and World Bank Prescriptions," *International Studies Quarterly* 34 (1990): 477-92.

20. Public Record Office, Foreign Office (hereafter F.O.) 371/163811, No. CS 1102/5, 22 August 1962.

21. State Department National Archives (hereafter SDNA) 781.00/7-1158, No. 39.

22. Ulises Humala Tasso, *Subdesarrollo o Camino al Colapso: Desarrollo del Subdesarrollo en el Peru* (Lima, 1987); pp. 130-33; Kofas, *Foreign Debt and Underdevelopment*, pp. 188-90; Raul Garcia Heras, "La Argentina y los organismos financieros internacionales," *El Trimestre Economico*, 67/268 (2000): 523-56.

23. Joseph Love, *Crafting the Third World* (Stanford, 1996), pp. 213-18; Raymond Vernon, *Two Hungry Giants: The United States and Japan in the Quest for Oil and Ores* (Cambridge, MA, 1983), 1-18; Michael Tanzer, *Race for Resources* (New York, 1981).

24. A. C. Robles, *The Political Economy of Inter-Regional Relations: ASEAN & the EU* (Aldershot, 2004); Derek McDougall, *The International Politics of the New Asia Pacific* (Boulder, 1997), pp. 199-210.

25. R. L. Curry, Jr. "Challenges of Asymmetry Associated with ASEAN's Evolution to a Lager-sized group," *Journal of Third World Studies*, 14/1, (1997): 13-36; K. P. Thomas and Mary Ann Tetreault (eds), *Racing to Regionalize: democracy, capitalism, and regional political economy* (Boulder, 1999); Saburo Okita, "Japan's Role in Asia-Pacific Cooperation," *Annals AAPSS,* 513 (1991): 25-37.

26. Robert Kagan, "The Benevolent Empire," *Foreign Policy*, 111 (1998): 24-35; Kofas, *Under the Eagle's Claw*, pp. 246-48

27. J. L. Gaddis, *The Long Peace: Inquiries into the Cold War* (Oxford, 1987); Patrick Brogan, *The Fighting Never Stopped: A Comprehensive Guide to World Conflict since 1945* (New York, 1990); T. G. Patterson, *On Every Front: The Making of the Cold War* (New York, 1979); Iriye, *Global Community*, pp. 3-8.

28. Charles A. Beard, *The Economic Basis of Politics* (New York, 1957); William Appleman Williams, *The Tragedy of American Diplomacy* (New York, 1962). A. J. Bacevich, *American Empire: the realities and consequences of U.S. diplomacy* (Cambridge, MA, 2002); Walter Lafeber, *Inevitable Revolutions: The United States and Central America* (New York, 1984); Gabriel Kolko, *Confronting the Third World: United States Foreign Policy, 1945-1980* (New York, 1988); Noam Chomsky, *Hegemony or Survival: The Quest for Global Dominance* (New York, 2003).

29. World Bank Archives (hereafter WBA) General Negotiations, Box 15, 15 October 1991, Speech of the Minister of Portugal.

Chapter 1

Historical Overview of Models of Integration

Inter-dependent, Patron-Client Integration Models, and the State in the Early Cold War

The emergence of the capitalist world-economy in northwest Europe in the 16th century gave rise to international economic integration which has always entailed uneven social and geographic distribution of wealth within nation-states and globally. Though Spain and Portugal played an important historic role in the integration of Latin America, Africa, and Asia, the Iberian countries were intermediaries as part of the semi-periphery in the world capitalist system. Owing to their dominant economic roles by the 17th century, northwest European countries used Spain (port of Cadiz) and Portugal (port of Lisbon) to sell manufactured products intended for domestic and global distribution, while purchasing raw materials from the Iberian colonies. Consequently, Spain and Portugal established a dependency relationship with northwest Europe, one that would last until the present.[1]

Along with the rest of the Balkans, Greece was underdeveloped by the semi-feudal Ottoman Empire at the same time that the Iberian peninsula and its colonies became dependent on northwest Europe. Like much of the Ottoman-ruled Middle East after the Treaty of Kutchuk-Kainardji in 1774, Greece became a satellite of the British empire from the 1830s to the end of World War II. The Industrial Revolution and institutional modernization that changed northwest Europe in the 19th century left the Iberian peninsula and the Balkans more dependent on northwest Europe. A catalyst to external dependence, in the 19th century foreign loans became a major tool for the advanced capitalist countries to exercise preponderate financial, commercial, and political influence in southern Europe and other underdeveloped countries around the world, including Latin America where British businesses dominated until the Great Depression.[2]

Replacing northwest Europe's traditional role, the U.S. became the preeminent force behind the policies of the IFIs that managed the world capitalist economy after the Second World War. The astronomical rise in U.S. GNP during the war, when the rest of the world experienced precipitous decline, combined with the experience of the

Lend-Lease program, and managing the hemispheres war-geared economy, afforded the U.S. the opportunity to design plans for global management. Based on the plans drafted in 1943 and 1944 by special assistant to the secretary of state Leo Pasvolsky and assistant treasury secretary Harry Dexter White, the U.S. had determined to impose its own transformation policy that would create a dependent relationship based on the asymmetrical patron-client model with the Third World. At the Bretton Woods conference, some Europeans and Latin Americans backed John Meynard Keynes who argued for a more equitable relationship between creditor and debtor nations. The U.S. rebuffed all proposals and implemented its own.[3]

Pursuing integration on the basis of the long-standing doctrine of Pan-Americanism in Latin America, the U.S. designated western Europe to help reintegrate southern Europe, Africa, and the Middle East to some extent, while Japan would help integrate Asia where South Korea and Taiwan would be deliberately strengthened owing to special geopolitical considerations as front-line countries in the fight against Communism. A continuation of a historical global integration process, globalization, which became identified with the post-Cold War rapid integration under a deregulated economy, has its origins in the Bretton Woods system. After the war the state in the developed and underdeveloped countries became increasingly a support mechanism for international finance capital. This does not mean, however, that there are not institutional differences between capitalist countries like the U.S. and Sweden, Spain and Nigeria, etc. in fiscal, monetary, trade, labor, and other policies, although in all cases the state is a tool for capital accumulation and in all cases they operate under the umbrella of a single world system.[4]

As part of a managed global system emerging from Bretton Woods, and the race to prevail over the Communist countries, the U.S. economic inter-dependent relationship with western Europe and Japan included political and military components, supported by a liberal ideology. U.S. foreign policy was institutionalized through the IMF, World Bank, OECD, GATT, regional military blocs like NATO and OAS, and international trade unions. To make certain that global integration under the aegis of the U.S. succeeded without problems arising from radical trade unions around the world after the creation of the pro-Communist World Federation of Trade Unions (WFTU) in 1945, the Truman administration helped to create the International Confederation of Free Trade Unions (ICFTU) funded by the U.S. and pro-U.S. governments. A docile, pro-capitalist labor movement in every country was as indispensable as NATO and the IFIs in managing the world capitalist system which targeted Communism and nationalism as enemies.[5]

To contain the spread of Communism, prevent economic nationalism, and buttress capitalism at home and abroad, the U.S. helped to revitalize the western European and Japanese economies and helped to shape their institutions. Re-industrializing western Europe and Japan was an ideological, political, military, and economic decision, largely at the expense of keeping Latin America, Africa, and most of Asia perpetually dependent on raw material exports to finance manufactured imports from the industrialized countries. Though southern Europe and large Third World countries like India, Indonesia, Brazil, Mexico, and others evolved into a dependent capitalist mode where foreign companies eventually dominated manufacturing and financial services, foreign capital rapidly penetrated periphery economies that were historically far less inward oriented or self-sufficient than the advanced capitalist countries.[6]

By providing billions of dollars in grants, sustaining massive balance-of-payments deficits, directing the World Bank to offer development and balance-of-payments loans, and subsidizing trade with western Europe and Japan, the U.S. made it possible to attract direct foreign investment and forge a solid foundation for a fairly symmetrical relationship with its junior partners compared with the asymmetrical relationship between the U.S. and the rest of the world. However, western Europe was obligated to open the markets of its colonies and spheres of influence to the U.S. and there was no doubt who was the hegemon. Moreover, U.S. wholesale prices rose sharply in the late 1940s, accounting for massive transfer of capital from around the world to the U.S.[7]

While western Europe and Japan were pursuing Keynesian policies, the IMF, World Bank, U.S. Export-Import Bank, and Washington were advising underdeveloped countries to pay their past debts in order to qualify for new loans, adopt laissez-faire measures affecting everything from trade and currencies to foreign investment, and abide by GATT which favored the U.S. and its junior partners. Semi-developed and underdeveloped countries indirectly provided the subsidies for western Europe's and Japan's re-industrialization, while also offering markets for the U.S. to sell surplus products. Besides being relegated to the raw materials export sector where the value of labor was substantially lower than in manufacturing, semi-developed and underdeveloped countries historically suffered from capital flight, deteriorating terms of trade which entailed billions of dollars in losses, service on foreign loans that far exceeded the principal, and dividend and profit repatriation. The net result of perpetual decapitalization and financial dependence entailed permanence under the patron-client integration model.[8]

Discouraging Keynesian policies and national capitalism in favor of global integration under its aegis, the U.S., the IFIs, and Wall Street discouraged state-owned companies in underdeveloped countries from venturing into areas like steel which they could purchase from American firms, or providing special protection for domestic textile firms, or from having their own merchant marine. A number of European firms, including UK's Rio Tinto, lobbied the State Department for a share of Spain's business under Eximbank credits, but U.S. firms were given preference. Just as the U.S. demanded that Latin American countries must use U.S. shipping companies instead of their own for inter-American trade financed by IFI loans, in 1953 the State

Department blocked Spain from drawing a $12 million Eximbank credit for cotton purchases, because Madrid insisted on using national lines for transport.

In the late 1940s-early 1950s the State Department and U.S.-based multinationals did their best to prevent *Flota Mercante Grancolombiana* (Colombia, Venezuela, Ecuador), and other Latin American lines from taking any business away from U.S. shippers. From the early 1950s to early 1970s, the U.S. prevented Peru from strengthening its own merchant fleet, arguing that Lima had no right to demand that half of all imported goods must be shipped on Peruvian vessels. While the U.S. discouraged a mixed economic model that included nationalism in Spain, Peru and other underdeveloped countries, it permitted it in western Europe, Japan, Canada, Australia, Taiwan, and South Korea.[9]

To qualify for aid, the U.S. during the past sixty years has always demanded that governments make accommodations to U.S.-based multinational corporations. In the 1950s the U.S. and western Europe decided that underdeveloped countries must focus on increasing raw materials exports to finance imported manufactures and capital goods from the U.S., western Europe, and Japan. In 1957 prime minister Jawaharlal Nehru appealed to Washington for a $500-600 million loan, but the Eisenhower administration and the World Bank refused any money for state enterprises.[10]

Where the Third World needed farm machinery, petroleum refineries, and other capital goods, western Europe was initially interested in exporting luxury products, though gradually it began to sell capital equipment. Admonishing underdeveloped nations about quasi-statist policies that impeded private enterprise and global integration, the U.S. government's policy of not allowing industrialization of the Third World was based on general policy but also corporate pressures. Among others, General Electric (GE) demanded and received assurances from Washington that Brazil, Argentina, Turkey, and other Third World governments would not receive U.S. loans to form publicly-subsidized electric industries that competed with GE. The same rules did not apply to western Europe and Japan where the state fostered national capitalism.[11]

While loans to underdeveloped countries were designated for the foreign-dominated primary sector and infrastructural development, the U.S. directed the World Bank and Eximbank to make loans for western Europe's and Japan's manufacturing with a focus on rebuilding national capitalism. Encouraging a multilateral inter-European clearing system to stimulate trade and raise living standards, while discouraging the same in the rest of the world, the U.S. supported the Schuman Plan that led to the Treaty of Rome in March 1957 and the formation of the EEC and its initial four sub-agencies. Two years later, Britain led the European Free Trade Association (EFTA) designed to eliminate trade barriers.

The historical significance of European integration was that the political and business elites chose this route as a means of strengthening national capitalism and protecting national sovereignty from the U.S. The massive injection of capital from the U.S. to western Europe and Japan, the preferential interest rates and long-term loans targeting industrialization, and the trade, monetary, and fiscal policies that they pursued resulted in full employment of males in high paying manufacturing and professional (white collar) jobs. By contrast, the political economy in southern Europe and the Third World shaped by the asymmetrical patron-client model entailed low-wage jobs in the primary sector, high unemployment and underemployment, and mass emigration that provided cheap labor for the G-7.[12]

Import-Substitution and Dependent Development

Import substituting industrialization, which had its roots in the Great Depression and continued through the 1970s from Turkey and Taiwan to Brazil and Argentina, posed no threat to global integration. Though many underdeveloped and semi-developed countries used import-substitution to counterpoise U.S. transformation policy thinly veiled in the legitimacy of the Bretton Woods system, the policy did not achieve its intended results. Like southern Europe, South Korea, Taiwan, Turkey, Brazil, among other larger Third World countries pursued import-substitution to protect jobs and national capital.[13]

To circumvent national laws and take advantage of cheap labor, proximity to regional markets, and less regulation than they faced in the advanced capitalist countries, multinational corporations, with the help of their governments and the IFIs, set up subsidiaries and merged with local capital. Under the guise of free enterprise, they established plants and assumed dominant roles in national economies. Regardless of import-substitution or export-oriented growth strategies, semi-developed and underdeveloped countries remained dependent on U.S., Japanese, and west European capital and technology that dominated not just extractive industries, but gradually all the major sectors from finance to communications. Hence, either import substitution policies ostensibly designed to develop national capitalism, or export-oriented strategies actually strengthened international capital because the patron-client integration model was the superstructure within which national policies functioned.[14]

After president John Kennedy enunciated the Alliance for Progress, the World Bank advised countries around the world to better integrate all underutilized regions within their countries, to foster capitalist agriculture which entailed importing machinery and argo-chemicals, to liberalize trade, to provide more incentives for direct foreign capital investment, and to keep wages low as a means of checking inflation.

To provide agricultural loans, the World Bank demanded local and foreign capital financing for large operations, thereby making a political decision to strengthen the agrarian elites and foreign agrochemical companies at the expense of the small farmers. While the European Community Common Agricultural Program provided subsidies for farmers, the U.S., EEC, and IFIs advised underdeveloped and semi-developed countries to embrace the Green Revolution by purchasing agrochemicals and machinery from the advanced countries. Though production increased, such a policy helped only the large domestic and foreign operations, and drained precious resources which added to foreign debt.[15]

Though the process had started in the 1950s, during the 1960s the industrialized countries began to move more manufacturing plants into southern Europe and larger Third World countries like India, Indonesia, Brazil, and others. Larger underdeveloped countries were the first targets for a foreign-owned manufacturing sector that would be the basis for the new phase of dependent development. But underdeveloped countries, including Greece, Portugal, Peru and others developed the primary sector and light manufacturing under the dependent development model. Despite tensions between national capitalists and foreign capitalists, dependent development entailed the participation of local capital not just in manufacturing, but in all areas from consumer to producer goods.

Postwar Portugal is unique because the cotton supplied by its African colonies to the textile factories at home became a justification for remaining a colonial power in the era of globally-managed neo-liberalism. Spain's and to a lesser degree Portugal's case among others, accounted for dependent development in no small measure owing to the promising automobile sector. Unlike western Europe and Japan, and eventually South Korea where the state buttressed indigenous manufacturing development, such was not the case in southern Europe and the Third World. In other words, Spain, Portugal and Brazil did develop multinationals like Hyundai or Samsung.[16]

Just as there are structural variations between developed countries, similarly, there are differences in dependent societies. Indonesia as a dependent society during the past half century is very different than southern Europe where capital accumulation is derived in part as a result of exploiting other underdeveloped countries, and which underwent significant transformation from the patron-client model to EU integration. In all cases, however, the level of development and living standards are lower in semi-developed and underdeveloped countries than in the G-7, the informal economy represents a much higher percentage of the total than in developed nations and inordinate dependence on foreign capital remains essential for the economy.[17]

Because the integration process evolves within its own structural limitations, dependent development is symptomatic of systemic dynamics, which entails that a country would go from processed food production in the 1950s to high tech production in the 1990s. In all cases the IFIs, the state, the multinationals, and the local business and political elites played salient roles in forging the nexus of dependent development under the patron-client model. Considering that the U.S., western Europe, and Japan took out more capital from underdeveloped countries than they invested in public loans and private foreign investment, the patron-client integration model contributed to higher living standards in the advanced capitalist countries to the detriment of debtor nations. Capital transfers from the poor countries to the rich ones was an issue that first arose at the Bretton Woods conference, and one that is still debated today. Keynes proposed providing liquidity to underdeveloped nations to avoid recessions and secure low unemployment, but the U.S. objected to fostering a symmetrical financial-trade relationship across the entire world.[18]

Throughout the 1950s there was massive capital transfer from the underdeveloped countries to the industrialized ones, and from the U.S. to western Europe and Japan. Making the point that the EEC had become an economic rival at the expense of the U.S., Kennedy informed the world in 1961 that since the end of the war the U.S. had invested $1.5 billion in western Europe, but received back $1 billion. U.S. investment in underdeveloped countries amounted to $200 million, but the return was $1.3 billion, a trend that would remain steady throughout the second half of the 10th century.

Equally revealing, in 1963 Kennedy administration officials acknowledged that IMF monetarist policy, which was pro-U.S., was partly responsible for perpetually low living standards and weak economies in southern Europe and the Third World. For the U.S. to continue its global competitive advantage and for the inter-dependent integration model to remain viable under international competition owing to Japan's and western Europe's economic recovery, the patron-client model needed to evolve under the new phase of dependent development of more thorough process of capital accumulation which entailed multilateralization of foreign aid and investment. In short, America's junior partners would play a more active role in the patron-client model reflecting the trend of trade multilateralization in the Third World and the Communist bloc since the late 1950s.[19]

U.S. Transformation Policy and Foreign Aid in Southern Europe and Third World

The combination of changing socioeconomic, cultural, and educational conditions in the industrialized countries, and the rapid diffusion of technology and modern means of communication influenced young people in semi-developed and underdeveloped countries. To end the dichotomy and close the gap between the G-7 experiencing rapid technological-industrial modernization, while persistence of underdevelopment in the rest of the world entailed social and geographic polarization, various groups from academics to trade unionists and UN agencies called for an end to authoritarianism and external dependence. Achieving such a goal meant restructuring the model of integration within the world system that the U.S. upheld.

President Charles de Gaulle challenged Pax Americana and offered an opportunity to southern Europe to question the patron-client model. Limiting U.S. take-over of French firms, and challenging U.S. financial hegemony, de Gaulle posed a symbolic threat to the patron-client model. In January 1963 the Foreign Office and the State Department complained that General Francisco Franco was pro-de Gaulle, that he was strengthening diplomatic and commercial ties with Paris and Bonn, and that Spain was using France and Germany to counterpoise or gain leverage with the U.S. and the U.K.

Madrid vehemently denied the accusation, but it was no accident that Francisco Franco strengthened ties with de Gaulle amid Spain's and Portugal's negotiations for the U.S. military base agreements which carried political and financial conditions. A few months later, Washington was concerned that liberal prime minister George Papandreou was using Gaullist tactics to loosen his country's dependency relationship with the U.S. and to justify multilateralizing its relations. Because the U.S. enjoyed such preponderate influence, none of these tactics worked, but they laid the groundwork for southern Europe's realignment in the 1970s.[20]

Before the mid-1970s southern European governments had little in common with western Europe and much more with Third World regimes that survived largely by accepting U.S. tutelage. Dependent on U.S. military and economic aid, Spain, Portugal, and Greece made various military, economic, and political accommodations to Washington. For its part, the U.S. lobbied its allies to help integrate southern Europe into the EEC and EFTA. Similarly, the U.S. lobbied for greater integration of the Third World, especially in countries where significant geopolitical interests were at state, like Indonesia after Suharto adopted a pro-U.S. policy.[21]

From Truman to Nixon, the U.S. had no problem aiding its southern European dictatorships, although western Europeans demanded an end to authoritarianism. From CIA-engineered coups in Iran and Guatemala in the early 1950s to the CIA-aided coup in Greece in 1967 and the overthrow of Salvador Allende in 1973, the U.S. supported authoritarian regimes in patron-client states. Were all these countries threatened by Communism and were the dominoes falling from Tehran to Santiago de Chile throughout the Cold War, or was the U.S. interested in preventing regimes from asserting their sovereignty which clashed with the patron-client integration model? To strengthen capitalism which Washington, many western academics, and the mass media invariably equated with democracy, the U.S. eliminated political obstacles to global integration, even at the cost of condoning egregious human rights violations.[22]

"Democracy" American-style was well served in the Dominican Republic in 1966 where the U.S. marines and CIA made certain that an authoritarian regime was put in power, the same year that the U.S. helped back Suharto in Indonesia and U.S. military commitment to Vietnam was deepening. Favorably disposed to covert operations in its sphere of influence, in 1966 the Johnson administration encouraged Peruvian president Fernando Belaunde Terry, who started out as a well-intentioned reformist, to suppress a popular revolt that ended in the death of more than 8000 people. And all in defense of the International Petroleum Company (IPC), a subsidiary of Standard Oil of New Jersey, for the sake of complying with the IMF, and for the overriding protection of the patron-client integration model.[23]

Just as Peru was rewarded with IMF and World Bank loans for defending the IPC, so were Indonesia, Nigeria, and southern Europe for accepting IFIs' policy advice leading toward greater integration. In exchange for receiving military and economic aid, and political support, Spain, Portugal, Greece, and Indonesia offered to help the U.S. in its war against Vietnam. Both Iberian countries, however, demanded that the U.S. oppose UN pressures for Africa's decolonization. A politically embarrassing issue for Washington that tried to project a pro-civil rights image while backing apartheid in southern Africa, this is another clear demonstration of how the patron-client model took precedence over other considerations.

Portugal welcomed integration into the EEC, but it had doubts about the political aspects, especially with regard to colonial policy which entailed that the U.S. and the EEC wanted to integrate Africa without inefficient intermediaries. Unlike Charles de Gaulle who did not believe that French political or economic interests would be jeopardized after allowing Algeria its freedom, especially given the reality of multinationals operating in there already, Portugal and Spain suspected that decolonization would negatively impact their regimes and economies while benefiting the U.S. which wanted direct integration.[24]

Following the passage of a UN Security Council resolution on Rhodesia, Salazar threatened to reexamine Portugal's relations with Washington, including the U.S. base in Azores. After April 1966, the UN began to apply pressure on the IFIs not to provide loans for Portugal until it reconsidered decolonization. Ignoring the UN, in June 1966 the World Bank approved $30 million for Portugal's power projects. Because of the U.S. military bases agreement with Lisbon, the Johnson administration pressured the World Bank to make the loan. More significant, the U.S. approved more direct aid for Portugal, after the Salazar government agreed to sell USAID-financed pharmaceutical supplies to South Vietnam. The linkage between economic integration and geopolitical concerns was at the core of the patron-client model, whether in Portugal, Indonesia, or any other country.[25]

Though the Cold War afforded U.S. aid recipients some political leverage, under the patron-client model capital had been transferring from southern Europe and the Third World to the advanced capitalist countries. U.S. and IFI loans to the rest of the world entailed that a large percentage of direct foreign investment was financed by the taxpayers of the recipient countries through service payments and repatriated profits. From the end of the war to the accession into the EEC, southern European countries constantly feared lapsing into marginal status in the world economy by failing to keep pace with the west. Heeding the IMF admonition, southern European governments knew that EEC associate membership and supplier credits did not entail eradication of structural problems. Like Third World countries, southern Europe used inter-bloc and intra-bloc competition to secure foreign aid which accounted for greater foreign dependence and further consolidation of the patron-client model, rather than alleviating their structural problems.[26]

Until the early 1970s the UN, World Bank, and IMF considered Portugal, Spain, and Greece underdeveloped, as reflected by vital economic and social statistics. Though the foundations for dependent development in southern Europe, as in Taiwan and South Korea, and to a degree Israel and South Africa, were established in the 1950s, all countries had special military agreements with the U.S. which accounted for some preferential treatment in comparison with other underdeveloped countries.[27]

From the 1940s to the 1980s southern Europe's national identity as reflected by their governments, political and social elites, and divisions of labor remained more closely linked with the Third World than western Europe or the U.S. In three separate visits to Latin American countries in 1971, Spain's foreign minister Gregorio Lopez Bravo noted that Spain had much more in common with the Third World, opposed big power domination, and regional blocs. Concerned about sovereignty, prime minister Andreas Papandreou would repeat that statement even after Greece was a full member of the EEC. Like the Third World, southern Europe during most of the Cold War was aware of its marginal status in the world system. Providing cheap emigrant labor of about three million people for the advanced capitalist countries, southern Europe's integration accelerated after its associate membership in the EEC in the early 1960s.[28]

Despite their pro-western foreign policies, EEC and EFTA membership, and proximity to western Europe, Spain, Portugal and Greece retained close links to the Third World and actually had more in common with Soviet-dependent Eastern Europe than the west. Though gradual shifting of identity with western Europe was a reflection that the positive effects of the EU integration process on southern Europe took many years to trickle down to the middle classes, there was no doubt that regional bloc identity had an overall uplifting impact on many professional and business people, though not necessarily on unskilled labor. Reflecting the patron-client model, the identities of Third World societies like Nigeria, Indonesia, and Peru remained unaltered.[29]

Consortium Aid as a Tool of Dependency and Integration

In the postwar era the U.S. encouraged countries around the world to allow the World Bank, IMF, OECD, and western economists to help them draft long-term (3-7 years) development plans which were linked to foreign loans approved only after the applicant agreed to adopt neo-classical monetary measures, like trade liberalization and investment policies that the IFIs and the U.S. recommended. Ultimately designed to forge greater integration on the basis of an asymmetrical relationship, uniform policy recommendations were made to semi-developed and underdeveloped countries, regardless of their unique circumstances, political economy, and stages of development. Always justifying austerity policies on the basis of trying to stabilize the currency and achieving external equilibrium, the IMF fostered global integration by devaluing the currency of loan recipients and opening their undervalued markets to foreign capital.[30]

Besides the IFIs as instruments of imposing uniform monetary, trade, and investment policies, U.S. national security interests always transcended any other consideration in bilateral and multilateral foreign loans. That precedent was set in May 1947 when the International Bank for Reconstruction and Development (IBRD) approved a $250 million loan to France just after prime minister Paul Ramadier ousted the Communists from the government. Coincidentally, the Truman Doctrine set off a series of anti-Communist policies targeting politicians, trade unionists, and intellectuals across Europe and Latin America. In 1948 the IBRD offered Chile a loan as reward for pursuing pro-U.S.-anti-Communist and anti-labor policies. Nehru, Tito, Augusto Pinochet, and a host of others who adopted pro-market and pro-U.S. policies received multilateral and bilateral foreign loans. Such examples abound in the past half century when U.S. foreign policy has been guiding the IFIs hand.[31]

The IMF, the World Bank, and the U.S. proposed that semi-developed and underdeveloped countries from India to Yugoslavia become full members of GATT, consult with the IFIs on development plans and foreign borrowing, and adopt monetarist policies and liberalization programs to allow for free flow of capital across national borders. Whereas the G-7 fiscal structures were designed to strengthen the state and national capital that would expand into the rest of the world, southern Europe and the Third World could not possibly compete with the types of incentives provided by the state to large corporations in the advanced capitalist countries. Deviating from the patron-client model principally for geopolitical considerations related to Communist China and North Korea, the U.S. allowed South Korea and Taiwan under dictatorships to provide high tariffs and special incentives to strengthen their large corporations that competed with the G-7. While the corporate welfare structure was becoming stronger in the G-7, South Korea, and Taiwan, protectionist or quasi-statist policies were not allowed in the rest of the world because the patron-client integration model required compliance with IMF, GATT, and accommodations for foreign capital.[32]

Where the advanced capitalist countries have pursued stimulative fiscal and monetary policies amid recessionary cycles to better manage the contracting economy and mitigate its impact, the IFIs and the G-7 have vigorously opposed the same course of action for the rest of the world which has many structural disadvantages, including unfair terms of trade, limited access to G-7 markets and lack of domestic market protection, dependence on the U.S.-dominated IFIs for loans linked to adherence of IMF policies designed to strengthen the international corporate sector at the expense of labor and small businesses, and reliance on the dollar as a reserve currency. Thus when cyclical recessions hit the developed countries, they are not under the IMF austerity gun, and their policy options are more flexible, in no small measure because they are the core of the world system. The G-7 national economies remain strong relative to the rest of the world which suffers derivative effects of inflation and recession stemming from the core. Cyclical recessions, therefore, that create greater social polarization across the world, also result in greater geographic polarization.[33]

The first challenge to the Americentric patron-client integration model was in the mid-1950s when a number of Asian and African countries, joined by China and USSR, called for equal and mutual economic benefits in international economic relations. After the Bandung Conference hosted by Indonesia in April 1955, a number of Third World countries were eager to affirm their position in the global political and economic arenas, thus protesting American-style global integration. Fearful that the nascent non-aligned bloc offered alternatives with China and USSR vying for influence in Asia and Africa, the U.S. and its junior partners moved swiftly to prevent any plan from threatening the patron-client integration model. Because there was a split in Bandung between those advocating Socialism against those advocating reformist capitalism, the local political, military, and business elites collaborated with the U.S. and its junior partners to reconcile the two sides, thus coopting non-aligned states.[34]

Very prominent at the Bandung conference, in 1958 India became the first country to receive a World Bank-coordinated consortium loan that included the U.S., western Europe, Japan, and Australia as donors. India reciprocated with incentives for foreign capital, and foreign investment rose from $1 billion in 1957 to $2.1 billion in 1965. The Development Loan Fund provided $350 million and the U.S. $1 billion to "Aid-to-India-Club" for 1961 and 1962, and an additional $1 billion in agricultural surplus exports. Financial dependence under the patron-client model proved a resounding success even in the largest Third World country that tried to use East-West competition as leverage.

Two years after the formal aid coordination for India which had been suffering from high balance-of-payments deficits, a Pakistan consortium was created. This was as much for economic as for political considerations to counterbalance India. The same model was followed by a U.S.-west European aid consortium for Aegean rivals Greece and Turkey, also for economic and geopolitical considerations amid the controversies of Cyprus' independence and U.S. deployment of nuclear weapons in both countries. Meanwhile creditor countries had created the Paris Club in May 1956 to address Argentina's debt restructuring, operating with the IMF's and World Bank's considerable influence in determining the terms for the debtor countries.[35]

Consortium loans assumed a new phase in 1961 when the OECD was created to coordinate foreign aid programs, promote trade, and compile country studies for development plans among other tasks. A year later a number of debtor countries requested consortium aid which became the standard method of integration under the patron-client model between the developed countries belonging to OECD and the rest of the world. In 1963 the consultative groups for Nigeria, Colombia, Tunisia, and the Sudan were established, as much for economic as for domestic political and foreign policy considerations. Along with other Third World countries in 1966, Peru and South Korea came under the consortium umbrella, but Indonesia's was one of the most important that critical year that Washington was trying to help Suharto consolidate power.

Indonesia's consortium split between a Paris-based group, and a Dutch-led group, both dealing with debt rescheduling and new loans, mostly at the Johnson administration's urging amid reluctant OECD members. The World Bank invariably provided pre-investment studies for consortiums which then negotiated appropriate levels of assistance. Grants and publicly-guaranteed loans were almost always linked to corporate contracts from the aid donor's country, many of which were tainted with bribery. Therefore, both the donors and the recipients used public funds to generate businesses benefiting mostly multinational corporations.[36]

Among the first to receive consortium assistance, Turkey offers a fair representation of how the U.S. and OECD used loans as part of the patron-client integration model that took into account poignant geopolitical considerations. Amid a famine in eastern Turkey in 1962, the U.S. agreed to supply 80,000 tons of wheat, while the IMF announced extra drawing rights of $31 million, and the OECD $45 million. In July 1962 Turkey was approved for EEC associate membership, at the strong urging of the U.S. which considered Turkey along with Iran and Greece strategic zones of the Northern Tier umbrella against the Soviet bloc. Once an OECD-sponsored consortium was created to coordinate loans, the USAID approved $10 million for diesel railway engines purchased from U.S. firms, $5.3 million to the U.S. Royal Lastik company for the construction of a plant in Turkey, $1.78 million for American Home Products to build a pharmaceutical plant, $31.2 million for the purchase of electrical equipment, and $383,000 given directly to U.S. companies interested in exploring business opportunities in Turkey's plastics industry and to study a dam project in the Euphrates and Sakarya rivers.[37]

During an aid consortium meeting, the U.S., France, West Germany, Italy, and Belgium agreed that Turkey would receive aid from all participants and the European Fund. Though the U.S. and Germany would provide most of the financing for the plan, Ankara asked that the UK be included in the consortium, largely because London was sympathetic to Turkey during the Cyprus negotiations. Because of the special relationship of Greece and Turkey with NATO and the U.S., a broader working consortium was created to coordinate their tasks between military and civilian projects. The Swiss vehemently objected to the fact that NATO, and by implication the U.S., instead of the OECD, had such a dominant role in planning a consortium. In short, diplomatic and military considerations in certain cases were more significant in the consortium's role than economic factors.

To weaken the OECD's role, the U.S. backed World Bank-sponsored consortia, thereby continuing to relegate western Europe to a junior partner role. The IMF and the consortium urged Turkey to comply with the stabilization program, otherwise there would be more difficult times ahead, but Ankara used its geopolitical leverage to lessen the IMF's pressures. Though the Turkish regime complied with the conditions that the multilateral banks and the consortium had imposed, it was at the expense of labor and widespread disillusionment about the country's future as a U.S. satellite, especially after the Cuban missile crisis that left Turkish leaders feeling vulnerable amid the U.S.-Soviet nuclear chess game.[38]

Besides the geopolitical dimensions of consortium loans, official corruption was another significant dimension associated with multilateral and bilateral loans. Contrary to their claims, western companies trying to secure government contracts in southern Europe and the Third World were deeply involved in official corruption, whether they used consortium loans or private financing in their bribery and embezzlement schemes. It was especially embarrassing that corrupt businesses were frequently beneficiaries of government and IFI loans often tainted by scandals. More blatant in Suharto's Indonesia than in Franco's Spain, corruption extended from the corporate board rooms of New York and London to the presidential palaces of Third World loan recipients. Considering that Washington used money throughout the Cold War to secure elections of pro-U.S. politicians and trade unionists around the world, official corruption extended from corporations paying bribes to secure contracts-financed IFI loans to government pay-offs.[39]

Shortly after Robert McNamara became World Bank president in 1968, officials argued that it was embarrassing for the institution to know that many well-informed leaders around the world perceived the World Bank as a vehicle for western corporations to secure development-loan contracts for projects in underdeveloped countries. Under McNamara, who introduced some institutional reforms including an environmental assessment component to project loans, the World Bank requested that companies no longer approach the Bank directly as they had been doing for contracts, but instead go to their governments and bid in accordance with their respective country's laws and regulations, thereby shielding the Bank from corruption scandals and legal liabilities.[40]

McNamara's reforms notwithstanding, in May 2004 a U.S. senate investigation revealed that up to $130 billion of World Bank development loans may have been part of a corrupt pattern since Bretton Woods. The total amount rises to $200 billion when other multilateral bank loans are included. Senator Richard Lugar pointed out that: "In the starkest terms, corruption has cost the lives of uncounted individuals contending with poverty and disease." Nor is corruption an ephemeral problem that is "cleaned up" and things are "back to normal," because according to the World Bank, in 2001 an estimated one trillion dollars was devoted to bribes, kickbacks, etc. in a world economy estimated at $30 trillion. Suharto's Indonesia, one of America's and Japan's most important Asian satellites, was listed among the countries with the worst corruption record, though the problem is global and runs deep in the corporate culture from the advanced countries to the Third World.[41]

Besides rampant corruption linked to consortium aid and corporate bribes to politicians, an equally serious problem was the areas that the IFIs targeted for development. Rather than making the loan recipient more self-reliant, public foreign loans were mostly intended to strengthen the multinational corporations that lobbied to receive the contracts or to export products to the borrowing countries. For example, because of the high balance-of-payments deficit, in May 1966 Greece requested foreign aid from the OECD consortium to help with its investment program. Opposed to Greece's request for commercial credits, London was flexible in allowing funds for the purchase of British telecommunications, electrical, port-handling, and other equipment. The U.S. and other OECD members adopted the same position toward Nigeria, Indonesia, Portugal, Philippines, and other consortium-loan recipients, thereby strengthening the multinationals while undercutting national capitalism in the client states.[42]

Though the Foreign Office noted that Greece along with the Iberian countries were semi-developed and did not need as much aid as the Third World, there was no doubt that only through loans could British firms compete with other foreign companies to secure contracts. Because Europe and Japan offered high-interest-rate, short-term loans linked to purchases of products in their countries, Greece, Portugal and other underdeveloped countries protested to the IMF that consortium aid was invariably linked to those industries that the advanced countries wanted strengthened rather than focusing on the loan recipient's most urgent needs. Not only were consortium credits more favorable to the donor's private sector than to the loan recipient's economy, but the latter had the responsibility for infrastructural development, irrigation, and programs that the private sector would not undertake. Hence, there was a question of the foreign loans' cost-benefit ratio to the taxpayers in the recipient countries.[43]

Over 90 percent of World Bank loans to the Third World from 1948 until 1960 were devoted to infrastructure and the primary sector, while direct private foreign investment targeted mining, manufacturing, and financial services. Though U.S.-based multinational corporations benefited from IFI loans, they adamantly opposed credit for foreign public enterprises, unless there was partial private investment involved from one of the OECD members. The World Bank had complained on numerous occasions during the 1950s and 1960s that despite official U.S. policy of trying to strengthen the private sector at home and abroad, various U.S. administrations made loans that strengthened foreign public enterprises in exchange for political and military concessions.

Similarly, throughout the Cold War the Eximbank engaged in such practices to buttress U.S. foreign policy while strengthening U.S. corporations. In 1963 a pro-market study called the Clay Report noted that the U.S. was assisting foreign publicly-owned industrial and commercial firms competing with private enterprises. Arguing that state-run companies had dubious economic value in underdeveloped countries whether in southern Europe or Third World, the report recommended that with the exception of Greece and Turkey, no other European government should receive U.S. economic or military aid. To counterpoise Eximbank loans, OECD countries used their own state bank loans to compete with the U.S., especially by the end of the 1960s when western Europe and Japan had accumulated sufficient dollar reserves to afford them more leverage in international lending.[44]

After the Clay report stressed that the Eximbank, USAID, and all IFIs should tighten borrowing terms, the U.S. congress cut aid to southern Europe sharply, though bilateral and multilateral bank loans rose in the second half of the 1960s, especially where Washington was trying to effect policy changes. For example, Eximbank loans to Portugal amounted to $81 million in the 1960s, as U.S. companies and banks were becoming more involved in Portugese Africa. More development and balance-of-payments loans were devoted to the Third World after Kennedy, partly through the newly-established International Development Association (IDA) and the World Bank. At the same time, there was a transition toward multilaterization of U.S. development policy, largely because western Europe and Japan had accumulated dollars at a time that the U.S. was experiencing balance-of-payments deficits.

Besides consolidating the patron-client integration model to suit the realities of the increasingly multipolar world economy, the rise in foreign aid to the southern hemisphere was in large measure a response to the rising U.S. concern about revolutionary and non-aligned threats in the Third World. After the Cuban Revolution and radical African anti-colonial movements following the CIA overthrow of Congo's Patrice Lumumba, the nexus between multinational corporations, U.S. foreign policy, and client states tightens even more than it was during the early Cold War.[45]

U.S. Balance-of-Payments Deficits and Multilateralization of the Patron-Client Model

Chronic U.S. balance-of-payments deficits were partly responsible for the gradual transition during the 1960s from public loans that carried lower interest rates and were long-term, to commercial loans that were short-to-medium term carrying higher rates and contributing to the Third World debt crisis in the early 1980s. Linked to numerous policies designed to facilitate greater capital penetration of the recipients' markets, consortium loans were gradually supplemented by commercial bank credit and multilateralization of foreign aid that necessarily entailed the multilateralization of the patron-client integration model.

Starting in the late 1950s when western European and Japanese economies were becoming competitive, the multilateralization process of the patron-client model as reflected in the OECD consortium system was inevitable. Western Europe and Japan had deep roots in Africa and Asia, and the U.S. could no longer carry the burden of empire alone amid Third World radicalization, escalating arms race and Vietnam war, and rising costs to keep the domestic economy strong. The U.S. used multilaterization as a mechanism to keep its G-7 junior partners in line amid Charles de Gaulle's nationalist challenge to the U.S.[46]

Though the balance-of-payments crisis boiled over in the late 1960s, U.S. gold reserves were about equal to the foreign dollar balances by 1959. The IMF warned the Eisenhower administration about the impact of trade deficits and depleted gold reserves on the dollar. Thereafter, deficits increased, owing in part to business investment and capital transfers, and military expenditures arising from the arms race and global commitments from South Korea and South Vietnam to West Germany. Besides subsidizing Europe's, Japan's, South Korea's and Taiwan's trade, the U.S. permitted discriminatory practices against the dollar zone in exchange for exercising influence of the former's policies in all areas from trade to interest rates. While western Europe accumulated Eurodollars used for loans to the Third World, Africa and Latin America combined received less U.S. aid than South Korea during the 1950s.[47]

Given the integrative and concentrated nature of international capital, and considering that Washington poured billions of dollars into defense and space programs, the dollar crisis was inevitable by 1970. During the 1960s U.S.-based multinationals absorbed billions of dollars to finance expansion, mergers, and acquisitions. Private banks increased their Eurodollar borrowing, while the government increased its short-term liabilities to about $50 billion against gold reserves of $17 billion. After Kennedy promulgated the ambitious Alliance for Progress, the U.S. had been asking its junior partners to provide Eurodollar loans to Third World countries, a move that gave Europe and Japan the opportunity to capture greater market share of world trade, to enjoy more economic policy leverage, and reap the benefits of the patron-client integration model. As EEC-Latin American trade and financial relations took off in the 1960s, the U.S. expected western Europe to provide more aid that would alleviate pressure on the dollar.[48]

Although the U.S. enjoyed a net trade surplus as the world's largest exporter from the mid-1940s to 1970, it also exported more capital than was invested in its borders.

While the U.S. was a net exporter of capital to the advanced capitalist countries during the Cold War, underdeveloped countries transferred capital to the U.S., thereby deflecting some of its costs to maintain Pax Americana. By 1970-1971 the protracted U.S. balance-of-payments deficit exploded into an international monetary crisis, amid high inflation and high unemployment, the stagflation phenomenon. Holding only $13 billion in foreign exchange reserves against $88 billion in foreign hands, the U.S. Federal Reserve and major European central banks adopted floating rates, thereby unleashing a flood of their own currencies to stabilize the dollar and international financial system. The result of the overvalued dollar came at the expense of the semi-developed and underdeveloped countries, considering that EEC average wages and living standards had reached parity with the U.S. by 1970.[49]

At the annual IMF-World Bank meeting, French finance minister Valery Giscard D'Estaing argued that the U.S. had been exporting inflation primarily because the dollar as a reserve currency was unstable owing to chronic balance-of-payments deficits since the 1950s. Calling on the industrialized countries to stabilize their currencies, Giscard D'Estaing noted that debtor countries were hardest hit. His statements after the December 1969 EEC decision to create a European monetary unification were intended to formalize the competition with the dollar as a reserve currency. Harmonizing EEC economic policies would entail that Europe would exert greater control not only over its own policies, but over Third World debtor countries and southern Europe that were associate members.[50] The IMF and World Bank shared the EEC's concern about global monetary stability and the need for renewed confidence in the Bretton Woods system.

But OECD members, especially France and Germany, had differences on strategic and monetary policy issues as far back as the Kennedy administration. Hosting 350,000 U.S. troops on its soil, Germany was Europe's largest economy, just as Japan was dominant in the Asian economy. Because neither Germany nor Japan absorbed the full costs for its own defense, the U.S. had been pushing both to be more active in the multilateralization process of foreign aid. Partly because of its new strength within Europe and its concern about the U.S. determining the regional and global balance of power under the pretext of the East-West conflict, France was the first junior partner to pose a challenge to Washington's hegemony. Despite the Franco-German Treaty of 1963, de Gaulle vetoed England's entry into the EEC, and later the U.S. proposal for Multilateral Nuclear Force.[51]

While the U.S. wanted multilateralization of aid, or more burden sharing by western Europe, de Gaulle contended that America was living beyond its means, forcing the EEC to finance America's global empire under an anachronistic bipolar world model to Europe's detriment. By 1969 the National Security Council (NSC) was concerned that Europe and Latin America were worried about U.S. economic expansion and the appearance that U.S. foreign policy was in the service of Wall Street. Knowing that the

EEC would use its dollar surplus to influence the management of the world economy, secure a larger share of world trade, and increase capital investment in the Third World, the U.S. was resigned to the reality that the patron-client model would be multilateralized in some fashion.[52]

Besides EEC and Japan concerns about the U.S. dollar and its undue influence in macroeconomic global policy, 95 underdeveloped countries condemned U.S. foreign economic policy at a UN Conference on Trade and Development held in Lima in 1971. Besides a number of Third World representatives dismissing U.S. aid as furthering U.S. interests, Swedish economist Gunnar Myrdal noted that given the large military component of U.S. aid and conditions that recipients buy American products and services, it was not aid but payment for global claims of U.S. foreign policy and rewarding Wall Street. The Nigerian press noted that the U.S. Agency for International Development (USAID) was pressuring all of Africa and developing nations to surrender their sovereignty in exchange of meager assistance. The problem was that debtor countries had few options within the patron-client model.[53]

Though the IFIs, OECD, and the U.S. were advising southern European and Third World governments that they must seek loans from commercial banks and not rely as much on public loans, commercial banks were just as eager to compete with the IFIs. As inflation rose globally after 1968 and energy prices skyrocketed after the Yom Kippur War in 1973, non-oil producing underdeveloped countries fell deeper into debt. Nigeria, Indonesia, Mexico, Venezuela and other petroleum producers enjoyed modest balance-of-payments surpluses, but they failed to diversify their economies, they resorted to heavy foreign borrowing at high interest rates in the 1970s, thus paying a high price from the 1980s to the early 1990s.[54]

To a great extent, the weak dollar as a reserve currency undermined Third World economies whose currencies were pegged to the dollar. Seeking greater leverage, semi-developed and underdeveloped countries pursued multilateral trade and financial relations, relying more on the EEC and Japan for loans and direct investment. While the U.S., western Europe and Japan increased their share of world trade from 50 percent in 1960 to 60 percent in 1970, that increase came at the expense of the semi-developed and underdeveloped countries. This was partly because of deteriorating terms of trade, discriminatory tariffs on Third World exports by the G-7, especially the EEC and Japan, decapitalization in the form of debt service, dividend payments, and repatriation of profits, and the domestic elites invested their capital in the U.S. and western Europe.[55]

To strengthen the dollar and stimulate their exports, after August 1971 the industrialized countries deliberately limited the appreciation of their own currencies. Owing to divisions within OECD, differences between U.S. and individual European countries about the dollar's value, and U.S. excessive spending, there were sharp disagreements on how to best pursue a coordinated effort to deal with the exchange rate crisis. Warning about the possibility of currency and trade warfare, the IMF urged international coordination to integrate the world's economies more closely. But the question was whether to allow the dollar as a fixed currency that would benefit the U.S. at the expense of other countries. To curtail outflow of gold and to curb the demand for the dollar, and to prevent western Europe and Japan from putting restraints on U.S. macroeconomic policy, the Nixon administration abandoned the fixed rate exchange system, thereby recognizing multilateralization of patron-client integration as a fait accompli.[56]

Having to share macro-economic policy decisions with the G-7, the U.S. was still the number one economy in the world and the leader in multiple areas from military to technological. With the dollar as the standard world currency, it was in the interest of the G-7 to back U.S. leadership. In cooperation with Japan, western Europe, Australia, and Canada, in 1970 the U.S. formed an interagency foreign private investment group that would promote more direct investment in Latin America, Asia, and Africa by having Third World governments share in the costs of investment guarantees.

Though such a move would hurt pro-U.S. regimes like Indonesia, others like South Korea and Spain had made sufficient progress that they could assume the guarantee contracts. Carried out with the assistance of the donor countries and the IFIs, the taxpayers paid for the new insurance program. After 1970, therefore, the multilateralization phase of globalization is consolidated with the U.S. remaining hegemonic. The deregulation, privatization, trade liberalization, anti-trade union wave of the Thatcher-Reagan decade in the 1980s had its origins in the previous decade.[57]

An indication that multinational corporations were increasingly interested in closer global integration and in locating factories in the Third World to take advantage of low-wage labor, fewer environmental law restrictions, and less regulatory scrutiny, the proposed foreign investment guarantee program was designed to transfer the burden of corporate welfare from the state in the advanced capitalist countries to the public sector in the periphery. The program became widely used, although initially Chile and Kenya among others did not go along with the investment guarantee, and a number of European and U.S. politicians questioned the scheme as burdensome on taxpayers.[58]

Besides investment guarantee as a method of continuing to accumulate and transfer capital from the periphery to the center, and for maximizing corporate profits while reducing risk, multinational corporations were entering into partnerships with government-owned enterprises especially in mining operations. A means to safeguard against nationalization, such co-ownerships afforded multinationals greater state protection from trade unions that were less likely to cause problems for the government than a foreign company that was a political target. Meanwhile, manufacturing de-industrialization of the U.S. economy entailed the loss of at least 30 million jobs in the 1970s alone. While the government was lowering corporate taxes and providing incentives for mergers and acquisitions, there was gradual downward pressure on wages. De-industrialization of the G-7 continued as Taiwan, Hong Kong, South Korea, Brazil, Singapore, and Spain during the 1970s, eventually joined by China and India during the 1980s, gradually shifted from labor-intensive to technology-intensive industries.[59]

Because of the patron-client integration model, de-industrialization which put downward pressure on wages in the U.S. did not mean that workers in underdeveloped countries achieved wage levels comparable to their counterparts in the advanced counties. This was in large measure due to the IFIs' constant pressures on all governments to keep wages low and corporate incentives high as a means of keeping inflation low. While the U.S. was exporting inflation from 1968 to 1980, it was in the process improving its current account deficit with a cheaper dollar. Because IMF-imposed stabilization programs weakened the underdeveloped countries' currencies against the dollar, they did not improve their economies, while western Europe and Japan did. Given that the U.S. prescription to lower inflation at home included lowering the tax burden on the upper income groups and limiting wage increases, IMF stabilization programs mirrored that policy in southern Europe and Third World.

The Nixon administration proposed that U.S. banks absorb dollars by discouraging repayment of liabilities by their branches overseas. Strengthening the dollar at the expense of the rest of the world had its limitations, especially considering that U.S. foreign policy and defense spending contributed to rising international monetary instability. This was evident in November 1973 when secretary of state and NSC advisor Henry Kissinger backed Israel against its Arab neighbors, although France and the rest of Europe warned about the destabilizing consequences on the world economy. Besides the U.S. defense spending and balance-of-payments deficit as catalysts in the dollar crisis, a UN study noted that multinational corporations and U.S. investors speculated in various currencies and played a key role in global currency instability, a process that would be repeated until the present.[60]

On the eve of the Yom Kippur War and the oil crisis that ensued, IMF Managing director H. Johannes Witteveen reported to the UN Economic and Social Council that the global recession of 1971-1972 ended in 1973. Accelerated inflation spurred by demand growth in the industrialized countries, a rise in primary commodities, and a weak dollar would spread from the core to the rest of the world after 1973. Having held consultations with 85 of 126 IMF-members in 1972, the IMF recommended anti-inflationary measures that resulted in downward pressure on wages and redistributed income toward the upper income groups and toward the industrialized countries. Intended to achieve external equilibrium and currency stabilization, IMF measures accomplished neither goal for the duration. Instead, they contributed to lowering the value of labor in all countries, especially in countries exporting non-oil primary commodities, and to maintaining the patron-client integration model on a multilateral basis.[61]

Though inflation rates differed among industrialized countries, the IMF and the World Bank acknowledged that it was beyond question that the G-7 were exporting inflation to the rest of the world. Nor was there a question that inflation from the metropolis was a means of lowering the balance-of-payments deficits and strengthening the G-7 currencies at the expense of debtor nations. Urging stabilization programs for southern Europe and the Third World, the IMF and the Ford administration reiterated that wage increases and lack of incentives for business investment were at the heart of inflation.

The combination of the weak dollar, high oil prices, high defense, and the high costs of the corporate welfare state amid the economic ascendancy of western Europe and Japan were at the heart of U.S.-based multinational corporations' desire to globalize the economy at a more rapid pace. By the late 1970s and early 1980s the effect of stabilization programs was sharp reduction in real wages and massive redistribution of wealth geographically toward the metropolis. This was partly because the real value of the dollar was artificially high, multinationals accumulated capital locally, and local elites took capital out of their countries.[62]

Multipolar World Economy, Multipolar Patron-Client Integration Model

During the global inflationary climate of the late 1970s, the EEC had become more guarded of the multilateral banks than the U.S. whose role was relatively weakened. To retain U.S. dominant influence in   patron-client relationships, the Carter administration pursued bilateral financial policies when it deemed it prudent to serve its larger foreign policy goals. For example, after the IMF announced assistance for Portugal in April 1977, Washington proposed a package of $1.5 billion over three years to assist with Portugal's external payments. Insisting that the IMF's role must not be compromised, Germany and other EEC members objected to U.S. bilateral approach for external payments. The Europeans charged that this was a transparent effort to redefine the traditional integration (patron-client) model under U.S. unilateral policies. For its part, the IMF proposed linking any bilateral aid to the Fund's conditionality terms, though the EEC demanded that Washington remains bound by the multilateral institutions and agrees to equitable sharing of the benefits of global integration.[63]

Besides opting for bilateralism to preserve the optimal privileges of patron-client integration at the expense of its G-7 competitors, the Carter administration diverted some of the loan operations from the IMF, World Bank, and Eximbank to commercial banks. Apparent in the late 1960s, by the mid-1970s it was an open secret that the Federal Reserve Bank and U.S. government had been encouraging private banks to make foreign loans at a greater rate than ever, thus using commercial banks as a catalyst to integration.

As OPEC money flowed back into U.S. financial markets and was then reinvested abroad, the trend of heavy Third World borrowing in the 1970s led to the global debt crisis of the 1980s and to a massive transfer of real resources from the less developed countries to the G-7. Anticipating a crisis, in September 1977 the IMF cautioned that the economic sluggishness in the advanced capitalist countries must not result in the transfer of resources from the Third World back to the G-7. Nevertheless, the IMF's stabilization whether in Latin America, Asia, Africa, southern Europe, and even Eastern Europe were catalytic in such transfer of wealth from the semi-periphery and periphery to the metropolis.[64]

Within the G-7, however, there was a fierce power struggle for control of markets and resources in the Third World, and a parallel struggle to redefine the patron-client model in an increasingly multipolar world economy. In a quest to solidify control of the tumultuous Third World and isolate or coopt Communist and pro-Communist regimes, the Carter administration introduced "human rights" as a cornerstone of its foreign policy. Reluctant to cooperate with the UN on human rights, the U.S. used the policy against not only historic enemies, but against countries like Peru and Brazil where the national bourgeoisie, and political and military elites were eager to gain greater leverage in a multipolar world economy by strengthening ties with western Europe and Japan.[65]

Besides the obvious hypocrisy in the application of U.S. human rights policy, a significant issue was how the policy was manipulated to maintain U.S. hegemony under the patron-client model that had evolved to reflect a multipolar world economy. By definition the patron-client model was inherently contradictory with human rights and social justice. Nevertheless, the U.S. coopted the concept to project a facade of promoting democracy when the only goal was Americentric globalization.[66]

Partly because of the energy crisis and sluggish world trade, OECD countries, including Spain and Portugal went from a balance of payments surplus in the early 1970s to deficits in the late 1970s. With the exception of oil producing countries, the Third World also experienced a sharp rise in current account deficits in the aftermath of the Yom Kippur War, largely because of deteriorating terms of trade. To qualify for balance-of-payments loans from abroad, southern Europe along with a host of underdeveloped nations in the late 1970s implemented IMF stabilization programs, only to find themselves in a cyclical debt crisis and greater dependence on the G-7.[67]

The U.S. Treasury Department acknowledged that the combination of higher energy prices, inflation, and stagnation in the world economy during the 1970s compelled IMF members to borrow $225 billion between 1974 and 1976, of which only 7 percent was financed by the IMF, while 75 percent of balance-of-payments deficits were financed by commercial bank loans that carried much higher costs than public loans. Washington and the IFIs were encouraging the private market orientation as the panacea, though such orientation resulted in the Third World debt crisis, banking crisis in the U.S., and massive transfer of capital from labor to corporations.

In September 1977 under-secretary of the Treasury Anthony M. Solomon reassured the sub-committee on Foreign Economic Policy that underdeveloped countries were in no danger of a debt crisis, because OECD countries were the heavy borrowers. While that was certainly the case in terms of absolute dollars, OECD countries were never in danger of a debt crisis. Even the smaller southern European nations, which ran deficits and increased their foreign borrowing, were shielded from a crisis as a result of their association with the EEC that provided heavy subsidies, though the trend resulted in redistribution toward the upper income groups.[68]

Blaming the Iranian Revolution and Arab oil producers, especially Lybia, for America's double-digit inflation and sluggish economic growth throughout the world, in June 1979 Brzezinski argued that Japan and Germany had a competitive advantage because the dollar had depreciated and oil was priced in dollars. By mid-summer U.S. foreign policy became much more hawkish, and the U.S. media continued to press for a more aggressive foreign policy after the Soviets sent troops to aid Afghanistan in December 1979. Against the background of a weak U.S. economy and rising revolutionary activity in Africa, Central America, and the Middle East, the Carter administration worked with the IFIs and OECD to stabilize volatile economies by enforcing more stabilization programs that would only push many underdeveloped economies into a crisis during the Reagan administration.[69]

One of the most significant developments in the contemporary world economy, in 1978 China resolved to modernize by allowing capitalism and foreign investment to take root as part of its ten-year development plan costing $600 billion. Anxious to counterpoise the Soviet Union and gain access to the most populous country in the world, both the Carter administration and Wall Street backed the policy of integrating China into the world economy, a move that would prove very beneficial economically to the faltering capitalist system in the last quarter of the 20th century. Japan, however, had concerns about how China's integration would impact the Asian economic and political balance of power, and whether U.S.-China rapprochement would undercut Japan's regional hegemony. Similarly, Asian and Latin American countries were justifiably concerned about China's new "open door policy" on their economies.[70]

The combination of high interest rates, sluggish growth in world trade resulting in about one percent drop in GNP in the 1970s, and growth-by-debt policies that the IFIs reinforced accounted for serious problems toward the end of the decade. At the Venice summit of the seven industrialized countries in June 1980, discussions centered around the high price and low supply of energy and its implications on global trade, inflation, and unemployment in the industrialized countries, and lack of economic growth in underdeveloped nations.

The U.S. and its G-7 partners agreed that top priority was to reduce inflation while guarding against further rises in unemployment and underemployment, and world-wide recession. To achieve this goal, it was agreed to shift resources from government spending to strengthening the private sector, lessen dependence on oil by increasing coal and nuclear energy, and shift policy from encouraging consumption to investment. Acknowledging the Third World's special problems, the G-7 concluded that greater global integration by strengthening GATT and affirming free market principles would help the entire world.[71]

The U.S.-G-7 commitment to strengthen GATT and the private sector was no comfort to the Third World about to undergo the most serious debt crisis since the Great Depression. The third largest in Latin America, Peru's foreign public debt jumped from one billion dollars in 1970 to $8.5 billion in 1981, representing 77 percent of GDP. Chile was no better off with $20 billion foreign debt at a time that the minimum wage was $38 per month in the mid-eighties. Third World debt service payments amounted to $1.5 trillion between 1982 and 1992, or double the amount of foreign indebtedness in 1982. The massive transfer of capital from the periphery and semi-periphery to the G-7 during the 1980s helped to further consolidate the patron-client integration model during the globalization decade of the 1990s. Considering the massive defense spending during the Reagan decade, combined with the Savings and Loan bail-out that cost billions to the U.S. Treasury, and real growth rate drop from 3.8 percent to 2.7 percent, the Third World debt crisis subsidized the U.S. economy.[72]

Debt Crisis of the 1980s and Capital Accumulation

One of the most ideological and militaristic regimes in history, the Reagan administration's response to the Third World debt crisis was to strengthen the Overseas Private Investment Corporation (OPIC) and the USAID Bureau for Private Enterprise. Both were designed to buttress U.S.-based multinationals and help strengthen the patron-client model with the financial and political support of the state. Though Reagan and Thatcher contended that their goal was to reduce the state's role in the economy, such limits did not include large tax breaks and subsidies of all types for businesses.

Governments unwilling to liberalize their economies and to provide incentives to U.S.-based multinationals would receive less aid. Under pressure from the U.S., IFIs, and multinationals, Third World governments needing debt rescheduling and new injection of capital went along with U.S. policy to cut social programs, weaken the public social sector, and strengthen the private sector and defense. The result was that capital accumulation in the 1980s entailed a substantial downward pressure on real wages not just in the Third World, but in southern Europe and in the G-7 where trade unions were under attack by the Reagan-Thatcher anti-labor policies.[73]

Far from helping to revitalize weak economies as neo-liberals preached, the Third

World had not experienced a more severe crisis since the Great Depression. The Third World debt crisis was the result of sharp rise in interest rates from the low single digit in 1970 to mid double digit in 1980, a sharp drop in commodities prices and sluggish world trade, imprudent investment decisions and corruption associated with foreign loans, and liberal lending policy by private commercial banks in the advanced countries. World Bank studies have confirmed that devaluations result in capital flight and currency speculation which exacerbate the crisis. Far from alleviating structural problems, debt adjustment and renegotiation along with IMF conditionality entailed massive capital outflow from the Third World to the G-7. The result was that the Third World collectively was in deeper debt in 2000 than in 1980, largely because the outflow of capital exceeded the inflow. Whereas capital outflow amounted to $22 billion from Latin America in 1981, capital inflow was $2 billion less, of which 85 percent was in the form of loans to service debts.[74]

With more than $1.3 trillion foreign debt, the Third World and Eastern Europe were paying $95 billion annually in service through the 1990s. Like all the Third World recovering from debt crisis shock, Peru, Nigeria, and Indonesia endured sharply lower living standards, sustained very high debt-GNP ratios, failed to make economic progress, and suffered sociopolitical instability under authoritarian regimes opposed by insurgent groups. Resulting in 30 to 70 percent wage reductions in the Third World, the debt crisis entailed that 60 million more Latin Americans lived in poverty, affecting especially children and women living in slums. To help meet foreign debt obligations, Third World countries ignored environmental concerns like deforestation and strip mining, thus environmental degradation was exacerbated. More than half of Latin Americans lived below the poverty line in the 1980s, and a much higher percentage of Africans. By contrast, southern Europe were rapidly closing the per capita income gap with western Europe, and making rapid progress in education, health, and social welfare.[75]

Under the auspices of the EEC and with the help of grants, Spain, Portugal, and Greece were able to establish representative institutions that reflected the changing division of labor. Southern Europe was as concerned as most of the world not just about U.S. resolve to impose Reaganomics on other countries, but to preserve U.S. hegemony and escalated arms race to the point of destabilizing the world. Despite U.S.-IFI pressures, southern Europe's dependency relationship with the U.S. lessened after the mid-1970s, the state was strengthened despite Reaganomics, labor unions were free from authoritarian control, and society became more pluralistic. However, foreign capital actually played a larger role in the last quarter of the century, and capital accumulation was actually facilitated not curbed by EEC integration.[76]

Politically the 1980s was a decade of polarizing trends between southern Europe whose voters backed Socialist parties, and the U.S. and UK which had ultra-conservative governments and advocated patron-client relationships become even stronger amid the Third World debt crisis. Though the U.S. tried to take credit for spreading democracy by spreading Reaganomics across the world, authoritarian regimes in the Third World, from the Philippines to Argentina, actually fell victim to the debt crisis. Primary producers had to export more surplus to service the foreign debts, while their workers and peasants paid the price under hyperinflation, followed by austerity which entailed currency devaluation and drop in wages.[77]

Because the U.S. dollar was overvalued by 35 percent in the first half of the 1980s, the Third World which was paying foreign debt in dollars experienced decapitalization that was artificially high, especially given the dollar's inconvertibility into gold under such conditions. Because of IMF austerity programs that weakened foreign currencies and kept the dollar artificially high, the sale of Third World assets during the contracting cycle was a bonanza for U.S. investors. The combination of the artificially strong dollar that precipitated deteriorating terms of trade for the Third World, and debt readjustment amid recessionary conditions were partial reasons for Latin America's debt jumping from $100 billion in 1980 to $464 billion in 1986.[78]

The Reagan administration's macro-economic policies of tax reductions for the wealthy, massive spending devoted mostly to defense and domestic security like prisons and the phantom "war on drugs," $500 billion to bail out the savings and loan banks, and a sharp rise in private spending resulted in the U.S. becoming the world's largest debtor. Though the overall U.S. deficit as a percentage of GDP during the 1980s was higher than Indonesia's and almost equal to non-oil-producing countries, the massive transfer of capital from the Third World to the G-7, especially to the U.S., helped finance higher defense spending, the savings and loan crisis, and corporate mergers and acquisitions.[79]

Because the EEC and Japan were challenging and in some cases prevailing in international political and economic issues, the U.S. used its dominant economic and military position in the world and its patron-client relationships with the Third World to compete effectively within the G-7. While the U.S. government deficit spending and trade deficit benefited western Europe and Japan, only the U.S. with the strongest economy and reserve currency could determined macroeconomic policy in the world. Though western Europe and Japan could influence the modality of the patron-client integration model, the U.S. still had the power to pursue a unilateral course at will, to distribute the benefits and costs to different countries within the G-7, and to instigate competition and rivalries among them, and between them and their Third World trading partners. Hence, southern Europe, like the Third World, remained very respectful and obsequious of America's hyperpuissance, in no small measure as leverage within the EU.[80]

In the 1980s southern Europe under Socialist regimes followed the U.S. lead in deficit spending and greater allocations for defense, but it was not affected by the wild fluctuations of Third World financial and trade trends. This was in large measure because southern Europe was no longer under the patron-client model, and enjoyed stability through its EEC association not afforded to Third World or East European debtors. Despite the leftist populist rhetoric designed for domestic consumption, Socialist Spain, Greece, and Portugal, were more interested in economic development through greater integration with the west under a more equitable and a symmetrical integration model, rather than in addressing maldistribution of wealth and social inequality by introducing welfare programs comparable to northwest Europe.

Merely an affirmation of a centrist orientation, southern European Socialism did not entail going the route of Norway or Sweden. Deradicalizing the masses by co-opting them through trade unions and various wings within the larger umbrella Socialist parties, southern European Socialists were aided by Euro-Communism's reformist platform, by a wide perception that the Soviet bloc was declining as evidenced by its increasing economic integration with the capitalist west, and by the orientation of France under Socialist president Francois Mitterand.[81]

When the Socialist regimes opted for economic development and cooperated with the IFIs to strengthen capital at the expense of labor while rationalizing the economy and modernizing social institutions to conform to EEC standards, there was no place politically for the lower middle class or trade unions to turn. By contrast, Indonesia, Nigeria, Peru and underdeveloped countries operating under the patron-client model did not have southern Europe's regional safety net. Whereas the G-7 and IFIs historically imposed sectoral restrictions on how Third World countries could utilize loans, such restrictions were absent for southern Europe once it was part of the EEC. Is it any wonder, therefore, that perceptions of U.S. foreign policy in Africa, the Middle East, Latin America, and southeast Asia range from malign neglect, to aggressive unilateralism based on military power, to failed implementation of publicly-stated policies like helping to fight widespread epidemics and famine?[82]

During the 1980s market liberalization accelerated after prime minister Thatcher and president Reagan pursued an ideological foreign policy based on military solutions, empowering the private sector by various means ranging from tax breaks to subsidies, and weakening trade unions and social services. Whereas in Europe and in most of the world the meaning of the word "democracy" includes social, economic, and environmental justice, Thatcher-Reagan-style democracy was equated with the supply-side economics and the culture of consumerism, globalization under the patron-client model, and coercive diplomacy for countries resisting. After the era of authoritarianism in Portugal, Greece, and Spain, and in the aftermath of the Third World debt crisis, the U.S., Japan, the EEC, the IFIs, and the corporate media inculcated into the masses the notion that democracy can only be achieved through integration that entails suspending social and environmental justice. Besides the IMF and the World Bank, Anglo-American think tanks played salient roles in influencing the political economies of the world.[83]

After Greece joined the EEC in 1981, followed by Spain and Portugal in 1986, European integration entailed strengthening international capital. But there were also benefits across the board, a case that cannot be made for Indonesia, Nigeria, and Peru operating under the patron-client model. Because it was EEC policy to improve the basic infrastructure and human capital of its weaker members, and to elevate them in many socioeconomic indicators to western Europe's level, Spain, Greece, and Portugal benefited from EEC budget transfers and hundreds of policy directives as a prerequisite to membership. Though EEC agricultural subsidies concentrated in Southern Europe's richest regions, some stability was injected into the rural economy. Whereas Spain had a regional development policy since the late 1960s, Portugal and Greece did not, despite their official claims to the contrary. Once they joined the EEC, funding helped all three countries to develop more robust regional policies, though they do not compare favorably with those of the G-7.[84]

The global economic, social, and political consequences of liberalization, privatization, and integration ultimately affected income redistribution from the lower classes to the upper income groups, not just in the Third World, but in the entire world. Wage inequality during the debt crisis of the 1980s amid greater global integration, privatization, and liberalization naturally entailed that labor in the Third World did not fare well in comparison with their southern European counterparts where job security, relatively strong unions, the welfare state, and minimum wages were higher. Regardless of integration models, from 1980 to the mid-1990s labor's share of income declined across the entire world, as disinflationary policies went into effect.

The IFIs, U.S., and EEC advised countries to strengthen the private sector by either selling public enterprises, using them to strengthen the private sector, or making them operate on the basis of the private business model. This was the case with both Portugal's *Investimentos Comercio e Turismo de Portugal* (ICEP) and Spain's *Instituto Nacional de Industria* (INI), which operated some 80 companies, including the domestic auto manufacturer SEAT. To qualify for loans, INI and ICEP cooperated with the World Bank, IMF, EEC, and U.S. in strengthening the private sector and internationalizing the economy.[85]

The IMF made no secret that its policies in southern Europe and the Third World joined by former Communist countries were designed to engender stabilization largely by restraining wages to curb consumer demand, restrain credit and the money supply, liberalize imports, and keep national currencies low to stimulate exports and invite foreign capital investment. In the end, the net result was massive income transfer from labor to capital, again affecting women and children more than adult males, and from the semi-developed and underdeveloped countries to the G-7. As income disparity rises between northern and southern hemispheres, contraband trade also rises, especially narcotics. From the coca farmers of Peru and poppy farmers of the Golden

Crescent, the fight against illegal drugs results in higher defense costs for the G-7 and their allies, largely because drugs in some cases like Afghanistan under the Taliban fund anti-U.S. regimes, while others like Colombia fund guerrilla groups.[86]

The escalating global militarization led by the U.S. during the Cold War absorbed 6 percent of global GNP by 1980, only to skyrocket after the Reagan administration accelerated the arms race by adding the Strategic Defense Initiative (SDI). By the end of the century U.S. defense spending was 40 percent of the world's total and heading much higher. U.S. defense spending entailed that other countries rich and poor had to spend more thus diverting resources from the civilian economy. A testament to the Cold War's detrimental impact on semi-developed and underdeveloped countries, from 1960 to 1980 military spending rose 4.5 times, while GNP rose 3 times. The economic and social consequences of militarization entailed that resources were diverted from the civilian sector to parasitic defense areas that helped keep Third World authoritarian regimes in power while enriching weapons manufacturers mostly in the G-7.

Whether in Portugal, Spain, Greece, Indonesia, or Turkey, U.S. economic aid was invariably linked to negotiations on U.S. military bases, strategic, diplomatic, and economic interests. Defense spending in underdeveloped and semi-developed countries historically was linked either to a regional conflict as in Greece and Turkey, or to domestic developments caused by external shocks rather than external military threats. Indonesia, Nigeria, Philippines, and other underdeveloped countries suffered political and social instability during the 1980s when IMF stabilization programs precipitated labor strikes and social unrest that turned violent in some cases, thereby prompting governments to raise national security spending.[87]

Throughout the Cold War, but especially during the Reagan administration when "containment militarism" based on NSC #68 returned as an integral part of the Reagan Doctrine of interventionism and coercive diplomacy, defense spending across the globe reinforced the patron-client integration model. Not just Indonesia, Nigeria, and Peru which always had a strong military presence behind the government, but even Socialist southern Europe devoted billions of dollars to purchase aircraft and other hardware mostly from companies in the G-7 countries.

Even when East-West tensions eased after Mikhail Gorbachev and Reagan held the Reykjavik summit in 1987, regional conflicts whether between India and Pakistan over Kashmir, Israel and the Arab states, South Africa and its neighbors, and Greece and Turkey meant high defense expenditures, G-7 defense contractors lobbying and government loans to purchase the weapons exacerbated the process. An integral part of foreign borrowing, defense-related loans contributed to financial dependence, lower living standards, monetary inflation, and rising foreign debt, and wealth redistribution toward upper income groups and the G-7.[88]

Globalization under American Hyperpuissance

During the late 1980s and 1990s the trends of deregulation, privatization, and above all globalization, a euphemism for accelerated integration and mergers of multinational corporations and selling publicly-owned assets, undercut the modest socioeconomic progress of workers and peasants in the past fifteen years across southern Europe and the Third World's ability to lessen its foreign dependence, and provide for its people while protecting the environment. In the late 1980s the EEC, supported by the IMF, World Bank, OECD and U.S., demanded that public sectors like petroleum comply with "single-market" requirements. Consequently, publicly-owned companies from oil and natural gas to industrial entities were partially sold to private domestic and foreign shareholders. The same model was applied to the Third World. In the process, such companies which had minority state ownership downsized their labor force and curbed wage and benefits for their workers.[89]

Some results of capital concentration included heightened radicalism in the form of militant anti-Americanism and widespread resistance to globalization identified with the IFIs and Americanization, though the EU and Japan are U.S. partners in globalization. World public opinion notwithstanding, there is hardly a shortage of neoliberal apologists arguing that globalization will result in lower unemployment, higher living standards, and freedom and democracy across the world, arguments repeated since Bretton Woods. Without considering the history of global integration under the patron-client model which exacerbates poverty and socioeconomic inequality, while it gives rise to authoritarianism and violates national sovereignty, during the 1990s many scholars, politicians, and journalists became euphoric about the U.S. winning the Cold War and securing even more frontiers in Eurasia to integrate under its hegemony. Was there any alternative for underdeveloped countries to the patron-client model in a world of a single superpower that declared a New World Order was upon us?[90]

Globalization entailed that neither southern Europe operating under the EU interdependent model in the 1990s, nor the Third World under the patron-client model could escape the more systematic method of capital accumulation. Nor did the end of Communism entail the triumph of democracy either in Eurasia or Third World as neo-liberals contend. Authoritarian rule, mobster-based economy composed of oligarch monopolists, about half of the population living in poverty, old ladies selling drugs in the street corners of Moscow, international prostitution rings from Kiev to Singapore, and polarizing socioeconomic conditions throughout the former Communist countries as a triumph of the market-system are hardly worthy of celebration. Far from a panacea for semi-developed and underdeveloped areas or for workers in the G-7, globalization is merely a higher stage of capitalism.[91]

With the reorganization of GATT into the World Trade Organization (WTO) that would integrate former Communist countries and China, the new frontiers of capitalism expanded substantially during the Clinton administration's new version of "Dollar Diplomacy." Because the superiority of the market economy and by implication of Pax Americana triumphed over Communism, the U.S. and its junior partners earned the right to re-impose hegemony on the rest of the world. Though India's embrace of globalization was a major factor in strengthening the patron-client model in the 1990s, China's integration was by far the most significant development, as hundreds of billions in foreign investment poured from all over the world to take advantage of cheap labor, the largest market, and fastest growing economy in the world. Though Japan clearly benefited from China's and India's rapid integration and deregulation in the 1990s, the U.S. reinforced the patron-client model, ignoring not only child labor abuses, but everything from low-wage labor to environmental degradation. Because of low wages in China's factories and India's outsourcing office complexes, downward wage pressures were felt on a global scale after 1990.[92]

Critical of public enterprises in the Third World and Europe, the IFIs and the U.S. wanted governments around the world to pass legislation to streamline and privatize public enterprises. But there was no mention of taxpayers bailing out the savings and loan banks, providing guaranteed loans to private corporations like Chrysler and Harley-Davidson, or offering massive tax breaks in addition to those by local and state governments to strengthen capital. Amid the disintegration of the Communist bloc, the privatization euphoria was so sweeping that it was simply assumed that any public enterprise in any country and under any circumstances was contrary to public interest, while anything privately held was the only solution. A blatant hypocrisy of the advanced capitalist countries since Bretton Woods, they directly and indirectly through the IFIs imposed liberalization on underdeveloped countries, while preserving circuitous privileges of protectionism for themselves.[93]

Rather than acquiesce to the IMF-U.S. prescription of mass firings of public employees, southern European and Third World governments were asking for help to secure employment for the dismissed workers. It is no secret that in southern Europe and even more so in Indonesia, Nigeria and Peru, politicians use public enterprises to reward their constituents with jobs, not much differently than mayors in Chicago or Philadelphia. Many public firms operated very inefficiently, there was systemic corruption, and they contribute to public debt which lowers living standards. From 1980 to 1990 the Third World suffered capital outflow of between $100 billion and $200 billion. In 1993 Spain's public foreign debt was $90 billion, Portugal's $13.1 billion in 1997, and Greece had a $41.9 billion debt.

The larger issue associated with public foreign debt is who benefits and who loses, literally who lives and how or whether they live. And what are the immediate and long-term costs and benefits to the national economy and to a country's institutions and social structure? Despite the persistence of patronage networks and crony capitalism in southern Europe, even after becoming full members of the EEC, their institutions and policies reflected those of the G-7, while no comparable structural changes took place in Nigeria, Indonesia, Peru, or in the rest of the Third World.[94]

Debatable whether the privatization solution was socially, economically, or politically prudent for all advanced capitalist countries from Sweden to Japan with private sector job opportunities, it was certainly clear that in semi-developed and underdeveloped countries privatization entailed mass unemployment and lower living standards. Even in Great Britain privatization was far from the ideal alternative to public enterprises considering the record of the railroad system since privatization, and there were major social and economic costs without any social benefits that had been promised. Transferring public wealth into private ownership, thereby lowering costs by lowering wages was a trend that the U.S., multilateral banks, and to a lesser extent the EU were advising, but the result was greater global integration, more capital concentration, and socioeconomic and geographic inequality.[95]

Characterized by intense economic integration on a world scale, sharp rise in trade, stronger roles of multilateral institutions and multinational corporations in society, and weaker role by the sovereign state, especially in underdeveloped and semi-developed countries, globalization is a transformation policy that precludes plausible options for different countries with unique needs. An example of the bad public policy choices resulting from globalization is the sale of the Ukrainian steel company sold for half of its assessed value. Though U.S. Steel and British LMN Group, owned by Indian billionaire Lakshmi Mittal, offered $1.5 billion for the company, the government sold the company to corrupt oligarchs led by the president's son-in-law. Typical of the capitalist system in former Communist bloc countries where the line of legal and subterranean economies are non-existent, the IFIs along with the EU and U.S. had been urging the former Communist countries to privatize public enterprises.

Seeking to dominate steel in the former Communist countries, in 2002 LMN purchased the Romanian steel company SIDEX, one of the worst polluters in the Balkans. Faced with the choice of selling its largest steel company to foreign investors or local oligarchs in the name of economic nationalism, the Ukrainian government was deprived of the option of statism which has been an anathema to globalization advocates, though exceptions are made for advanced capitalist countries. Public companies and key industries in the former Communist bloc, southern Europe, and Third World have been sold to foreign investors at a very high cost to workers who lost jobs, to consumers who pay higher prices, and to the environment.[96]

Globalization has had a similar impact on the pharmaceutical and food industry. A tragic result of the patron-client model can be illustrated in the manner that the U.S. and the pharmaceutical industry have been operating to preclude competition, and to literally condemn millions of patients to death. Because of the giant drug companies' resistance to permit generic drugs manufactured by companies in Brazil, Argentina, and India among others, 98 percent of HIV-aids African patients do not have access to drugs. Where the state can subsidize generic manufacturers to save millions of lives, the U.S. and its junior partners have fought such efforts which are antithetical to globalization, and all in the name of preserving drug patents, technological superiority, and immense profits against unauthorized use by foreign competitors.

By contrast, the U.S. has been lobbying to sell more genetically-modified foods around the world, much to the concern of scientists who have raised concern about the health consequences of such foodstuffs. Moreover, processed foods, agrochemicals, and hybrid seed business dominated by multinationals have been displacing small farmers throughout the World and driving food prices higher. In addition, the demand for meat and processed food products in the advanced capitalist countries drive agricultural prices higher as more land is devoted to animal feed and export commodities. The products/services demand in the advanced capitalist countries for the latest medical care, technology, wearing apparel, foodstuffs, automobiles, etc., determines what Third World people produce, what they consume, and how they live.[97]

The triumph of markets over the state has had a profound impact on the nature of the media that serves not merely as a passive conduit, but actively promotes the corporate and state policies and goals in preserving the domestic social order and international system. Besides the consolidation of corporate giants owning media outlets that control what news is reported and how it is reported, there has been a disturbing trend of corporations dependent on government contracts receiving for public works and defense owning all types of media outlets. Besides GE, Time Warner, News-Corp, among the more well-known names that illustrate this case, in France much of the media is owned by billionaire Serge Dassault, of the aircraft company of the same name, who is linked to the Bouygues group specializing in public works. In Italy the Berlusconi family which owns almost half of the country's media is also in politics with Silvio Berlusconi as premier. Because media companies are part of defense and public works companies that receive government contracts, or benefit from government legislation, the interests of the state and corporate capital are more intertwined than ever.

News organizations in the G-7 are homogenized and increasingly tabloid-like designed to promote the market system and socioeconomic and political status quo, deflecting from serious issues confronting people's lives and increasingly focusing on entertainment and sensationalist stories. The tabloid populist influence has spread to semi-developed and underdeveloped countries, including the former Communist countries, which emulate the media in the G-7. Instead of critically analyzing all facets of social, economic, and political issues, examining the root causes of conflicts from all perspectives, holding political and business leaders up to public scrutiny and accountability, the corporate media reflects, serves, and legitimizes the power structure and the world economy of which it is an integral part.[98]

Whether it is steel, pharmaceuticals, foodstuffs, or the media, the patron-client model precludes serving the best interests of people in the client countries. Redefining the patron-client and interdependent models, globalization has entailed greater concentration of existing markets from media to hotels and restaurants. While west European and U.S. companies took control of key sectors in Spain's economy, within five years after EEC membership, there were 1,800 Spanish enterprises in Portugal, controlling key industries in the 1990s. Forty percent of Portugal's bank assets were under the control of Spanish banks. Portugese businessmen, politicians and intellectuals feared that membership in the EEC entailed subordinating the economy and Portugese identity to Spain. Such fears were shared by Peru which had sold off key assets to Spanish companies as well. Because foreign capital dominated major sectors of the economies in Portugal and Greece, both countries sought more underdeveloped markets to exploit.

Greece looked to the Balkans and the trans-Caspian region, while Portugal sought greater market share in Africa and Brazil, and to a lesser extent in eastern Europe. Therefore, the inter-dependent model the geographic polarization was carried onto a new phase during the 1990s. With the aid of the state and the backing of the EU, the weaker EU countries maintained their semi-periphery role by exploiting smaller markets in underdeveloped countries. By the end of 2000, popular opposition to globalization synonymous with U.S. foreign policy was more than 75 percent across southern Europe. It was much higher in many Third World countries, like Muslim Indonesia where Suharto, his cronies, and the multinationals had raped the country's wealth and left behind a massive debt before he stepped down in 1998.[99]

Southern Europe has been able to cope with globalization much better under the EU umbrella than Third World countries remaining under the patron-client model, despite enclaves of opulence in large cities. As institutions in Spain, Portugal, and Greece evolved to resemble those of western Europe economically, politically, socially, and culturally in the last quarter of the 20th century, their development, governments, and popular attitudes toward foreign policy and the U.S. have reflected a European identity. Even before the Maastricht Treaty in 1992 and the European Monetary Union in 1999 paving the road toward convergence and the bid of a number of former East European countries to join the EU, there were multiple signs of competition and divergence between Washington and its junior partners across the Atlantic.

In areas ranging from foreign policy, trade, the environment, and the degree to which fiscal policy must serve a social component, European governments to a degree reflect public opinion and regional bloc interests. EU corporate interests and the conservative political and military elites, however, are more closely aligned to the U.S. As the GNP of the ever-expanding EU is fast approaching that of the U.S., antagonisms at various levels from foreign policy and defense to trade and the environment have intensified since Charles de Gaulle first challenged Pax Americana, but cooperation remains a matter of mutual self-interest. Many countries enthusiastically await to join the EU and others wish to emulate its success. By contrast, regional integration schemes based on the patron-client model that the U.S. has helped to forge have not met with comparable success for the client states.[100]

Celebrating the triumph of capitalism and western bourgeois political system, Francis Fukuyama's *The End of History and the Last Man* became one of many neoliberal bibles in the 1990s. Projecting the impression that the world has no choice but to accept the Americentric world system, all focus was on the core states and successes of the elites, without taking into account the billions suffering as a result of a polarizing world system.[101]

Teleological historiography from euphoric ideologues notwithstanding, the triumph of neoliberalism and globalization have been reserved for the socioeconomic elites and wealthy nations, especially the U.S. as the leader. Though the end of the Cold War entailed reconfiguration of the global power structure that has been evolving toward economic polycentrism since the 1960s, few people around the world disagree with French foreign minister Hubert Vedrine that the U.S. achieved *hyperpuissance* in all categories from economic to military, all sources of its power to superimpose transformation policy.[102]

Regardless of how the Europeans and the rest of the world view U.S. *hyperpuissance*, the empire has been displaying signs of aging, and the historical dialectic of the patron-client model may not have the kind of future that globalization advocates imagine. The end of the Cold War has changed the justification for the patron-client model, while new power centers are seeking influence for macroeconomic policy. Challenging the Americentric patron-client model in which the G-7 participate, the EU has forged an integration model designed to rationalize the economy, harmonize sociopolitical interests, and lessen international tensions within the hierarchical regional bloc.

In addition, China uses its leverage with the G-7 to ensure its regional and global influence poses a challenge to the U.S., as does Japan at the core of the Pacific Rim. The Russian Federation has also been attempting to forge its own regional bloc and prevent erosion of its position by the EU and the U.S. competing for influence and raw materials in the trans-Caspian region. The political price paid for the patron-client model is perpetual instability and turmoil where the American Leviathan has the opportunity to superimpose its authority unilaterally and/or in cooperation with its G-7 partners, depending on the situation. A world system operating under different integration models and different sets of rules for the rich and poor nations is doomed to fail.[103]

Notes

1. Immanuel Wallerstein, *The Capitalist World-Economy* (Cambridge, 1979), pp. 37-48; Immanuel Wallerstein, *The Modern World System: Capitalist Agriculture and the Origins of the European World-Economy* (New York, 1980).

2. A. D. Lignadis, *E Xeniki Exartisis kata tin Diadromin tou Ellinikou Kratous, 1821-1945.* [Foreign Dependence in the course of the modern Greek state, 1821-1945] (Athens, 1975).

3. Neil Smith, *American Empire: Roosevelt's Geographer and the Prelude to Globalization* (Berkeley, 2003); F. L. Block, *The Origins of International Economic Disorder* (Berkeley, 1977), pp. 40-55.

4. Toyoo Gyohten, "The United States in the Global Financial Arena," in D. M. Malone and Yuen Foong Khong (eds), *Unilateralism and U.S. Foreign Policy* (Boulder, 2003), pp. 285-96; J. H. Makin, *The Global Debt Crisis: America's Growing Involvement* (New York, 1984), pp. 173-75.

5. Gabriel Kolko, *Confronting the Third World: United States Foreign Policy, 1945-1980* (New York, 1981); J. V. Kofas, "U.S. Foreign Policy and the World Federation of Trade Unions," *Diplomatic History*, 26/1 (2002): 21-61; Jose Luis Rubio, *Dependencia y liberacion en el sindicalismo iberoamericano* (Madrid, 1977), pp. 125-50; Pedro Reiser, *L'Organisation Regionale Inteameriaine des Travaileurs de la Confederation Internationale de Syndicats Libres de 1951 a 1961* (Paris, 1962).

6. Eric Helleiner, *States and the Reemergence of Global Finance: From Bretton Woods to the 1990s* (Ithaca, NY, 1994), pp. 52-60; Shigeto Tsru, *Japan's Capitalism: Creative Defeat and Beyond* (Cambridge, 1993), pp. 49-70; Rogelio Frigerio, *La Integracion Regional Instrumento del Monopolio* (Buenos Aires, 1968), pp. 28-30; F. L. Block, *The Origins of International Economic Disorder* (Berkeley, CA, 1977), pp. 79-82; Kofas, *Foreign Debt and Underdevelopment*, pp. 48-50; D. Dowd, *Capitalism and its Economics: A Critical History* (London, 2000), pp. 146-47.

7. Dwight D. Eisenhower Library, *Oral History Interview*, Eugene Black, pp. 21-4; E. S. Mason and R. E. Asher, *The World Bank since Bretton Woods* (Washington, D.C., 1973), pp. 112-15; Melvin P. Leffler, *A Preponderance of Power: National Security, the Truman Administration, and the Cold War* (Stanford, 1992), pp. 463-69; Joyce and Gabriel Kolko, *The Limits of Power: the World and United States Foreign Policy, 1945-1954* (New York, 1972), pp. 519-28; Alfred Eckes, Jr., *The United States and the Global Struggle for Minerals* (Austin, TX, 1979), pp. 155-60; Paul Baran and Paul Sweezy, *Monopoly Capital* (New York, 1966), pp. 159-93; F. S. Northedge, *Descent from Power* (London, 1974), pp. 40-50.

8. J. V. Kofas, *Dependence and Underdevelopment in Colombia* (Tempe, Arizona, 1986), pp. 92-3, 117-18; Bela Kadar, *Problems of Economic Growth in Latin America* (New York, 1980), pp. 90-2.

9. SDNA 852.10/1352, No. 270; SDNA 852.10/10-2352, No. 296; SDNA 852.10/2952, No.

330; SDNA 852.10/10-3152, No. 2070; SDNA 852.10/8-2853 No. 9649; J. V. Kofas, *Colombia*, pp. 103-08; Kofas, *Foreign Debt and Underdevelopment*, pp. 157-58; Nixon Project, WHCF, Box 60, Peru, C0-119, 10 February 1970.

10. Eisenhower Library, U.S. Commission on Foreign Economic Policy, Box 44, Staff Report, Area 2, No. 1, Alfred Neal to Commission, 19 November 1953; State Department, National Archives (hereafter SDNA), FN 3- OECD, 28 February 1973; Ibid., 28 June 1973; Payer, *The Debt Trap*, p. 170.

11. S. G. Hansen, *Economic Development in Latin America* (Westport, CT, 1974), pp. 428-30; Dowd, *Capitalism*, pp. 147-48; Kofas, *Foreign Debt and Underdevelopment*, pp. 27-8.

12. R. Solomon, *The International Monetary System, 1945-1976* (New York, 1977), pp. 18-25; S. B. Clough and C. W. Cole, *Economic History of Europe* (Boston, 1966), pp. 879-83; W. Diebold Jr., *The Schuman Plan* (New York, 1959); Alan Milward et al., *The European Rescue of the Nation-State* (London, 1992); Stuart de la Mahotiere, *Towards One Europe* (Baltimore, 1970), pp. 20-22; R. K. Schaeffer, *Understanding Globalization* (Lanham, MD, 2003), p. 23

13. Theotonio Dos Santos, "Latin American Development: Past, Present, and Future," in *Underdevelopment of Development*, op cit., pp. 158-59; Amin, "Economic Catastrophe in Africa," pp. 201, 207.

14. Ching-yuan Lin, *Latin America vs East Asia: A Comparative Development Perspective* (Armonk, NY, 1989), pp. 70-5; Gustav Ranis, "Why Latin America Borrowed when East Asia Exported," in R. J. Salvucci (ed), *Latin America and the World Economy* (Lexington, MA, 1996), pp. 154-64.

15. J. V. Kofas, *The Sword of Damocles: U.S. Financial Hegemony in Colombia and Chile* (Westport, CT, 2002), pp. 13-14; Nick Butler, *The International Grain Trade* (New York, 1986), pp. 30-130.

16. Pitcher, M. Anne, *Politics in the Portugese Empire* (Oxford, 1993); A. Glen Mower, Jr., *The European Community and Latin America* (Westport, CT, 1982), pp. 39-43; Ernst Mandel, *Europe vs. America* (New York, 1970), pp. 80-84; Peter Evans, *Dependent Development: The Alliance of Multinational, State, and Local Capital in Brazil* (Princeton, 1979).

17. Nicos Poulantzas, *The Crisis of Dictatorships* (Atlantic Highlands, NJ, 1976), pp. 10-11.

18. Furtado, *L'Amerique Latine*, pp. 93-4; Melvin Gurtov, *The United States against the Third World* (New York, 1974), pp. 88-90; Rafael Urriola, *Crisis: FMI y neo-liberalismo* (Quito, 1984), pp. 10-23.

19. Kofas, *Foreign Debt and Underdevelopment*, pp. 68-9; IMF C/Greece/420.1, Exchange Restrictions Consultations, 1962/63, Article XIV, 24 June 1963, Xenophon Zolotas and Ernst Sturc.

20. Andrew Shennan, *de Gaulle* (London, 1993), p. 119; F.O. 371/179305, No. 36, 1 February 1963; F.O. 371/179305, No. MRD127, 31 January 1963; F.O. 371/179305, No. 1035, 5 February 1963; F.O. 371/179305, No. CS1022/4, 6 March 1963; F.O. 371/179305, No. CS 1022/5, 7 March 1963.

21. Semih Vaner, "La Turquie, la Grece et les Grandes Puissances: L'une contre l'autre, trois contre une ou chacune pour soi?" in Semih Vaner (ed), *Le Differend Greco-Turc* (Paris, 1988); Walker, *Cold War*, pp. 191-92; Kofas, *Under the Eagle's Claw*, pp. 69-70; Payer, *Debt Trap*, pp. 79-80; F.O. 371/152120, No. SC 60/38, 11 October 1960.

22. Richard Immerman, *The CIA in Guatemala* (Austin, TX, 1982); Kofas, *Under the Eagle's Claw*, pp. 87-93; Osvaldo Silva Galdames, *Breve Historia Contemporanea de Chile* (Mexico City, 1995), pp. 300-15.

23. E. S. Herman and F. Brodhead, *Demonstration Elections: U.S. Staged Elections in the Dominican Republic, Vietnam, and El Salvador* (Boston, 1984); Anibal Quijano Obregon, "El Peru en la Crisis de los Anos Treinta," in Luis Antezana E. et al. (eds), *America Latina en los Anos Trienta* (Mexico, 1977), pp. 119-21.

24. Hartmut Elsenhans, *La guerre d'Algerie, 1954-1962* (Paris, 1999); Joao de Melo, *Os Anos da guerra, 1961-1975: os portugeuses em Africa* (Lisbon, 1988).

25. F.O. 371/185744, No. CP1022/1, 16 February 1966; Ibid., No. 10274, 14 April 1966; *New York Times*, 17 March 1966; Nixon Project, NSC, Box 701, 20 August 1972. SDNA AID (US) 15-11 PORT, No. A-396, 24 June 1966.

26. Ford Library, Arthur Burns Papers, Box 69, IMF-IBRD Meeting, Nairobi, No. 73/20, 13 September 1973; IMF C/Greece/420.1, Exchange Restrictions Consultations, 1965/66, Final Statement, 9 June 1966; SDNA FN 15 Greece, A9, 8 July 1966.

27. WBA, General Negotiations, Box 3, Vol III, J. A. Holsen to Balassa, 1 May 1968. Even in 1984 the World Bank classified Portugal and Greece as developing, after analyzing all indicators from per capita income to health care, education, and foreign debt. WBA, General Negotiations, Box 3, V. N. Rajagopalan to E. F. Lari, 22 May 1984.

28. Giovanni Arrighi, "Fascism to Democratic Socialism: Logic and Limits of a Transition," in Giovanni Arrighi (eds), *Semiperipheral Development: The Politics of Southern Europe in the Twentieth Century* (Beverly Hills, 1985), pp. 264-66; Schaeffer, *Globalization*, pp. 313-14; Nixon Project, Country Files, Box 701, 7 March 1972, Helmut Sonnenfeldt and Bob Hormats to Kissinger.

29. Poulantzas, *Crisis of Dictatorships*, pp. 11-15; Kofas, *Under the Eagle's Claw*, pp. 184-85.

30. Teresa Hayter, *Aid as Imperialism* (New York, 1971), pp. 130-40; Emmanuel, *Unequal Exchange*, pp. 44-7.

31. David Gisselquist, *The Political Economics of International Bank Lending* (New York, 1981), pp. 109-12; Kofas, *The Sword of Damocles*, pp. 96-7; Guy de Carmoy, *The Foreign Policies of France, 1948-1968* (Chicago: University of Chicago, 1970), pp. 23-4.

32. Gyohten, "Global Financial Arena," pp. 285-90; R. Z. Lawrence, "Emerging Regional Arrangements: Building Blocks or Stumbling Bocks," in *International Political Economy: Perspectives on Global Power and Wealth* (New York, 1995), pp. 404-14; Schaeffer, *Globalization*, p. 290.

33. Urriola, *FMI y neo-liberalismo*, pp. 7-31; Kofas, *Sword of Damocles*, pp. xii-xvi.

34. Iriye, *Global Community*, pp. 64, 79; Walker, *Cold War*, pp. 106-07; Aseniero, "Asia and

the World System," op cit., p. 179; Samir Amin, "On the Origins of the Economic Catastrophe in Africa," in S. C. Chew and R. A. Denemark (eds), *The Underdevelopment of Development* (Beverly Hills, 1996), pp. 204-05; H. W. Brands, *Into the Labyrinth: The United States and the Middle East* (New York, 1994), p. 57; Payer, *Debt Trap*, pp. 170-75.

35. SDNA FN 3-OECD, 28 February 1973; Ibid., 28 June 1973; J. P. Lewis, *Quite Crisis in India* (Garden City, NY, 1964), pp. 269-286; Dos Santos, "Latin American Development," 162; Kofas, *Under the Eagle's Claw*, pp. 40-44; A. F. P. Bakker, *International Financial Institutions* (London, 1996), pp. 100-104.

36. OD 39/103, 12 September 1969; Payer, *Debt Trap*, pp. 28-31, 171-73; Kofas, *Sword of Damocles*, pp. 57-61; Harold Molineu, *U.S. Policy Toward Latin America* (Boulder, 1990), pp. 107-11; Evan Luard, *International Agencies: The Emerging Framework of Interdependence* (London, 1977), pp. 245-48.

37. F.O. 371/163653, AID-44, 2 March 1962; Ibid.-AID 105, 6 June 1962; Ibid., AID-174, 13 August 1962; Ibid., AID-193, 6 September 1962; Ibid., AID-220, 17 October 1962; Ibid., AID-251, 18 December 1962; F.O. 371/169514, No. 1, 2 January 1963.

38. F.O. 371/163846, No. 1112/40, 15 June 1962; Ibid., No. 79, 27 June 1962; Ibid., No. CT 1114/37, 6 July 1962; Ibid., No. 46, 10 July 1962; Ibid., No. 47, 10 July 1962; OD 34/332, 26 August 1970; Ibid., 28 August 1970; Ibid., 21 August 1970; G. S. Harris, *Troubled Alliance: Turkish-American Relations* (Washington, D.C., 1972), pp. 90-99.

39. SDNA 852.10/12-1758, No. 370; SDNA 852.131/1-2159, No. 441; Payer, *Debt Trap*, pp. 7, 88; J. V. Kofas, *The Struggle for Legitimacy: Latin American Labor and the United States* (Tempe, 1992), pp. 354-56.

40. SDNA, OD 39/103, 4 December 1968.

41. Reuters, 13 May 2004; World Bank, <www.worldbank.org> "The Costs of Corruption," 8 April 2004; Douglas Dowd, *Capitalism and its Economics* (London, 2000), pp. 208-09.

42. F.O. 371/185671, CE 1151/17, 27 August 1966; David Zenoff, *Private Enterprise in the Developing Countries* (Englewood Cliffs, NJ, 1969), pp. 104-110.

43. IMF, C/Greece/420.1 Exchange Restrictions Consultations, 1965/66, L. A. Whitcomme to Managing Director, 9 June 1966; Sophie Boutillier and Dimitri Uzundis, *La Grece Face a L'Europe: Dependance et indusrtialization truquee* (Paris, 1991), pp. 39-45.

44. WBA, Box 6 General Negotiations Vol. III, 16 April 1963, B. M. Cheek to Files; Kofas, *Colombia*, pp. 91-3; Mason and Asher, *World Bank*, pp. 500-14.

45. J. A. Rubin, *Your Hundred Billion Dollars* (New York, 1967), pp. 50-70; Rogelio Frigerio, *La integracion regional instrumento del monopolio* (Buenos Aires, 1968), pp. 26-29; Eduardo Galeano, *Las Venas obrietas de America Latina* (Madrid, 1993), pp. 40-46; R. J. Barnet, *Intervention and Revolution* (New York, 1968), pp. 143-235; Kofas, *Foreign Debt and Underdevelopment*, pp. 47-8; Tony Monteiro, "The CIA in Africa," in Howard Frazier (ed), *Uncloaking the CIA* (New York, 1978), pp. 130-33; William Minter, *Portugese Africa and the West* (New York, 1972), pp. 110-15.

46. Kofas, *Sword of Damocles*, pp. 12-14; Gavin, "American Monetary Policy," pp. 61-3.

47. Aseniero, "Asia and the World System," p. 179; Kofas, *Foreign Debt and Underdevelopment*, pp. 50-52; Payer, *Debt Trap*, pp. 28-30; Little, *Boom, Crisis, and Adjustment*, p. 14.

48. Ford Library, Arthur Burns, Box B69, IMF-IBRD Meeting-Nairobi, September 1973, Ashby Bladen, "The Collapse of the International Monetary System: Causes & Consequences"; M. S. Wionczek, "Integration and Development," *International Journal* 24 no. 3 (1969): 449-62; R. L. Genillard, "The Eurobond Market," in H. V. Pronchow (eds), *The Eurodollar* (Chicago, 1970), pp. 315-35.

49. Theotonio Dos Santos, "The Structure of Dependence," in K. T. Fann and D. C. Hodges (eds), *Readings in U.S. Imperialism* (Boston, 1971), p. 232; Rafael Urriola, *Crisis: FMI y neo-liberalismo* (Quito, Ecuador, 1985), pp. 3-30; Kofas, *Foreign Debt and Underdevelopment*, pp. 72-3; R. B. Du Boff, *Accumulation and Power: An Economic History of the United States* (Armonk, NY, 1989), pp. 110-13.

50. Ford Library, Arthur Burns Box B68, IMF-IBRD, no. 8, 25-27 September 1970; Ibid., no. 27, 22 September 1970; Ibid., "European Monetary Unification," 14 September 1970.

51. Dowd, *Capitalism*, pp. 147-49; M. M. Mochizuki, "To Change or to Contain: Dilemmas of American Policy Toward Japan," in K. A. Oye et al. (eds), *Eagle in a New World: American Grand Strategy in the Post-Cold War Era* (New York, 1992), pp. 347-50; Andrew Shennan, *de Gaulle* (London, 1993), pp. 117-19.

52. Francis J. Gavin, "The Gold Battles within the Cold War: American Monetary Policy and the Defense of Europe, 1960-1963," *Diplomatic History*, 26 (2002): 61-94; Schwartz, *States versus Markets*, pp. 222-29; National Archives, Nixon Project, WHCF, Box 60, Peru, CO-119, 13 February 1969, Willard Braker to *Time* & Henry Kissinger.

53. SDNA AID US-Nigeria, No. A-47, 25 June 1971; Ibid., No. A-106, 10 December 1971.

54. Ford Library, Arthur Burns Box B68, Federal Reserve File, 27 September 1971, IMF-IBRD Meetings, Press Release No. 2; Ibid., Box 65, International Monetary Crisis 3, 5 November 1971, David Willey to Coombs; Anne O. Krueger, "Origins of the Developing Countries' Debt Crisis, 1970-1982," *Journal of Development Economics*, 27/1 (1987): 165-86.

55. Glen Mower, Jr., *The European Community and Latin America* (Westport, CT:, 1982), pp. 39-45; Raymond Aron, *The Imperial Republic* (Englewood Cliffs, NJ, 1974), pp. 194-97.

56. Ford Library, Arthur Burns, Box 65, International Monetary Crisis 3, 5 November 1971, David Willey to Coombs; Robert Gilpin, *The Political Economy of International Relations* (Princeton, NJ, 1987), pp. 120-165.

57. Iriye, *Global Community*, pp. 128-29; Dowd, *Capitalism*, pp. 159-61.

58. SDNA, FN 11, 17 September 1970; Ibid., 8 September 1970; Ibid., A-109, 14 May 1973.

59. Kofas, *Sword of Damocles*, pp. 157-58; Peter Evans, "Shoes, OPIC, and the Unquestioning Persuasion: Multinational Corporations and U.S.-Brazilian Relations," in R. R. Fagen, *Capitalism and the State in Latin America* (Stanford, 1979), pp. 302-36; Barry Bluestone and B. Harrison, *The Deindustrialization of America* (New York, 1982), pp. 9-10; W. Adams and J. W. Brock, *The Bigness Complex* (New York, 1986), pp. 206-10; 26; Okita,

"Japan's Role in Asia," p. 26.

60. Ford Library, Arthur Burns Box B65, International Monetary Conference, 21 March 1971; Ibid., Box B69, IMF-IBRD Meeting, Nairobi, No. 73/20, 13 September 1973.

61. SDNA, FN 10 IMF, No. 1427, 16 October 1973.

62. Ford Library, Arthur Burns Box B72, International Monetary Meeting, 22 September 1977.

63. IMF, C/Portugal/1760, Stand-by Arrangements, 26 April 1977, L. A. Whittome to Managing Director.

64. Fold Library, WHCF, Box 23, FO3-2/CO 139, 6 January 1978, John J. Cavanaugh; IMF Press Release No. 77/78, 24 September 1977.

65. D. L. Cingranelli, *Ethics, American Foreign Policy, and the Third World* (New York, 1993), pp. 172-86. Jerry Sanders, *Peddlers of Crisis: The Committee on the Present Danger* (Boston, 1982), pp. 240-55.

66. Kofas, *Under the Eagle's Claw*, pp. 155-58; Dos Santos, "Underdevelopment," pp. 163-65.

67. Ford Library Arthur Burns, Box B61, 4 January 1978, Irene Cavanagh to Siegman; I. M. D. Little et al. *Boom, Crisis, and Adjustment* (Oxford, 1993), pp. 29-54.

68. Ford Library Arthur Burns, Box B72, IMF Wittenveen Facility, 21 September 1977, Anthony Solomon, Treasury under-Secretary to the sub-committee on Foreign Economic Policy.

69. Carter Library, Brzezinski Donated, Box 42, Weekly Report, File 3/79 to 6/79, Brzezinski to the President, 1 June 1979; Seth Lipski and Raphael Pura, "Indonesia: Testing Time for the New Order," *Foreign Affairs*, 57/1 (1978): 186-202; Mansoor Moadel, *Class, Politics, and Ideology in the Iranian Revolution* (New York, 1983), pp. 187-210; S. T. Hunter, *Iran and the World* (Bloomington, IN, 1990), pp. 54-9; McDougall, *Asia Pacific*, p. 76.

70. Saburo Okita, "Japan, China, and the United States," *Foreign Affairs*, 57/5 (1979): 1090-1110.

71. 110. Carter Library, NSA Staff, Horn/Special, Box 108, No. 3, Declaration of the Venice Summit, 22-23 June 1980; Carter Library, NSC Staff, Horn/Special, Box 108, 26 June 1980, Spanish Government's Statement on President Carter's Visit.

72. Otto Kreye, "The Debt Crisis Revisited," in "The Underdevelopment of Development," in Chew and Denemark, op. cit., pp. 119-20; Virgilio Pineda Roel, *Proceso y Crisis de las Economias Peruanas y Norte-Americana* (Lima: Editorial el Alba, 1984), p. 48; R. L. Ground, "A Survey and Critique of IMF Adjustment Programs in Latin America," in *Debt Adjustment and Renegotiation in Latin America*, Economic Commission for Latin America and the Caribbean (Boulder, 1986), pp. 128-33; Kofas, *Sword of Damocles*, pp. 178-82; Aseniero, "Asia and the World System," p. 171.

73. R. E. Feinberg, "Reaganomics and the Third World," in K. A. Oye et al. (eds), *Eagle Defiant* (Boston, 1983), pp. 148-58.

74. Little, *Boom, Crisis, and Adjustment*, pp. 92-3; Ariel Buira, "La promocion financiera y la condicionalidad del FMI," *El Trimestre* 50/197 (1983): 117-49; Cingranelli, *American Foreign Policy*, pp. 193-96; Rafael Urriola, *Crisis: FMI y neo-liberalismo* (Quito, 1985),

pp. 10-30; R. Devlin, "Private Banks, Debt, and the Bargaining Power of the Periphery: Theory and Practice," in Economic Commission for Latin America and the Caribbean (ed), *Debt, Adjustment, and Renegotiation in Latin America* (Boulder, 1986), pp. 5-28; Schaeffer, *Globalization*, pp. 95-6.

75. Kofas, *Under the Eagle's Claw*, pp. 15-6; Schaeffer, *Globalization*, p. 140; Little, *Boom, Crisis, and Adjustment*, pp. 94-6; Schwartz, *States versus Markets*, pp. 266-68; S. C. Chew and R. A. Denemark, "On Development and Underdevelopment," in S. C. Chew and R. A. Denemark, *The Underdevelopment of Development* (Beverly Hills, 1996), pp. 6-8.

76. Joseph Nye, Jr., "Understanding U.S. Strength," *Foreign Policy*, 72 (1988): 105-29; Sanders, *Peddlers of Crisis*, pp. 277-311.

77. Kofas, *Under the Eagle's Claw*, pp. 182-84; Schaeffer, *Globalization*, pp. 286-88.

78. Ricardo Alagia, "The External Debt," in M. A. Morris (ed), *Great Power Relations in Argentina, Chile and Antarctica* (London, 1990), pp. 133-35.

79. Schaeffer, *Globalization*, pp. 86-91; Little, *Boom, Crisis, and Adjustment*, pp. 318-20.

80. Miyohei Shinohara, "Japan as a World Economic Power," *ANNALS AAPSS*, 513 (1991): 12-26; Schwartz, *States versus Markets*, pp. 233-34.

81. Desmond Dinan, "The Transformation of the European Community," in Desmond Dinan (ed), *Ever Closer Union?* (Boulder, 1994), pp. 129-56; Alfonso Guerra, *Felipe Gonzalez: de Suresnes a la Moncloa/recuerdos e impresiones de Alfonso Guerra* (Madrid, 1984); T. A. Couloumbis, "Andreas Papandreou: the Style and Substance of Leadership," in T. C. Kariotis, *The Greek Socialist Experiment: Papandreou's Greece, 1981-1989* (New York, 1992); Bettino Craxi, *Il Progresso Italiano* (Milano, 1985-1989); Jean Lacouture, *Mitterand: Une histoire de Francais* (Paris, 1998).

82. WBA General Negotiations, POR-General, 27 August 1982, Jane Loos to Files; Francois Heisbourg, "American Hegemony? Perceptions of the U.S. Abroad," *Survival* (Winter 1999-2000): 5-19; C. Landsberg, "The United States and Africa: Malign Neglect," in *Unilateralism and U.S. Foreign Policy*, op cit., pp. 347-52; Yvonne Haddad Yazbeck, "Islamist Perceptions of U.S. Policy in the Middle East," in D. W. Lesch, *The Middle East and the United States* (Boulder, 1996).

83. Geoffrey Smith, *Reagan and Thatcher* (New York, 1991); Jeff McMahan *Regan and the World: Imperial Policy in the New Cold War* (New York, 1985).

84. WBA General Negotiations, Box 3, PO-Leap 15 June 1988, Ken Kwaku to Files; Fischer, *The United States and the European Union*, p. 108; *New York Times*, 14 June 1992; Francesc Morata, *La Union Europea: Procesos, actores y politicas* (Barcelona, 1998), pp. 378-82.

85. Juan F. Jimeno et al., "Integration and Inequality: Lessons from the Accession of Portugal and Spain in the EU," in The World Bank (ed), *Making Transition Work for Everyone: Poverty and Inequality in Europe and Central Asia* (Washington D.C. 2000), pp. 1-28; WBA General Negotiations, Spain-Leap 16 June 1983; Ibid., Portugal-Leap, 16 February 1994, Helena Cordeiro W. P. Thalwitz; Ibid., 25 October 1994, Elia Rodriguez to Julius Varallyay.

86. IMF Archives, C/Spain/810, Mission, 8 November 1979, L. A. Whittome to Managing Director; Schaeffer, *Globalization*, pp. 347-50; Meno Vellinga, "The War on Drugs and Why it Cannot be Won," *Journal of Third World Studies*, 17/2 (2000): 113-28; Mario Arrubla, *Estudios sobre el subdesarrollo colombiano* (Bogota, 1971), pp. 15-50.

87. SIPRI, *World Armaments and Disarmament*. (London, 1980), pp. xvii-xix; M T. Klare, and Cynthia Arnson, "Exporting Repression: U.S. Support for Authoritarianism in Latin America," in R. R. Fagen (ed), *Capitalism and the State in U.S.-Latin American Relations* (Stanford, 1979), pp. 138-168.

88. Jurgen-Heinz Axt and Heinz Kramer, *Entspannug im Agaisonflikt? Griechiesch-turkische Bezeihungennach Davos* (Baden-Baden, 1990), pp. 210-15,   Reagan Library, Nelson Ledsky Files, Box 92081, Turkey: An Increasing Strategic Asset for the U.S., 14 October 1987; J. M. Scott, *Deciding to Intervene: The Reagan Doctrine and American Foreign Policy* (Durham, 1996).

89. WBA, Box 328, Spain-General Negotiations, ES-LEAP, 12 March 1995, Richard Soto to Akin Oduolowu.

90. Schaeffer, *Globalization*, pp. 10-12; J. Micklethwait and A. Woodbridge, *A Future Perfect: The Challenge and Hidden Promise of Globalization* (New York, 2000).

91. S. E. Flynn, "Beyond Border Control," *Foreign Affairs*, 79/6 (2000): 61-2; Jennifer Turpin and L. A. Lorentzen, *The Gendered New World Order: Militarism, Development, and the Environment* (London, 1996); Schaeffer, *Globalization*, pp. 304-05.

92. John Stremlau, "Clinton's Dollar Diplomacy," *Foreign Policy*, 97 (1994): 18-35; Edward Hermann, *Triumph of the Market* (Boston, 1995); Asiniero, "Asia and the World-System," pp. 191-97.

93. Magnus Wijkman, "U.S. Trade Policy: Alternative Tacks or Parallel Tacks," in D. M. Malone and Yuen Foong Khong (eds), *Unilateralism and U.S. Foreign Policy* (Boulder, 2003), pp. 251-79.

94. Andre Gunder Frank, "The Underdevelopment of Development," in S. C. Chew and R. A. Denemark (eds), *The Underdevelopment of Development* (Beverly Hills, 1996), pp. 34-5; Kreye, "The Debt Crisis Revisited," in Ibid., pp. 115-25.

95. IMF C/Greece/420.3 Article IV Consultations 1990, Secretary to Members of the Executive Board, 25 May 1990.

96. *Financial Times*, 16 June 2004.

97. T. Barnett and A. Whiteside, *Aids in the Twenty-First Century: Disease and Globalization* (New York, 2003); M. M. Silverman et al. *Bad Medicine* (Stanford, 1992); Stavrianos, *Global Rift*, pp. 812-13; Peter Pringle, *Food Inc* (New York, 2003);   Schaeffer, *Globalization*, pp. 153-59, 223-25.

98. Joaquin Roy and Aimee Kanner, "Spain and Portugal: Betting on Europe," in E. E. Zeff and E. B. Pirro (eds), *The European Union and the Member States* (Boulder, 2001), p. 241; R. J. Barnet and R. E. Muller, *Global Reach: The Power of the Multinational Corporations* (New York, 1974), pp. 170-75; E. S. Herman and R. W. McChesney, *The Global Media:*

The Missionaries of Global Capitalism (London, 1997); R. W. McChesney, *Rich Media, Poor Democracy: Communication Politics in Dubious Times* (Champaign, IL, 1999).

99. *New York Times*, 14 June 1992; Kofas, *Under the Eagle's Claw*, pp. 127-28; Kyung Won Kim, "Trade Monetary Policy, and Democracy," in M. F. Plattner and A. Smolar (eds), *Globalization, Power, and Democracy* (Baltimore, 2000), pp. 126-27.

100. Luciano Monti, *I Fondi Strutturali per la coesione Europea* (Roma, 1996), pp. 33-9; Z. M. Beddoes, "From EMU to AMU," *Foreign Affairs*, 78/4 (1999): 8-13; P. H. Gordon, "Their Own Army?" *Foreign Affairs*, 79/4 (2000): 12-7; Fischer, *Globalization*, pp. 128-31.

101. Francis Fukuyama, *The End of History and the Last Man* (New York, 1993).

102. Martin Walker, "What the Europeans Think of Americans," *World Policy Journal*, 17/2 (2000): 26-38; Hubert Vedrine, *Face a l'hyperpuissance: textes et discours, 1995-2003* (Paris, 2003).

103. J. M. van Brabant, *Remaking Europe* (Lanham, MD, 1999), pp. 1-39; McDougall, *International Politics*, pp. 29-30, 37-42; Fischer, *The United States and the European Union*, pp. 6-7; Stephen Blank, "American Grand Strategy and the Transcaspian Region," *World Affairs*, 163/2 (2000): 65-79.

Chapter 2

Spain: From Patron-Client under Franco to Interdependent Integration under the EU

U.S. Aid and Spain Integration under Patron-Client, 1950-1957

Covering 195,988 square miles, Spain is approximately the size of Colorado and Wyoming combined, with a population of 35.5 million in 1975, or about three-and-half times larger than Greece or Portugal. On the eve to transition toward democracy in 1975, GNP was $74.6 billion, but the per capita income historically has been closer to its southern European counterparts. Spain spent about 3 percent of GNP on defense, proportionally about the same as Portugal and Greece. Though agriculture constituted the base of the economy, by 1970 Spain's manufacturing sector specialized in food processing, chemicals, rubber, footwear, machinery, textiles, and metal works. Industrialization was made possible largely by foreign investment that penetrated the Spanish economy after the first major round of liberalization in 1959 based on the advice of the IMF, World Bank, U.S., and EEC.[1]

General Francisco Franco seized power after the Civil War in 1939 and remained in power until his death in 1975. The ruling party provided jobs from the municipal level to the central government and for public enterprises, and rewarded certain firms beholden to the dictatorship. As in some Third World countries like Argentina, Brazil, and India, Spain's trade unions were an extension of the state until the mid-1970s. Headed by a government minister, the corporatist Spanish Syndical Organization included labor, employers, and government officials who collaborated with their Portugese counterparts. The Workers' Commissions posed a minor threat to the government-controlled labor central in a country where strikes were illegal. While large and medium-sized firms made considerable progress under Franco, labor did not fare nearly as well, especially as the IFIs were advising Madrid to fight inflation by keeping wages under control.[2]

The foundations of the U.S.-Spain patron-client relationship were laid during the Truman administration. On 18 January 1950 secretary of state Dean Acheson wrote to senator Tom Connally, U.S. representative to the UN, that Spain could not be a member of the western community in the absence of civil liberties, workers' rights, and basic freedoms. Despite Acheson's private reservations, U.S. policy was to integrate Spain for geopolitical and economic considerations. Leading the opposition against U.S. loans, the *Avanzadillas Monarchistas* accused London and Washington of aiding Fascism, because the loan would only serve Franco's political and financial ambitions and would not address starvation throughout the country.[3]

A few months after the top secret document NSC 68 promulgated a militaristic foreign policy, and a few weeks after North Korea invaded the south, the U.S. senate passed the proposed $100 million loan for Spain, despite domestic and international opposition. *Alianza Nacional de Fuerzas Democratica* officially protested the loan to the U.S. embassy, arguing that Washington was sending a message to the world that any anti-Communist regime was worthy of support, regardless of its human rights record or totalitarianism nature. Western conservative newspapers supported the loan on the grounds that Spain was of value to NATO. Besides bipartisan legislative backing, Chase and other commercial banks supported more loans, after senate reports that Spain's mineral exports could service commercial loans of up to $250 million.[4]

Because of U.S. business interests in Spain and Franco's desire to expand economic ties with the U.S., some American businessmen and congressmen argued that a $200 million loan would strengthen Spain's military and economy by integrating it into capitalist world-system. Despite U.S. efforts to strengthen Spain's private sector and open its markets to foreign investors, Franco, like Salazar, defended the corporate state. To protect *Compania Hispano-Americana de Electricidad* from foreign bondholders who wanted control, the government bought the shares of Spanish nationals. Juan March, reputedly Spain's wealthiest man and a beneficiary of public foreign loans, argued that Spain and Portugal could serve as America's clients to deter the USSR.[5]

The patron-client model actually afforded legitimacy to Spain that needed it as much as any Third World dictatorship. On 26 September 1953 Spain and the U.S. signed a ten-year Defense Agreement providing for the establishment of the Rota base. Of the $226 million loan over a four-year period, $141 million was for air bases at Torrejon and Zaragoza, and the rest for defense-related industries. Thoroughly integrated in the U.S.-dominated western bloc, Spain strengthened ties with Portugal and Greece, advocated inclusion in NATO, and cultivated closer ties with Latin America and the Arab world. As a show of western solidarity, a number of conservative European statesmen visited Madrid.[6]

To join the EEC, Spain like Greece needed to liquidate her prewar foreign debt, thus requiring another $100 million loan from Washington. Because of the Eisenhower administration's expectations for higher NATO spending, Madrid expected more aid for its role in the western alliance. The World Commerce Corporation of America, which had a long-standing relationship with Madrid, asked the State Department to provide more aid to support Spain's volatile currency. A combination of factors, including capital flight, inflation, and decline of exports resulted in the peseta's free fall. Despite the internal debate about the degree of Spain's western integration as a means of stabilizing the currency and modernizing the economy, Franco had no alternative but to accept integration under the patron-client relationship.[7]

The Politics of Inflation and Stabilization, 1957-1959

Confronting inflation and stagnation in the late 1950s, Spain accepted IMF conditionality to qualify for more IFI and commercial loans. Partly because rampant official corruption exacerbated the weak economy and finances, bankers pressured Franco to appoint Alberto Ullastres Calvo minister of commerce. A devout Catholic and monetarist determined to achieve greater western integration, Ullastres did not have much support within the government to be able to foster efficiency and clean up corruption, but there were modest changes in the ministry designed to crack down on the illegal import-export trade. His appointment marked the beginning of a trend of technocrats and western-minded economists that would remain influential until the late 1960s, not just in Spain but across southern Europe.[8]

Appointed to deal with inflation and scarcity of foreign exchange that were serious after the winter of 1956 and remained an obstacle in securing U.S. loans, Ullastres like his Latin American and southern European counterparts adopted stabilization. More significant, he yielded to U.S.-European pressures to allow up to 49 percent foreign participation in select domestic industries. In a meeting with the U.S. ambassador John Davis Lodge, Franco noted that student riots and labor in Barcelona, Asturias, and elsewhere were related to hard times, but the economy would benefit once Spain joined the IMF-World Bank, and became an EEC associate member. After considerable U.S. pressure on the EEC to accept Spain, in January 1958 the organization agreed. The state-controlled press hailed the EEC decision as a political victory, as did Ullastres who represented the financial elites and advocated monetarist orthodoxy and greater integration into the Common Market, EFTA, and IFIs.[9]

Behind U.S.-European resolve to integrate Spain were large multinational corporations. Fearing it would lose a $9 million contract, General Electric (GE) lobbied on Spain's behalf for an Eximbank loan that had been delayed because Franco failed to undertake the types of monetary, fiscal, and trade reforms that Washington demanded. French and English electrical firms competed with GE, but Washington used the loan as leverage so that Spain would adopt austerity measures and buy American products and services.[10]

From 1953 to 1957 Spain had received $600 million in U.S. economic aid and $400 million in military aid. Though Madrid clearly needed U.S. financial aid and diplomatic support, the official press criticized U.S. foreign policy for not supporting

Portugese colonial regimes in Africa. Presenting itself as Europe's bridge to the Third World, Spain, like Greece and Portugal, cultivated cordial ties with pro-west Arab governments. Having a substantial role in Portugal's economy, Spain also benefited by exploiting Third World markets. Gamal Abd al-Nasser's regional popularity, however, and his anti-colonial appeal among Moroccans entailed that Africans and Arabs alike regarded Franco with deep suspicion, especially amid the Algerian uprising.[11]

To strengthen his hand politically and economically, Franco was counting on Washington to lobby for Spain's induction into NATO, and to provide financial assistance. Considering the large U.S. loans to France, India, and even Poland, Ullastres complained that secretary of state John Foster Dulles had not responded to Franco's request for a $250 million loan. Though Ambassador Lodge argued that Spain's human rights violations caused the U.S. not to consider a large-scale loan, the reasons were related to a U.S.-EEC agreement that Madrid must meet certain fiscal, monetary, trade, and foreign investment criteria. To satisfy external pressures for monetarist orthodoxy, in July 1957 the banks raised interest rates, and in September the Bank of Spain tightened credit.[12]

Spain's tax rate on the mass consumer was much higher than on the wealthy that the government did not pursue for tax fraud and evasion. The U.S. urged fundamental tax reform, rather than the cosmetic reforms that Franco introduced to retain the elites on his side. Amid social unrest and protests demanding improved material conditions and social justice, in March 1958 the World Commerce Corporation of America, Chase Manhattan Bank, National City Bank, and Manufacturers Trust agreed to a $30 million loan for Spain, including a $10 million credit for petroleum imports. Franco resisted U.S. proposed austerity measures that would stifle growth. Because he needed U.S. cooperation on so many fronts, including the nuclear production of power, Franco went along with Washington on many policy matters.[13]

Stabilization Program of 1959 and Consequences

In 1959 finance minister Mariano Navarro Rubio and Ullastres persuaded Franco to pursue rapid western integration, and greater reliance on the IMF and World Bank for advice. Central planning designed to strengthen the private sector and stimulate the flow of capital across borders assumed a more important role in which the IMF, IBRD, and EEC would have a voice in helping Spain's integration. In January 1959 the EEC, U.S., and IMF urged Spain to adopt a stabilization program, focusing on curtailing spending by the central government and state-owned enterprises. Madrid went along with proposals to liberalize all imports of raw materials and spare parts, policies that Turkey, Peru and other Third World countries had adopted. Indicative of the prejudicial patron-client model, Spain signed an agreement for global import quotas affecting the dollar and EEC areas, and a different one affecting Latin America.[14]

Implemented in June 1959, the stabilization program set the peseta at 60 per dollar. The IMF provided $75 million in stand-by arrangement credits to strengthen Spain's reserves. Having received $1.1 billion in U.S. aid from 1951 to 1959, a few months before Eisenhower's visit, Madrid requested $100 million in PL 480 aid and an additional $20 million in defense aid. Eximbank approved $30 million line of credit for projects in the pipeline, $40 million already budgeted, and $10 million as a contingency. The IMF and State Department lobbied commercial banks to participate in Spain's stabilization program that required $355 million. Instrumental in trying to secure Spain's EEC associate membership, the State Department argued that Madrid should provide EEC members with favorable import quotas in exchange for free credit, just as Turkey had bilateral EEC credits to be used in Europe only.[15]

Though some businessmen questioned the negative impact of incentives for foreign investment on domestic firms, Franco promulgated Law 16/1959 of 17 July 1959 authorizing foreign capital participation in Spanish companies of up to 50 percent of their capital. In addition, foreign firms had access to local financing. The U.S. embassy acknowledged that the stabilization program afforded the U.S. a position comparable to the one it enjoyed in west Germany during the late 1940s when Americans controlled the country. Rewarding Spain for complying with stabilization guidelines and creating favorable foreign investment terms, Eximbank provided $10 million for the REPESA fertilizer project and $7.6 million for Abonos Sevilla fertilizer. Though stabilization lowered workers' living standards, the IMF wanted assurances that real wages would be kept under the inflation rate. Once Madrid pledged to follow the recommendations, the IMF raised its quota from $100 to $150 million.[16]

The U.S., western Europe, and IMF urged bilateral tariff reductions, less government intervention in the private sector, and more incentives to attract foreign capital. The only one willing to confront the powerful state-run *Instituto Nacional de Industria* (INI), Navarro Rubio failed to coordinate his policies with the ministers of industry, agriculture, and commerce so that he could be more effective against the INI. But even bankers who had confidence in Navarro Rubio complained that the stabilization program was choking off the economy. Nor was the U.S. helping to strengthen Spanish capitalism by awarding DLF loan contracts to U.S. and west European instead of Spanish companies.[17]

There was a split of opinion within the government, with old guard Falangists and some bankers supporting a strong public sector, while younger technocratic minded advisers belonging to the Opus Dei faction sided with the U.S., IFIs, and EEC. Embracing strict adherence of the Catholic faith in daily life, Opus Dei was founded in 1928. The secretive organization included the ministers of finance and commerce, businessmen, various government officials, newspapers publishers, and intellectuals who advocated modernization by preserving traditions.[18]

While some Spanish officials argued that the World Bank's proposal to integrate Spain was tantamount to handing the economy over to foreign corporations, World Bank president Eugene Black urged Navarro Rubio to embrace the future. Committed to IMF-World Bank policy guidelines, Navarro Rubio faced opposition by the Sindicatos and the INI. Because foreign investors opposed complex tax laws and cumbersome regulations, the IMF and U.S. encouraged Madrid to retain stabilization measures and further liberalize the economy. In February 1961, a month after Spain signed liberalization agreements with France and England, Ullastres assured the IMF that the government was committed to foreign investment incentives. With the exception of the military bases, Franco did not have much leverage with the U.S. on whether Spain would continue to be integrated under the patron-client model or the inter-dependent one applicable in western Europe.[19]

Though the U.S. had provided about $1 billion in economic assistance from 1954 to 1960, Madrid complained that meager foreign aid and its non-participation in the Marshall Plan accounted for economic weakness in comparison with western Europe. With unemployment at 13 percent in 1961, the Cortes approved an unemployment insurance and social security plan effective in October for all agricultural workers. Throughout the 1950 and 1960s, Spain like southern Europe and the Third World was pursuing monetarism at the expense of labor. Moreover, reliance on IFIs for loans entailed that development plans had to avoid inflation, weakening the public sector, and providing incentives for foreign investment.[20]

Twilight of Corporatism and Spain's EEC Associate Membership

Though the U.S. and UK backed Spain's bid for EEC membership at the Council of Europe in September 1961, Franco's human rights record made it very difficult defending the regime without appearing pro-Fascist. At the beginning of 1962 Spain agreed to EEC guidelines on economic, social, and political reforms. The World Bank recommended greater resources to modernize agriculture and infrastructure, remove obstacles to imports and foreign investment, and prevent the INI from playing a major role in the economy. Because Spain would industrialize by virtue of allowing foreign capital to dominate the economy, some ministers, businessmen, and intellectuals were concerned that integration could mean subordination to the EEC.[21]

Despite labor unrest amid continued rise in the cost of living, businesses were optimistic. Eximbank approved a total of $50 million in 1962, including $6.6 million to the *Empresa Nacional Siderurgica*, subsidiary of the *Instituto Nacional de Industria*, and $9.5 million to *Empresa Nacional de Electricidad*, to purchase equipment from GE which lobbied for the loan. To make it attractive for foreign corporations to invest, especially in manufacturing, the IBRD recommended that Madrid remove price controls, abolish subsidies and surplus workers in public enterprises, limit special incentives to industries, and eliminate cumbersome laws that hamper foreign capital. Besides advising Madrid to check the role of publicly owned entities, the World Bank and IMF favored curbing the costs of social programs.[22]

On 17 May 1962 Spain promulgated a decree lifting all limits on profit repatriation and allowing 50 percent of foreign investment in Spanish enterprises, regardless of economic and social contribution. The decree was part of the negotiations with the IMF, World Bank, U.S., and OECD. At an industry fair in Bilbao in August 1962, Ullastres stressed that Spain's economic future rested with EEC integration, though U.S. foreign investment accounted for about 60 percent of the total. Acknowledging that Spain needed to raise wages and foster greater geographic income equality, he argued that living standards must rise at the same pace as the cost of living and closer to EEC levels in order to curb emigration.[23]

Published on the eve of the Cuban Missile crisis, the World Bank report recommended similar policies for southern Europe as it did for the Third World, namely, infrastructural and mining development, and commercial agriculture linked to U.S. imports of agrochemicals and technology. Paris Eguilaz, secretary-general of the National Economic Council, protested the dismantling of INI enterprises and undercutting key industries by allowing foreign banks and foreign competition to undercut the agency, lowering tariffs, and ignoring labor's rights within the context of the corporate state. That Franco permitted the press to publish the most controversial aspects of the World Bank report calling for administrative and fiscal reforms signaled that he had finally sided with Opus Dei technocrats and against Falangists, INI, and bankers linked to INI.[24]

Multinational corporations positioned themselves to take advantage of Spain's new policies and market opportunities in every sector from the retail to manufacturing and financial services. Spain's low-cost labor was a selling point to attract foreign capital, while its emerging petit bourgeoisie, though much smaller than in the advanced capitalist countries, was sufficient to stimulate consumer demand, allowing the dictatorship to claim that social mobility was taking place. With over 32 million consumers whose living standards were rising, and abundant raw materials, Spain was in a propitious position to attract foreign loans and investment.[25]

A number of foreign companies, including Marathon Oil and U.S. Steel were investing in Spain, but overall capital inflows actually fell, despite a $50 million loan from Kreditanstalt fur Wiendenraufbau. By 1962 the U.S. was number one in foreign investments in Spain, leading with 57.2 percent, followed by France with 11.4 percent. Within a few weeks after an agreement that reduced tariffs on more than $50 million in imports, in August 1962 Eximbank approved $9.5 million for the *Empresa Nacional de Electricidad* to purchase a generator from a U.S. company, and an additional $6.6 million loan was for the *Empresa Nacional Siderurgica* for the purchase of a blast furnace.[26]

In 1963 Eximbank approved an $18 million loan for the Altos Hornos de Vizcaya (AHV), Spain's largest steel company with subsidiaries in chemical, engineering, iron, coal, and other industries. Banco de Vizcaya, Banco de Bilboa, and Banco Urquijo had substantial interest in AHV, which was partly owned by U.S. Steel. Given the over-supply of steel in the world, even the combined influence of Franco's crony capitalists and U.S. Steel was not sufficient to convince the World Bank that it should approve a loan to AHV.[27]

In March 1963 Madrid signed a tariff agreement with London, and on 30 April 1963 the European Council voted in Spain's favor, clearing the way to join the EEC. Besides Navarro Rubio and Ullastres, Laureano Lopez Rodo, chief of the Planning Commission, was the staunchest defender of implementing World Bank and IMF policies. Because Spain, like Portugal and Greece, continued to rely on a strong executive, the trend toward liberalization and integration was not threatening to Franco who had a firm grip on the country. As wages were rising in western Europe, Spain became attractive owing to its surplus labor force, abundant raw materials, large domestic market, and a regime that protected capitalists and did not tolerate dissent. Complying with EEC-IFI liberalization and foreign investment recommendations, Madrid invited foreign investment in steel and electricity among other sectors.[28]

European governments raised concern about Franco's human rights record, especially after the arrest of 50 Socialists accused of subversion, and the execution of Julian Grimau, a Communist activist from the Civil War era. Spain's financial, commercial, and diplomatic cooperation with the U.S. was linked to negotiations of the Rota military base agreement renewed in 1963 for five years.[29]

On 26 September 1963 Spain signed the new military base agreement with the U.S., and on 24 October the IBRD signed a $33 million loan agreement for road construction. Although Spain's annual economic growth rate from 1954 to 1962 was 4.5 percent, the four-year development plan (1964-67) envisioned a 6 percent annual growth rate. Madrid expected the World Bank and other foreign sources to raise their contributions to Spain's development plan from an annual average of 12.9 billion pesetas (60=$1) in 1962 to 35.8 billion in 1967.[30]

Economic growth in 1963 and 1964 entailed inflation that left workers demanding wage adjustments. The financial elites, Opus Dei technocrats, and the multilateral banks insisted that low wages kept Spain attractive to foreign investors. Though Franco continued to castigate western political systems as divisive and inherently unequal, foreign capital had a sense of safety under the regime and even the EEC maintained an economic relationship without accepting the regime. The Spanish government took regional development more seriously than Greece or Portugal. To absorb the unemployed in Seville's manufacturing sector, and to stimulate the local economy at the port town of Huelva, the government allocated funds to have a power plant built by GE and an oil refinery built and operated by Gulf Oil Company.[31]

To promote regional development in areas where there was high unemployment and sharp income inequalities, especially Burgos and Huelva, the government used the development plan to justify more investment. Special subsidies of up to 20 percent of capital investment and tax breaks of up to 95 percent of their obligations made it attractive to apply for projects in Burgos, Huelva, Seville, Vigo, Zaragoza, La Coruna, and Villadolid which absorbed most of the contracts and where subsidies amounted to 10 percent of capital. Until summer 1964, the applications submitted to the Development Commission totaled $1.1 billion, of which 18 percent were from U.S. and west European companies.[32]

Having committed $150 million to Spain, France complained that U.S. firms were usually rewarded contracts financed by World Bank loans, a general policy position that de Gaulle adopted to reflect dismay with U.S. hegemony. The World Bank threatened to cancel all French contracts unless it agreed to co-financing in Spain. In May 1964 Franco reiterated Spain's desire to be a part of the EEC, but threatened that de Gaulle's nationalist approach made sense. France, UK, and U.S. had been actively promoting closer ties between Spain and the EEC, but de Gaulle's flirtation with Madrid coincided with Franco's interest in improving relations with the Soviet bloc against the background of the Sino-Soviet split and global pressure on Portugal to give up its colonies. Because de Gaulle dared to challenge U.S. policies, Spain assumed a more significant role in the Apollo space program and as a military base. Nevertheless, anti-Americanism was as widespread in Spain as in France.[33]

In November 1964 Spanish officials met with GATT in Geneva for the first time to consult on balance of payments and import restrictions that Madrid reduced, arguing that it would ease inflationary pressures in the second half of 1964. Considering that Spain had reserves equal to seven months of imports, the U.S. asked that GATT demand much more rapid import liberalization than Madrid proposed. As was the case in Portugal and Greece, Spain's key industries came under increased pressure and many fell under foreign ownership, including U.S. Steel Corporation which had a major deal with Altos Hornos de Vizcaya. Like Salazar, Franco had to accept the preeminence of private domestic and foreign enterprise over public entities, and abided by the World Bank's recommendations on development. Approving over 1000 projects requiring $1 billion investment involving more than 100,000 workers, the government considered many of the projects only if European and U.S. capital were involved. France provided $150 million for suppliers' credits, Eximbank $17.6 million, and the World Bank $138 million for roads, railroads, and ports, but acknowledged that Spain needed about $150-200 million annually to carry out its development plan. Because annual per capita income in 1965 was $550, Spain was still eligible to borrow from western governments and the multilateral banks at the same low interest rates as Latin America.[34]

In June 1965 the Foreign Exchange Institute eased select restrictions on blocked peseta balances by non-EEC countries. Viewed as another liberalizing measure affecting repatriation of U.S. investors' profits, this measure followed a previous one that allowed EEC investors to repatriate profits without limits earned before 1959. In October 1965 the recommendations of a joint World Bank-U.S. mission resulted in the greater commercialization and liberalization of the agrarian sector. The idea was to reduce subsidies to those sectors where surpluses existed and to focus on large commercial operations that would serve the domestic market and potentially export as well. Hence, the World Bank and U.S. targeted large-scale farming for assistance, a policy applied globally.[35]

Indicative of Spain's appeal to multinational corporations, new foreign investment rose from $47 million in 1960 to $236.3 million in 1965. The U.S. embassy correctly predicted that foreign investment would rise sharply in the future.

Statistics on authorized investments show the United States as the leading source of outside investment in recent years with authorized annual investment by American firms having averaged 42.3% of total annual authorized foreign investment since 1960. Areas which have attracted the most investment interest have been services, chemicals, petroleum refining and food processing. Using available statistical material as a basis total American investment in Spain is estimated above $500 million.[36]

Like Greece and Portugal, Spain used its U.S. relationship as leverage with the EEC, though Washington and the IFIs coordinated policy with the EEC which discriminated against cotton textiles and olive oil. The French, British, German, and Italian governments noted that the EEC's agricultural policy was not intended to create unfavorable terms of trade at Spain's expense, but rather to protect the common market's integrity.[37]

As part of a stabilization deal, in March 1966 Spain signed an agreement with the U.S. and the aid consortium. The World Bank approved $138 million for roads, railroads and ports, while the Kreditanstalt provided Spain with $50 million to finance irrigation in the south. Madrid agreed to maintain a balanced budget, internal and external financial stability, a tight monetary policy, and wages below 8 percent, although inflation was over 12 percent. Promising to cooperate with Washington in diplomatic and strategic matters affecting the western alliance, Franco agreed that a U.S. economic mission would help assess Spain's economic and financial needs.[38]

Like other countries multilateralizing their commercial relations, Spain expanded trade with the EEC, and commercial and cultural relations with Moscow, Bucharest, and Warsaw. Dependent on the U.S. for about half of the foreign investment, U.S.-Spain relations were strained after 17 January 1966 when a U.S. aircraft carrying nuclear bombs crashed in the south, and the bomb was not recovered until 8 April 1966. In April foreign minister Fernando Maria Castiella signed two military agreements with the U.S.

and formalized the stationing of 54 USAF F-100 fighter aircraft at Todejon, with the understanding that they would rotate between Italy and Turkey.[39]

In November 1966 three banks suspended payments to depositors amid allegations of government investigations of illegal trafficking of foreign exchange, and fraudulent transactions. Critics blamed the lack of regulatory measures, lack of supervision, and inadequate capitalization. Exchange Institute (IEME) officials confided in the U.S. embassy that the government made an example of the three banks to send a message about the significance of enforcing exchange regulations. The State Department knew about the Spanish bankers' practice of failing to fully disclose operations involving foreign loans. Closely linked to Franco's patronage network, the banking scandal tarnished the IFIs reputation as well. Because Banco Urquijo had ties with Spain's industry, American exporters did not want Washington's skepticism about Spanish bankers to jeopardize losing market share to European firms.[40]

Amid controversial stabilization, banking scandals, and a popular referendum on the Organic Law, widespread labor unrest plagued major cities in December 1966 and January 1967. RENFE employees had been dissatisfied with conditions for a number of years, but conditions deteriorated when the company laid off 2000 workers in 1966 and wage increases fell below the legal minimum. Transport workers in all sectors went on strike as they had similar problems to the railroad workers. Mining and factory workers in the metal and electrical industries were also on strike in Madrid, Barcelona, Bilbao, Asturias, and Seville.

Joining the striking workers, Madrid University students clashed with police who struck indiscriminately, inviting unprecedented sympathetic editorials for the demonstrators. Student demonstrations and strikes continued throughout spring 1967, prompting the Cortes to approve new tougher penalties for political crimes, while the government adopted emergency measures to end social unrest. Though Luis Carrero Blanco ran the day-to-day government, Spain's policy was to cultivate closer ties with the U.S. and EEC, improved commercial relations with the Soviet bloc, and publicly support the Arabs just ahead of the Six-Day War, while privately going along with Washington.[41]

To qualify for new loans, in November 1967 Spain devalued its currency by 14.3 percent or 70 pesetas per dollar which was close to the minimum wage per day. With the trade unions' endorsement after promising job security, the government froze wages, prices and dividends for one year. Yet, it provided foreign banks and foreign investors with incentives to help fund the development plan. Because of a global economic slow down, stabilization did not have much impact, and as expected labor carried the burden of the sacrifice, with the consequences of higher unemployment and more social unrest.[42]

In a speech to the Cortes in November 1967, Franco admonished demonstrators and strikers, arguing that Communists were trying to disrupt national unity. Oblivious to widespread opposition to his regime, he reminded the Cortes that the armed forces were the guardians of law and order. Identifying his regime with other dictatorships, he added: "Simple minds fixed themselves on solutions for all, but the age of mirages was passed, and countries of the world from Argentine to Portugal, from Brazil to Pakistan, from Greece to Indonesia, were choosing their own roads."[43] Asserting that unity must take precedence over all other principles like human rights, he promised that by 1970 living standard would be equal to the EEC, although the OECD classified Spain as an underdeveloped country. Praising Madrid's military, political, and economic cooperation with the U.S., Franco also stressed that EEC integration was vital.

Desperate for foreign aid, the Franco dictatorship conveyed to the Johnson administration that military base negotiations could proceed on a quid-pro-quo basis with a U.S. aid package worth $1.2 billion. On 26 September 1968 Castiella formally invoked Article V of the 1953 Defense Agreement, calling for a six-month consultation period before the expiration on 26 March 1969. A World Bank mission had been examining Spain's education, livestock industry, ports, road projects, and RENFE to determine further reforms that the Franco regime must adopt to qualify for new loans and technical assistance. The World Bank concluded that public and private banks should be involved in financing the sector, and it recommended that the Spanish government support free market policies within the context of its development plan. The pro-IFI Opus Dei technocrats ran into some embarrassing scandals when it was revealed that the Matesa textile machinery factory had illegally obtained 10 billion pesetas in export credits with the aid of top administrators. Franco remained loyal to the technocrats who enjoyed the confidence of the IFIs as well.[44]

To improve the country's image abroad and satisfy both integrationists and nationalists, in October 1969 Franco appointed foreign minister Gregorio Lopez Bravo, the regime's best known technocrat. Renewing efforts to forge closer ties with the U.S. and EEC while pursuing a business-like policy toward the Soviet bloc, Lopez Bravo promoted industrialization. An integration proponent, he did not want Spain to be just a cheap tourist resort for the west like Portugal, Greece, and the Caribbean. Though he laid the foundation for Spain's transition from the patron-client model to interdependence, like Brazil and India, Spain was undergoing dependent development where foreign capital dominated.[45]

With $608 million of U.S. investment in Spain by 1970, primarily in manufacturing and petroleum refining, the U.S. led foreign investment in a country with a large domestic market, cheap labor, and close proximity to western Europe. Unlike the Third World which suffered a net capital outflow in the 1960s, on paper Spain appeared to have a net capital inflow but at the cost of much greater external financial-industrial dependence. Reaching a combined $2.5 billion by 1970, Spain's external public and private foreign debt repayable in foreign currency rose just as rapidly as the Third World's.[46]

During U.S.-Spain negotiations for the military base agreement in the spring of 1970, the EEC argued that a preferential trade agreement would help Spain's integration and stabilize the entire Mediterranean economy. The proposed EEC-Spain agreement resulted in Washington filing a complaint against Spain in GATT, and applying trade restrictions on Spanish shoe imports. Though the U.S. did not take any action before signing the military bases agreement in August 1970, the NSC, State Department and Defense Department realized that Madrid would retaliate. Insisting that the EEC-Spain arrangement violated GATT, the NSC allowed Lopez Bravo to believe that Washington would not oppose the agreement, but vehemently objected after the military base agreement was signed. The EEC-Spain agreement was another step of weakening the patron-client model at a time when the EEC and Japan demanded a role in shaping macroeconomic policy.[47]

Madrid formally protested U.S. restraints on shoe imports resulting from a Tariff Commission report, arguing that the trade quota was a violation of the friendship treaty signed in August 1970. The NSC and State Department advised Nixon to lift the latest trade restrictions on Spain, but domestic shoe manufacturers demanded protection. On the basis of the U.S.-Spain Friendship treaty, in February 1971 Madrid submitted to Washington a list of 130 projects costing $200 million. Because U.S. tariffs affected EEC and Japanese exports, and because Spain was so dependent on U.S. for capital, there was not much it could do except ask for favorable consideration with IFI loans.[48]

Spaniards hoped that the Third Development Plan (1972-75) was a way to reach 7 percent annual GNP growth. The new plan would reduce the share of public investment from 22 percent in 1971 to 15 percent in 1975, but it would require 65 billion pesetas of added public debt, and foreign capital inflow of $2 billion. Indicative of Spain's rapid industrial growth, McNamara decided to provide $220 million for industry, $90 million for agriculture, $40 million for port development, and $40 million for education. Advocating cautious stimulation amid price and wage rises, the IMF and EEC advised tax reform to generate more receipts and some public works spending to activate the recessionary economy. Because of the tremendous potential of its economy and geopolitical leverage with the U.S. at a time when Nixon was under criticism for backing the Greek Junta, Spain used all its leverage to secure as many concessions as possible.[49]

The U.S.-Spain trade dispute took place amid a domestic and international stagflation climate, impacting Spain's economy just ahead of the 1973 oil crisis. While select manufactured exports had increased during the 1960s, 30 percent of total exports were agricultural products. Like Portugal, Greece, and Third World countries suffering from deteriorating terms of trade, the value of Spain's imports rose by 26 percent in 1972, while the value of its exports went up by just 19 percent. As Spain's largest trading partner, the U.S. was also a significant source of foreign investment, accounting for $760 million of the $2.2 billion total foreign investment by 1970.

Despite some EEC inroads, the patron-client relationship was as solid in Spain as in Greece and Portugal.[50]

Despite the global stagflation, between mid-1971 and mid-1973 Spain's economy expanded largely due to housing construction and derivative industries. Official unemployment was a mere 1.2 percent, and prices and wages rose steadily amid modest expansion of the petit bourgeoisie that would become the nucleus for the post-Franco democracy. In July 1973 finance minister Antonio Barrera de Irimo cooperated with the IMF and the World Bank on policy, but he also advocated greater EEC integration. Backed by the World Bank and IMF, the EEC demanded that Madrid abolish 80 percent of tariffs on industrial products by July 1977 and 100 percent by 1980, while the community would reciprocate by abolishing all tariffs on Spanish products by July 1977. With $5.7 billion in reserves in 1973, the 10th highest in the world, the World Bank regarded Spain sufficiently wealthy not to require Bank development loans, though per capita GNP remained close to Third World levels. While regime change was imperative for the transition to the interdependent model, the patron-client model was waning before the dictator's death owing to socioeconomic changes.[51]

In a meeting with Kissinger on 4 October 1973, foreign minister Laureano Lopez Rodo stated that Spain concurred with the "Joint Declaration of Principles" affecting economic and geopolitical issues. Spain's willingness to renew the military agreement was predicated on economic cooperation with the U.S. Joining Greece, Portugal, and other NATO countries, Spain rejected U.S. proposals to use its bases in the Yom Kippur War. Concerned about popular anti-American sentiment, Madrid wanted to avoid taking sides in a conflict that only had negative consequences, especially given the strong protestations by Algeria and Morocco.[52]

On 20 December 1973 president Luis Carrero Blanco, who had been running the government's daily operations since 1967, was killed in an explosion two blocks from the U.S. embassy. Just two days prior, Kissinger had been holding talks with Lopez Rodo regarding the Middle East, NATO, and the renewal of the U.S. military bases agreements. The separatist group *Euskadi ta Askatasuna* (ETA) [Basque Homeland and Liberty] carried out the assassination to revenge the death of nine Basque prisoners, and to coincide with the opening trial of the "Carabanchel Ten" who had been accused of associating with ETA.[53]

The State Department conceded that along with the oil crisis, the U.S. and EEC were responsible for exporting inflation. Because of the growth and multilateralization of its economy, Madrid was not nearly as eager to make military, political, and economic concessions to Washington in the mid 1970s as it was in the 1950s. After Portugal's revolution and Nixon's resignation, Spain along with the rest of southern Europe was less inclined to go along with Washington and the IFIs. Commerce minister Luis Alcaide told the IMF that the inflation rate was about the same as the average for the EEC, and there was no evidence of accelerated demand or higher prices. Committed to extending a $150 million loan to Algeria for the construction of a natural gas facility in 1975, Madrid estimated current account deficit at $2.9 billion for which foreign loans were needed. Demanding that the U.S. reciprocate with aid and loans, the dictatorship was anxious to project a neutral foreign policy and that the military bases were leverage for loans, a strategy that Greece and Portugal pursued as well.[54]

Fearing isolation and deteriorating relations with Europe and even with the Vatican, many centrist pro-business elements wanted a democratic Spain that would take its place among EEC members. Living standards had remained low in comparison with western Europe, crime was high, and the Franco dictatorship was still in power after Portugal and Greece had adopted parliamentary regimes. Ford's attempt to enlist Spain's membership in NATO notwithstanding, the vast majority of the people believed that their future was in a more equitable political and economic relationship with Europe rather than an unequal one with Washington. Despite an obvious pro-EEC political wave across southern Europe, the NSC proposed a package of grants and loans for Spain. U.S. military bases remained at the core of discussions between President Ford and Prime Minister Carlos Arias Navarro in August 1975 at a meeting in Helsinki, but Spain was at the dawn of lifting itself from the patron-client model and embracing a European identity. This was made possible because the social elites viewed their future with EEC integration that could only be achieved under a representative regime with greater self-sufficiency and sovereignty.[55]

The Road to EU Integration

Like Portugal and Greece experiencing "democracy from above" in 1974, Spain managed the devolution of the authoritarian system with EEC and U.S. aid. When Franco died in November 1975, Ford sent condolences to head of state Prince Juan Carlos, but the NSC advised a low profile of the U.S. delegation at the funeral so as not to project the impression of Washington's backing for the notorious dictator. In the post-Vietnam, post-Allende era, the NSC was concerned that in addition to the Greek lobby that was vehemently anti-Kissinger, the Ad Hoc Committee for a Democratic Spain, headed by Barbara Tuchman and William Shirer, was projecting the image to the public that Washington supported dictatorships around the world. The Committee for a Democratic Spain called on the U.S. to reexamine its foreign policy and to promote democracy, amid a transition period that left in place Franco's totalitarian state structure. U.S. policy remained focused on preserving the strategic relationship with Madrid, preventing a leftist or a coalition regime similar to Portugal's after the Revolution, and greater integration with the western economies.[56]

Southern Europe's future, however, rested with the EEC as the patron-client model was to gradually be replaced by the interdependent model. By 1975, 45 percent of Spain's trade was with the EEC, European companies were entrenched in the Iberian peninsula, the Spanish people's identity was European, and the size and strength of the middle class entailed a representative political system under government that would not compromise its sovereignty to stay in power as it had under Franco. Washington was alarmed by reports that the *Junta Democratica*, founded in 1974 by a coalition that included Communists opposed any regime that did not include its members. Besides the Communists, the Basque separatists vowed to continued their struggle for a semi-autonomous state in the provinces of Vizcaya and Guipuzcoa.[57]

In January 1976 Kissinger and his Spanish counterpart, Jose Maria de Areilza, signed the Treaty of Friendship and Cooperation, which included a provision for military cooperation on western defense. Once the Senate ratified the treaty in June for five years, Spain received $150 million in grants, mostly in military aid, and $600 million in loans. In addition, Eximbank was considering $450 million, expanding the total aid package to $1.2 billion as part of the agreement. The new minister of finance Villar Mir, former CEO of Altos Hornos steel plant, promised to avoid radical reforms like those carried out by the Portuguese, and to abide by anti-inflation measures. He gained the IMF's confidence only after he agreed to devalue the currency and ignore widespread labor unrest and political clamor for immediate reforms. Pledging to bring Spain at par with OECD economic, political, and social standards, Villar Mir's policy reflected a much more conservative transition similar to Greece rather than Portugal after the Revolution.[58]

In February 1976 an IMF mission to Madrid worked with the new regime to implement a stabilization program, as a precondition for $276 million and other IFI loans. Besides increased European competition, the devaluation of Italy's lira was putting pressure on Spain's exports. Owing to the oil crisis and general deterioration in the terms of trade, Spain lost 20 percent of total income. Hence, it devalued the peseta by 10 percent to remain competitive, amid 12 percent inflation that would rise further because of devaluation. Faced with a $200 million balance-of-payments deficit in 1975, the government went along with IMF-OECD measures for higher indirect taxes and a rise in the minimum income tax. The new regime provided tax incentives for investment in select priority sectors, and it raised tax exemptions at the rate as social security contributions from 50 to 75 percent. Both the IMF and Madrid acknowledged that the devaluation would drive real wages lower by about 3 percent.[59]

King Juan Carlos appointed a cabinet composed of junior-level technocrats led by Adolfo Suarez who had served in Franco's civil service. In exchange for political reforms and amnesty for political prisoners, Suarez proposed that the leftist opposition acquiesce to wage restraint and public spending reduction. Because the transition from dictatorship to parliamentarism in Portugal had created economic instability, Spanish politicians were apprehensive about social unrest. Despite obvious differences in each case, negotiations of the U.S. military bases proved as difficult in Spain as in Portugal and Greece, because all three demanded fair compensation. Nevertheless, the agreement was signed and Spain received $600 million in guaranteed loans, $170 million in grants, and $450 million in Eximbank loans, bringing the total to $1.2 billion.[60]

An IMF report noted that from 1974 to 1977 Spain's economy was experiencing very slow growth, high inflation, rising unemployment, larger balance-of-payments deficits, and foreign debt of $11 billion. The Suarez cabinet acknowledged that some stabilization measures were inevitable after the elections, despite the expected massive opposition by labor groups and their political representatives. After lengthy negotiations with the IMF, on 12 July 1977 Spain devalued the peseta by 19.7 percent and allowed it float against the dollar and other currencies. Confronting 30 percent price inflation, the IMF contended that higher unemployment would force wages lower. In November 1977 Spain negotiated an IMF tranche for $143 million, after Suarez pledged to back stabilization, despite massive political opposition.[61]

Bringing together employers, labor, and all major political parties, the government forged the *Pacto Moncloa* designed to secure consent and inform all signatories of the new policies, in effect a corporatist approach to allow the regime political cover for conservative fiscal and monetary policies. Though leftists stressed the importance of labor's and parliament's role in all public enterprises, the state would in effect coordinate labor-management relations and enjoy a supporting role for private enterprises. By enforcing the compulsory wage guidelines for public employees and those working for state-assisted enterprises, the government hoped to reduce inflation. Firms that would exceed wage guidelines owing to trade union pressures were allowed to dismiss 5 percent of their workers. Despite an increase in unemployment, the government was determined to pursue monetarism.[62]

Subsidies and guaranteed prices for certain commodities through *Fondo Para la Regulacion de Precios y Productos Agrarios* entailed that Spain was emulating the policies of other countries. Suarez appointed a commission to coordinate the demand through subsidies, taxes, and other incentives. As in the case of Portugal, Greece and in the rest of the EEC, the state's role was becoming a facilitator and supporter of the private sector amid greater global integration and liberalization of the economy in accordance with IMF-World Bank advice. Suffering $1 billion annual trade deficit owing to agricultural imports, Spain was facing debt service commitments of $2 billion in 1978, and planned to increase foreign debt. Considering that all southern Europe and the Third World were accumulating larger foreign debt obligations in the late 1970s, Spain was following a trend. The IMF policy recommendations that Suarez accepted exacerbated the foreign debt, largely because stabilization occurred amid higher energy prices, decline in world trade, hyperinflation throughout the world, and increased global competition for markets.[63]

Though the Suarez cabinet turned to the right in spring of 1978 and the Socialist party and trade unions lost some influence, the IMF and OECD were encouraged that financial and monetary policies did not change. Anti-inflation policies that Spain was pursuing were not yielding the desired results, and the IMF acknowledged that most countries following similar policies on the basis of the Fund's advice would not likely achieve lower inflation, lower deficits, and higher rates of growth. Spain's challenge, argued the IMF and OECD, was to achieve higher rates of investment without triggering inflation, a scenario possible only if wages were kept from rising despite an inflationary price climate.[64]

Because elections were not scheduled until 1983, Suarez confided in the IMF and OECD that unpopular fiscal and monetary policies could be tolerated politically. He further contended that workers were fundamentally conservative and would not follow the reformist agenda of the Socialist and Communist leaders who opposed IMF stabilization. Leftist opposition to Suarez's policies notwithstanding, Spain had to raise its GDP at about 4 percent annually, or 2 percent higher than its trading partners in order to become full member of the EEC. In short, integration into the EEC necessarily obviated some IMF policies in Spain and across southern Europe whereas the same did not apply to the Third World in the 1980s.[65]

On 25-26 June 1980, president Jimmy Carter held talks with Juan Carlos and Suarez regarding the crises in Iran and Afghanistan, and Spain's progress toward EEC membership. They agreed on the need for western solidarity against Soviet aggression in Afghanistan, and Spain's support in trying to secure the release of the U.S. hostages. Reviewing the state of bilateral economic and trade relations, the two presidents agreed to erase the current commercial imbalance. Satisfied with the results of the Venice summit, Carter urged Spain to conserve oil and cooperate with other nations in research and development of alternative forms of energy.[66]

In 1980 Spain's external debt was $23.7 billion, of which $8.1 billion was public sector debt, representing a relatively modest percentage of GNP in comparison with the EEC, and very low in comparison with Latin America. In a meeting with IMF officials, Bank of Spain president Manuel Varela stressed the need to lower inflation and curb public spending. In a meeting with the vice president for Economic Affairs, Garcia Diez, the IMF pledged to support Spain's monetary policy, assuming that the money supply began to tighten and inflation kept under 12.5 percent. Moreover, the IMF advised keeping GNP at 2 percent growth in 1982, instead of 3 percent that Madrid preferred. Nor was the IMF optimistic about the budgetary deficit expected to reach near one trillion pesetas. That the dollar was depreciating against European currencies was the only positive development, though not for exporters competing with cheap Third World exports.[67]

In the early 1980s the Spanish economy was sluggish, averaging about one percent annual growth with an inflation rate exceeding the average for its European trading partners. But that was remarkable compared with the Third World. In March 1982 the IMF congratulated Spanish authorities for successfully holding down wages since 1979, while passing on the cost of higher energy to the consumers instead of subsidizing it. Equally pleased with the Suarez regime for pursuing a tight monetary policy, the IMF and World Bank providing policy advice acknowledged that GNP growth was flat, while inflation and unemployment remained high. Along with the OECD and World Bank, the IMF recommended that Spain cut budgetary spending and reduce real wages as indicated by the *Acuerdo Nacional de Empleo*.[68]

By the time that Socialist Party chief Felipe Gonzalez won the election in 1982, the Francoist patronage network had been dismantled, but Socialism in Spain was as pro-business and pro-west as in Portugal. In December 1982 the government devalued the peseta by 8 percent and tightened fiscal policy, but by 1984 total external debt jumped to $29.6 billion, of which public sector debt was $12.3 billion. Where real wages were rising in the second half of the 1970s amid the transition to democracy, a decline started in the early 1980s amid structural reforms designed to prepare Spain for full EU membership, and IFI, EEC, and U.S. pressures to pursue monetarism. More significant, after the devaluation of 1982, the result of the austerity entailed a jump in unemployment from 17 percent in 1982 to 22 percent in 1985.[69]

Fiscal tightening and currency devaluation as part of an IMF-recommended stabilization program resulted in economic sluggishness in 1983 and 1984, despite rapid export growth. In 1985 monetary policy shifted toward moderate stimulus, lowering personal income taxes, and offering fiscal incentives. Despite such measures, GDP rose a mere 2 percent for the year. More significant, to bring inflation down from double digits in the late 1970s to single digit in the late 1980s, Spain paid the price of 13-point higher unemployment. The net effect was that income inequality rose commensurately with unemployment, while the inflationary economy of the late 1970s had the opposite effect not just in Spain, but in southern Europe and in most countries around the world. In short, inflation had the net effect of redistributing income toward labor and lower middle class.[70]

In January 1986 Spain along with Portugal became full EEC members. In preparation for accession to the EU, Spain since 1980 was gradually implementing structural reforms including liberalizing trade and the capital market to allow greater foreign penetration, all on the basis of EU and IMF recommendations. Naturally, such structural shifts entailed steady inflation at relatively low levels in comparison with the EU, but chronic unemployment that was the highest in western Europe. Beginning in the 1980s, wage inequality also increased amid much higher structural unemployment, to be offset only modestly by the Socialist regime's welfare policies and the *Instituto Nacional de Empleo* which absorbed 170,000 people, or about one percent of the labor force, the same percentage as Denmark and Germany.[71]

During the second half of the 1980s, GNP growth averaged 4.8 annually, propelled by EEC integration and foreign investment, especially in manufacturing. In large measure, growth was driven by the tremendous manufactured exports which accounted for about three-quarters of total exports. Foreign direct investment and foreign loans reached an all-time high in 1988, representing continued financial dependence. Unlike the U.S., Japanese, or western European manufacturing sector, Spain's was predominantly foreign-owned, placing it in a category similar to Brazil and Mexico which were also technologically and industrially dependent on the advanced capitalist countries. The fundamental and very significant difference between dependent development in southern Europe under the interdependent model versus Latin America under the patron-client model is that in the latter wages were and still are well below those of the North American levels, whereas in the EU countries the wage gap among member countries is not nearly as great.[72]

On 7 July 1989 the government announced a series of stabilization measures that effectively slowed the economy and resulted in higher unemployment. Dismissing Gonzalez' Socialist Party as anti-labor and a tool of capital, the left wing of the party joined a Communist-led United Left coalition to make a bid for the elections in October 1989. Largely because the middle class backed him, Gonzalez won by a single seat in parliament. Transformed to resemble northwest Europe, Spain benefited from large injections of EEC grants. Inflation jumped from 4.8 percent in 1988 to an annual average of 6.5 from 1989 to 1991, which was closer to the European average. While per capita income rose close to the EEC average, unemployment remained at 18 percent, reflecting a decline in agricultural workers and a rise of women in the work force. Unemployment and underemployment would be Spain's most serious problem from the late 1980s to the present.[73]

Prepared to face a single European market by 1992, in March 1990 the IMF urged Madrid to curb sectoral demands in order to remain competitive. Stabilization implemented in July 1989 had already slowed the economy, but the IMF strongly advised against wage increases that exceeded the inflation rate. Though the current account deficit continued to grow, robust growth and long-term capital inflows indicated that foreign investors regarded Spain as an attractive market. One reason was the successful privatization program that included a number of companies, especially the lucrative state-owned petroleum company REPSOL and gas company ENAGAS in which domestic and foreign companies and private investors enjoyed majority control.[74]

During consultations with officials in Madrid in autumn 1993, the IMF insisted that despite suffering the highest unemployment in the EU, Spain needed to control wages, dismiss more redundant workers from public entities, and set hiring limits on public employees. To curb inflation hovering at 6.8 percent amid high unemployment, the government followed IMF-OECD advice gradually tightening monetary policy in the second half of 1988 and keeping a tight policy for the next three years. The combination of the stabilization program and the global recession of 1990-91 produced even higher unemployment, a decline in household income, and loss of domestic competitiveness as imports flooded the market.[75]

After experiencing rapid growth from 1986 to 1990, the economy reflected slower EU growth and global recession. Pursuant to discussions with the IMF in June 1992, the Spanish government announced significant tightening in monetary and fiscal policy. Arguing that budgetary receipts rose by 5 percent while expenditures rose 11.4 percent in the first half of 1992 compared with the same period in 1991, the IMF applauded a hiring freeze in public employment and a 10 percent reduction in the productivity premium paid to public workers. Besides cuts in public works, the government reduced disability benefits and raised taxes. Acknowledging that stabilization measures would slow an already recessionary economy and allow Spain to lag farther behind the core EU countries, the IMF noted that GNP would not rise above 2 percent for the year, while inflation would hover around 6.4 percent.[76]

Despite additional exchange rate adjustments in November 1992 and May 1993 reflecting a 20 percent decline in the peseta, the economy remained in recession and short-term interest rates hovered around 7-9 percent and unemployment was at 23 percent. The government conveyed to the EU and IMF that it would reduce spending by 0.8 percent of GNP in 1994, including imposing a wage freeze and reducing the public employment force. While raising alcohol and tobacco taxes, and imposing income and social security taxes on benefit recipients, the government refused to raise income taxes, providing instead income tax credits and business deductions. Because the government and the IMF tried to induce growth by reducing labor's share of income, it was not possible to achieve the savings necessary to reduce overall public debt which would rise from 54.3 percent of GNP in 1993 to 59.7 percent in 1994. Even a robust economic recovery, argued the IMF would not be sufficient for Spain to abandon fiscal and monetary tightening in order to achieve EMU convergence under Maastricht Treaty conditions like public deficit, interest rates, and inflation.[77]

In November 1994 an IMF mission in Madrid warned that Spain suffered from the combination of "persistent inflation, rapid wage growth with high unemployment and significant unused capacity indicated an urgent need to introduce measures to tackle structural rigidities."[78] In response to that report, in early January 1995 the government depreciated the peseta by 10 percent. Against the background of political uncertainty, short-term and long-term interest rates rose as reserves dropped from $44.5 billion to $44.1 billion.

In the euphoria of globalization and privatization of public enterprises, and to bring the public deficit down to 4.4 percent of GNP in 1996, the government agreed to reduce subsidies for public enterprises and cut social security programs. Amid social security cuts, unemployment was 24.2 percent in 1994, before dropping to 22.9

percent in 1995, while workers' share of national income dropped from 66.5 percent in 1990 to 63.6 percent in 1994. As the government had undertaken labor market reforms in conformity with the IMF and the EU guidelines, wage inequality continued rising in the second half of the 1990s. Along with Greece and Portugal, Spain was preparing for convergence under EU monetary rules, thus experiencing a decline in the peseta's value which was at the core of eroding labor income amid price inflation averaging 4.5 percent in 1994-96. Despite labor's setbacks, the average purchasing power gap between Spain and the EU dropped from 44 percent in 1985 to 23 percent in 1994, comparable to southern Europe.[79]

The IMF continued to admonish Madrid that persistent inflation and rapid wage growth accompanied by the highest unemployment in Europe and significant unused capacity was a prescription for economic problems. This was a rather curious assertion, considering that wage inequality was relatively steady in the first half of the 1990s while unemployment remained very high. To bring inflation at par with the EU and meet the goal of nominal convergence by 1997, the IMF and EU advised Madrid to reduce the budgetary deficit, despite an economic downturn and the highest unemployment rate in the EU. To improve the beleaguered social security system, the IMF recommended shifting toward a partially-funded public pension, thus resulting in greater public savings. Above all, the IMF and EU pressed hard for privatization, foreign investment incentives by the state, and participating in integration of Latin America and former Communist countries.[80]

Though the government deficit as a percent of GNP rose from 3.9 in 1990 to 5.9 in 1995, it was about average for Europe. Outstanding public debt as percent of GNP, however, was much higher than the European average at 50.8 percent in 1990, rising to 64.1 percent in 1995. Unemployment was Spain's most serious problem in the 1990s, to the degree that even the IMF was alarmed and recommended corrective measures. From 1975 to 1995 macroeconomic shocks created higher unemployment throughout the EU, owing in part to the oil crisis of the 1970s, and the recessions of the 1980s and early 1990s. Spain had higher unemployment than the rest of Europe, with 21 percent in 1985, 16 percent in 1990, and 24 percent in 1994. In contrast to the EU average employment drop from 65 percent in 1975 to 60 percent in 1996, Spain's employment plummeted from 57.6 percent to 47.2 percent during the same period.[81]

The IMF attributed Spain's hyper-structural unemployment problem to the oil crisis of the 1970s and 1980s, a significant rise in women entering the labor force, especially after Spain's EEC accession in 1986, and a sharp rise in real wages, despite an enormous slack in the labor market.

No country in Europe has as great an unemployment problem as Spain. From below 5 percent in the mid-1970s, the unemployment rate has peaked at above 20 percent in each of the last two economic slowdowns, without dropping below 15 percent in times of strong growth. From an analytical standpoint, the Spanish case is a fascinating extreme example of the pan-European unemployment problem. From the policy perspective, it is essential to understand and attack labor market problems successfully in Spain if the EU unemployment crisis is to be tackled, especially since the number of jobless in Spain in 1995 was higher than in the much larger EU countries of France, Italy, and the U.K., and nearly as high as Germany.[82]

Though more females entered the labor force in the post-Franco era, that was true throughout the western world after 1970. In the last three decades of the 20th century, wages barely kept pace with inflation in most countries. Contrary to IMF's wage theory, globalization had an impact on rising unemployment in Spain and across Europe. Nor did the IMF assume that its own policy advice to Spain and the rest of Europe had any impact on high unemployment.

On 3 March 1996, Jorge Aznar's Popular Party won the election and formed a coalition after failing to secure a sufficient majority of 156 seats in parliament. Besides the corruption scandals of the Socialists, the policies were quintessentially bourgeois that hardly paid much attention to workers' problems. Because most European Socialists were developmentalists and pro-west, substantive policy differences between them and the conservatives were not significant. During Aznar's regime, Spain reverted as far back to the Francoist era as possible, as it became much more closely aligned with the U.S. and the traditional elites that had backed Franco, while labor interests continued to lose ground.[83]

During consultations with an IMF team in Madrid, the finance ministry confirmed that Aznar's priority was to achieve nominal convergence as required under the Maastricht treaty, rather than focusing on lowering unemployment. As in the case of Portugal and Greece, the major political parties had come to a consensus on nominal convergence and on remaining competitive. Though the peseta was overvalued, the IMF had confidence in the Bank of Spain, which had become independent of the government, to maintain a tight monetary policy as Maastricht required. Tight monetary and fiscal policy translated into restraining the growth of spending on public health, social security, unemployment compensation, and wage increases. In short, the terms of Maastricht entailed that labor would pay a high price.[84]

Like Greece which benefited by integrating the Balkans and former Soviet republics under asymmetrical commercial relationships, Spain continued to expand in the Third World, especially Latin America by capturing key sectors from energy to telecommunications. Though the transition from the patron-client model to interdependent started even before Franco's death, it would not have been possible had the domestic elites not decided that their future rested with the EEC. Equally significant, the era of authoritarianism had proved anachronistic for Spain and for the rest of southern Europe as the division of labor had changed considerably since the end of the war. Finally, the remarkable economic advance of western Europe by the mid 1970s and the coincidence of the political and economic problems in the U.S. were contributing factors in the transition process.

Notes

1. U.S. Department of State, *Spain* (Washington, D.C. 1973); Teresa Lawlor, *Contemporary Spain* (New York, 1998); Robert Graham, *Spain: A Nation Comes of Age* (New York, 1984).

2. Public Record Office (hereafter F.O.) 371/130322, No. 11, 16 January 1957; Diego Abad de Santillan, *Contribucion a la historia del movimiento obrero espanol* (Mexico City,1971); Almendros Fernando Morcillo et al. *El Sindicalismo de clase en Espana, 1939-1977* (Barcelona, 1978); L. Suarez Fernandez, *Francisco Franco y su Tiempo* (Madrid,1984), V, pp. 250-60; Sheelagh Ellwood, *Franco* (London, 1994), pp. 160-64.

3. J. Cruz et al., (ed), *Franquismo y lucha de clases: una aproximacion historia*. (Barcelona: CEDOS, 1977); Jordi Garcia Gracia, *La Espana de Franco* (Madrid, 2001); F.O. 371/160266, No. 1, 2 January 1961; Ford Library, White House Central File, (hereafter WHCF) Box 46, Folder CO/39, Spain, Executive File, 19 November 1975, William Shirer and Barbara Tuchman to President Ford; SDNA 852.10/1-1950, No. 19; SDNA 852.10/1-1150.

4. Rodrigo Botero, *Ambivalent Embrace* (Westport, CT, 2001), 131, 148-58; SDNA 852.10/2-950; 852.10/3-1050; SDNA 852.10/6-1350, Francis Biddle to the President; SDNA 852.10/6-1350, Harold Taylor to the President; SDNA 852.10/6-1450, Robert Segal to the President; SDNA 852.10/8-1050, No. 163; SDNA 852.10/9-2750.

5. SDNA 852.10/11-2050, No. 536; SDNA 852.10/1-3151, No. 867; SDNA 852.10/2-751, No. 909; SDNA 852.10/5-451, No. 1299; 852.10/5-851, No. 1318; SDNA 852.10/5-2351, No. 1398; Ellwood, *Franco*, p. 158;

6. Botero, *Ambivalent Embrace*, pp. 162-63; F.O. 371/185779, No. CS 103145/5, 9 March 1966; F.O. 371/117860, 149/24/1, 2 March 1955.

7. SDNA 852.131/12-756, No. 596; F.O. 371/124138, No. 1451/23, 23 April 1956.

8. SDNA 852.10/2-2558, No. 624; F.O. 371/130322, No. 11, 16 January 1957; F.O. 371/136642, No. 10, 21 January 1958.

9. F.O. 371/13667, No. 70, 19 May 1958; SDNA 852.10/1-1757 No. 758; SDNA 852.10/1-3157, No. 829; F.O. 371/136542, No. 10, 21 January 1958; Ellwood, *Franco*, 179.

10. SDNA 852.107-857, No. 30; SDNA 852.10/8-257, No. A-26 SDNA 852.10/4-258, No. 717; F.O. 371/13667, no. 70, 19 May 1958.

11. SDNA 852.10/10-1557, Lodge to Christian Herter; F.O. 371/136642, No. 10, 21 January 1958; F.O. 371/136667, No. 70, 19 May 1958; F.O. 371/136642, No. 10, 21 January 1958.

12. F.O. 371/136667, No. 70, 19 May 1958; SDNA 852.10/2-1858, No. 597.

13. SDNA 852.10/11-3-2658, No. A-231; SDNA 852.11/11-2559, No. 383; SDNA 852.10/3-2458, No. 688; SDNA 852.10/6-3058, No. 945; F.O. 371/13669, No. 3853/58, 25 July 1958.

14. Eloy Fernandez Clemente, "Mariano Navarro Rubio artifice del Plan de Estabilizacion," <www.unizar.es/eheep/eloy7.pdf>15-20; The International Bank for Reconstruction and Development, *The Economic Development of Spain* (Baltimore,1963), pp. 3-4; IMF Archives, C/Spain/810, Mission Ferras, 9 April 1959, J. P. Salle to Gabriel Ferras; Ibid., 29 January 1959; SDNA 852.10/5-759, No. 3205; SDNA 852.10/5-2559, No. 717.

15. IMF Archives, C/Spain/Stand-by Arrangements, 15 July 1959, EBS/59/50 Secretary to Executive Board; Ibid., Mission Ferras, 29 July 1959; SDNA 852.10/6-1159; SDNA 852.10/6-1259; SDNA 852.10/7-259, No. 32; SDNA 852.10/7-1059, No. 93; Ellwood, *Franco*, p. 180.

16. SDNA 852.10/7-359, No. 2; SDNA 852.10/7-2359, No. 7; SDNA 852.10/8-1359, No. 139; SDNA 852.10/7-2359, No. 137; SDNA 852.10/9-2959, No. 33; WBA Box 6, Spain-General Negotiations Vol. II, 9 February 1960, Carelde Beaufort to J. Burke Knapp; IMF Archives, C/Spain/420, Stabilization Program, 6 July 1959, Jose Maria de Areiza to Per Jacobsson; Ibid., C/Spain/810 Mission, Gabriel Ferras, 20 November 1959, Ugo Sacchetti to Gabriel Ferras; IMF Archives, C/Spain/810, Mission Merwin, 17 May 1960, Irving Friedman and Ernest Sturc; Ferras; Botero, *Ambivalent Embrace*, p. 165.

17. SDNA 852.13/9-2559; SDNA 852.10/11-259, No. 306; SDNA 852.10/11-1059.

18. WBA, Box 6, General Negotiations II, 28 March 1960, J. H. Williams to Files; Ibid., 23 March 1960, J. H. Williams to Files; F.O. 371/153325, No. 63E 2 May 1960; F.O. 371/160266, No. 1, 2 January 1961.

19. IMF Archives, C/Spain/810 Mission Sacchetti, 23 November 1960; F.O. 371/163250, No. RS1102/9, 10 October 1960; F.O. 371/163250, No. C66, 2 December 1960; WBA, Box 6, General Negotiations Vol. III, 19 August 1960, Eugune Black to Navarro Rubio; Ibid., 19 August 1960, S. R. Cope to Files; Ibid., Spain-General Negotiations Vol. II, 20 October 1960; F.O. 371/160273, No. 9E, 12 January 1961; SDNA 852.00/3-661, No. 490; SDNA 852.00/1-2761, No. 407; SDNA 852.00/2-1461, No. 465; SDNA 852.00/2-2461, No. 489; IMF Archives, C/Spain/Stand-by Arrangements, 14 March 1961, Ullastres to Jacobsson; Ibid., 10 February 1961, Manuel Varela to D. Jose Aragones; Ibid., 28 February 1961, J. H. C. de Looper to Irving S. Friedman.

20. F.O. 371/163810, No. 19E, 9 February 1962 F.O. 371/163810, No. E.5, 21 January 1962; SDNA 852.00/3-1661, No. 547; IMF Archives c/sPAIN/810, Stabilization Program, Press Release No. 351, 1 May 1961; Ibid., 16 March 1960, G. Ferras to Sarda; F.O. 371163800, No. 1, 1 January 1962; WBA Box 6 General Negotiations Vol. II, 7 October 1962, S. R. Cope to Files.

21. F.O. 371/160770, No. CS1072/4, 21 August 1961; F.O. 371/160770, 15 September 1961; F.O. 370/160780, 26 September 1961; IMF Archives, C/Spain/810, Mission Ferras, 29 November 1961, Jacobsson to Ullastres; SDNA 852.00/10-261, No. 188; F.O. 371/169470,

No. 1 (1015), 1 January 1963.

22. F.O. 371/163810, No. 17, 22 January 1963; F.O. 371/163816, No. CS113145/1, 19 February 1962; F.O. 371/163816, No. CS113145/2, 2 June 1962; F.O. 371/163816, No. CS113145/3, 15 October 1962; IBRD, *Economic Development of Spain* (Washington, D.C.,1963), pp. 4-5.

23. F.O. 371/163811, c1116 22 May 1962; F.O. 317/163811, No. CS1102/5, 22 August 1962.

24. WBA Box 6 Spain - General Negotiations Vol. II, 17 October 1962, W. C. Baum to S. R. Cope; Ibid., General Negotiations Vol. III SLC/A/62-29, 14 December 1962 M. L. Lejeune to Distribution; F.O. 317/163811, No. 112E, 3 October 1962; F.O. 317/163811, No. C11012, 13 October 1962; SDNA 852.00/10-1962, No. 1-241; F.O. 317/163811, No. 134E, 23 November 1962; F.O. 317/163811, No. 137E, 30 November 1962; SDNA 852.00/3-1662; F.O. 371/169470, No. 1 (1015), 1 January 1963; FN 15 SPAIN No. A-913, 31 May 1963; IMF C/Spain/420.1, Exchange Restrictions, SM/63/65, 24 July 1963, Secretary to Executive Board.

25. Ibid.; F.O. 371/169488, No. CS1102/1, 25 January 1963; SDNA 852.00/12-462, No. A-352; F.O. 371/169487, No. E 25, 18 February 1963; WBA Box 6, General Negotiations, Vol. III, 30 October 1963, Bruce Cheek to Files.

26. F.O. 371/169491, No. 752, 31 December 1962; F.O. 371/169491, 19 February 1963; F.O. 371/169491, No. 4, 11 January 1963; SDNA, 852.05100/2-1061, No. 428; WBA Box 6 General Negotiations Vol. III, 7 July 1965, S. R. Cope to Distribution; Ibid., 17 January 1964, G.A. Torelli to Files.

27. WBA General Negotiations Vol. III, 14 February 1963, B. M. Cheek to Files.

28. F.O. 371/172334, No. 26, 14 May 1964; F.O. 371/172334, 6 March 1963; Gonzalo Fernandez de la Mora, "Lopez Rodo," *Razon Espanola* <http://galeon.com/razonespanola>; F.O. 371/172334, 3 May 1963; F.O. 371/172334, 7 May 1963; F.O. 371/171406, No. M10820/5, 14 February 1963; F.O. 371/171406, No. 42, 6 March 1963; F.O. 371/171406, No. C11012, 30 December 1963; FN 17-1 SPAIN, No. A-837, 10 May 1963; F.O. 371/169488, No. 10 April 1963; IMF C/Spain/420.1 Exchange Restrictions 26 August 1964, "Background Material for Article XIV Consultations, 1964."

29. Francisco Franco, *Discursos y mensajes del Jefe del Estado, 1960-1963* (Madrid, 1964), pp. 390-404; F.O. 371/169487, No. 150, 17 September 1963; F.O. 371/174942, No. 174, 12 December 1964; F.O. 371/169488, No. 87 E 7 June 1963; F.O. 371/174936, No. 1,7 January 1964; FN 11-1 SPAIN, No. 779, 18 April 1963.

30. F.O. 371/169488, No. C 11022, 21 October 1963; F.O. 371/169488, No. 177 E, 13 November 1963; F.O. 371/169488, No. CS 1102/11, 25 September 1963.

31. F.O. 371/174948, No. CS 1101/6, 2 October 1964; F.O. 371/174948, No. CS1101/3, 6 March 1964; F.O. 371/180777, No. 1, 4 January 1965; J. Sinova (ed), *Historia del Franquismo* (Madrid, 1985), II, pp. 589-93.

32. SDNA (Financial Files, hereafter FN)FN 9-1 SP, No. A-101, 5 August 1964; FN 9-2 SP, No. A-840, 15 May 1964.

33. WBA, Box 6 General Negotiations Vol. III, 7 February 1964, W. C. Baum to B. M. Cheek; Ibid., 17 June 1964, D. J. Fontein to L. J. Evans; F.O. 371/17939, No. CS1022/1, 20 May 1964; POL 17 SPAIN, 14 July 1964.

34. F.O. 371/180118, No. CS103145/13, 9 December 1965; F.O. 371/174948, No. CS 1101/6A, 30 December 1964; FN 12 SPAIN, No. A-333, 17 November 1964; F.O. 371/174948, No. CS 1101/1, 7 January 1964; F.O. 371/180777, CS1011/1, No. 1, 4 January 1965; FN 9-1 SP, No. A-306, 9 November 1964; WBA Box 6 General Negotiations Vol. III, EC/M/65-8, 23 April 1965 Acting Secretary to Economic Commission; Ibid., 27 April 1965, D. J. Fontein to S. R. Cope; WBA Box 6 General Negotiations, III, LC/O/65-46, 7 July 1965, S. R. Cope to Distribution.

35. FN 10-3 SPAIN No. A-56, 20 July 1965; WBA, Box 4 Spain - Mission Terms of Reference, 1 October 1965, D. S. Balantine to A. J. Macris.

36. FN 9 SP, No. 375, 29 December 1966.

37. F.O. 371/185797, No. C1166, 27 January 1966.

38. IMF C/Spain/420.1 Exchange Restrictions SM/67/45, 17 April 1967, Secretary to Executive Board; FN 10-2 SPAIN, No. A-856, 18 June 1966; FN 17 SPAIN, No. 478, 29 January 1966; FN 10-1 SPAIN, No. A-712, 11 May 1967; F.O. 371/185779, No. CS103145, 9 March 1966; F.O. 371/185797, No. 58, 10 March 1966; F.O. 371/185797, No. CS1111/8, 7 April 1966.

39. F.C.O. 91401, No. 59, 9 January 1967.

40. FN 6 SPAIN, No. A-367, 16 December 1966; FN 6-1 SPAIN, No. A-618, 19 March 1966.

41. IMF Archives, C/Spain/420.1 Exchange Restrictions/Consultation XIV, 23 January 1967; Ibid., 25 January 1967; Ibid., 29 January 1967; Foreign and Commonwealth Office (hereafter F.C.O) 9/401, No. C5/3, 11 January 1967; IMF C/Spain/420.1, Exchange Restrictions, SM/67/45, 17 April 1967, Secretary to Executive Board; F.C.O) 9/401, No. 68, 31 January 1967; F.C.O) 9/401 No. 541/67, 1 February 1967; F.C.O.9/401, No. 27, 5 January 1968.

42. IMF Archives C/Spain/810, Mission Ponsen, 21 February 1968, Whittome and Sturc; IMF Exchange Restrictions, SM/68/90, 10 May 1968, Acting Secretary to Executive Board; F.O. 1108/23, No. 47, 30 November 1967; IMF Archives C/Spain/810, Mission Pfeiffer, 27 June 1968.

43. F.C.O. 9/402, No. 1011/67, 23 November 1967.

44. WBA Box 4, Spain - Mission Terms of Reference, 26 February 1968, W. A. Wapenhaus to Ergas; Ibid., 17 October 1968, W. van Fleet to F. J. Lethem; Ibid., 30 October 1968, Don Stoops to C. P. McMeekan; Ibid., 5 November 1968, A. J. Carmichael to J. A. McCunniff; E, Alvarez Puga, *Matesa. Mas alla del escandalo* (Barcelona, 1974).

45. FN 12 SP, No. A-530, 11 October 1969; IMF Exchange Restrictions, SM/69/74, 29 May 1969, Secretary to Executive Board; IMF Archives, C/Spain/810, Mission Pfeiffer, 26 February 1969, "Spain 1968"; Ibid., 26 March 1969, Albin Pfeiffer to Managing Director; IMF C/Spain 420.1, Exchange Restrictions 4 February 1970, L. A. Whittome and E. Sturc;

Nixon Project, National Security (hereafter NSC) File, VIP visits, Spain, Box 938, January 1971; Ibid., SM/70, 13 April 1970, Secretary to Executive Board; Equipo Mundo, *Los 90 ministros de Franco.* (Barcelona, 1970), pp. 415-25.

46. IMF Archives, C/Spain/420.1 Article XIV Consultation, SM/73/96, 11 May 1973 Secretary to Executive Board.

47. Nixon Project, Country File, Box 701, 9 March 1970, C. Fred Bergsten to Kissinger; Ibid., 13 March 1970, Bergsten to Kissinger.

48. Nixon Project, Presidential Correspondence, Box 762, 6 January 1971, Helmut Sonnenfedt to Kissinger; Ibid., NSC Country File, Box 705, 25 February 1970, Bergsten to Kissinger; Ibid., 7 July 1971, Sonnenfeldt to Kissinger; Ibid., No. 581, 15 May 1971, U.S. Embassy/Madrid to State; Ibid., Box 701, No. 516, 11 May 1971, Embassy/Madrid to State; Ibid., No. 2115, 14 May 1971, Hill to Nixon.

49. WBA, Box 328, Spain - General Negotiations, 14 February 1972, A. David Knox to W. C. Baum; IMF C/Spain/420.1 Article XIV Consultations, Meeting No. 6, 26 October 1971; Ibid., Meeting No. 11, 28 October 1971; Ibid., Meeting No. 14, 29 October 1971; Ibid., 2 November 1971, Spain - 1971 Article XIV Consultation.

50. IMF Archives, C/Spain/420.1 Article XIV Consultation, 14 January 1972 L. A. Whittome to Sturc; Ibid., SM/72/9, 4 February 1972, Acting Secretary to Executive Board.

51. WBA, Spain - General Negotiations, Vol II, 16 July 1973, Wolfgang Wipplinger to Gregory B. Votaw; Ibid., 22 June 1973, J. L. Upper to G. B. Votaw; Ibid., 14 August 1973 S. Eccles to Benjeck; Ibid., October 1974, "1974 Briefing Paper"; IMF C/Spain/420.1, Article IV Consultations, 1 March 1973, Leo Van Houtven; Ibid., SM/74/129, 28 May 1974, Secretary to Executive Board.

52. Nixon Project, Country Files, Box 701, 4 October 1973, Memo of Conversation, Kissinger, Lopez Rodo et al.; Ibid., No. 428, 16 October 1973, Embassy/Madrid to State; Ibid., 24 October 1973, Embassy/Madrid to State.

53. Nixon Project, Country Files, Box 701, 20 December 1973; Ibid., 21 December 1973, Kissinger to the President; Ford Library, Office of Assistant for Defense and International Affairs, Box 66, No 299, 19 December 1973, Embassy Madrid to Sec-State; Ibid., No. 341, 19 December 1973, Embassy Madrid to Sec-State; WBA, Box 328, Spain General Negotiations, Vol. II, 7 January 1974, J. J. Stewart; Ellwood, *Franco,* 209-10; R. P. Clark, *The Basque Insurgents: ETA* (Madison, WI, 1984).

54. Ford Library, Office of Assistant for Defense and International Affairs Box 66, Spain, October 1974; IMF Archives, C/Spain/810, Mission Pfeifer, 17 November 1975, A. Pfeifer to Managing Director; Ibid., 3 March 1976, A. Pfeifer to Managing Director.

55. Ford Library WHCF, Central File, Box 46, Subject File CO-139 - Spain, 10 June 1975, Robert Goldwin to Donald Rumsfeld; Ibid., 17 June 1975, Clinton E. Granger to Scowcroft; Ibid., NSA Country Files, Box 12, 9 August 1975, Kissinger to U.S. Embassy/Madrid.

56. Sinova, *Historia del Franquismo,* I, pp. 160-66; John Logan "Democracy from Above: Limits to Change in Southern Europe," in *Semi-peripheral Development: The Politics of*

Southern Europe in the Twentieth Century, edited by Giovanni Arrighi (Beverly: Sage, 1985), 162-65; Ford Library, WHCF Box 7, Subject File, ME 1/CO-/39, 25 November 1975, Ford to Juan Carlos; Ibid., NSA Presidential File, Box 12, Spain, 22 December 1975, U.S. Embassy/Madrid to Secretary of State.

57. Ford Library, NSC 7812, 22 November 1975, Clift to Scowcroft; Ibid., Box 46, CO-39, 19 November 1975, Tuchman and Shirer to President Ford.

58. Ford Library, WHCF Box 47, Subject File, CO 139 - Spain, 753, 16 February 1976, Brent Scowcroft to the President; Ibid., 3 June 1976, Jon Howe to White House; Ibid., 4818, 3 September 1976, Brent Scowcroft to the President; Ibid., 16 June 1976, Scowcroft to White House; Ibid., 3588, 21 June 1976, Clift to Scowcroft; IMF Archives, C/Spain/810, Mission Pfeifer, 17 November 1975, A. Pfeifer to Managing Director; Ibid., 3 March 1976, Pfeifer to Managing Director.

59. IMF Archives, C/Spain/420.1 Article XIV Consultation, 19 February 1976, No. 3; Ibid., 20 February 1976, No. 4; Ibid., 18 February 1976, No. 1; Ibid., 18 February 1976, No. 2; Ford Library, Presidential Handwriting, Box 7, Spain, 14 May 1976, Brent Scowcroft to James Connor.

60. *The Economist*, 10 July 1976; Ford Library, WHCF Box 7, ME 1/CO-co/39, 28 June 1976, Juan Carlos to Ford; Ibid., 22 July 1976, C. Arthur Borg to Brent Scowcroft; Ibid., Permanent Operations Offices, Box 65, 19 October 1976, J. T. Lynn to the President; Ibid., NSC, Box 12, No. 497, 4 February 1976, Scowcroft to the President; U.S. House of Representatives, *Implementation of the Treaty of Friendship and Cooperation between the United States and Spain* (Washington, D.C.,1976).

61. IMF Archives, C/Spain/810, Mission Pfeifer, 2 March 1977, A. Pfeifer to Managing Director; IMF Archives, C/Spain/1760 Stand-by Arrangement, 18 October 1977 Whittome to Managing Director; Ibid., 28 November 1977 SEC-94/350; Ibid., 7 February 1978, EBS/78/36, Secretary to Executive Board.

62. IMF Archives, C/Spain/810, Mission, Pfeifer, 8 November 1977, Minutes of Meeting No. 1, Spain.

63. Ibid., No 2; Ibid. No 3; Ibid., 10 November 1977, Ibid, No. 5; Ibid., No. 7, 11 November 1977; Carter Library, NSA Staff, Horn/Special, Box 2, 10 November 1977, No. 4; IMF Archives, C/Spain/810, Mission Whittome, 11 December 1979.

64. IMF Archives, C/Spain/810, Mission Whittome, 9 March 1978, L. A. Whittome to Files; Ibid., 11 December 1979.

65. IMF Archives, C/Spain/810 Mission, 18 December 1979, L.A. Whittome to Managing Director; Ibid., 8 November 1979, L. A. Whittome and David Finch.

66. Carter Library, NSA Staff. Horn/Special, Box 108, 26 June 1980, Spanish Government's Statement on President Carter's Visit.

67. IMF C/Spain/420.3, Article IV Consultations, 11 December 1981, Brian Rose to Files; 14 December 1981, Brian Rose to Files; WBA General Negotiations, Spain-Leap, 16 June 1983, Eugenio Lari to A. W. Clausen.

68. IMF Archives C/Spain/810, Mission Rose, 19 March 1982, Executive Board Meeting 82/33.

69. Alfonso Guerra, *Felipe Gonzalez: de Suresnes a la Moncloa/Recuerdos e impresiones de Alfonso Guerra* (Madrid, 1984); IMF Archives, C/Spain/420.3, Article IV Consultation, SM/85/248, 26 September 1985, Acting Secretary to Executive Board; Juan F. Jimeno et al. "Integration and Inequality: Lessons from the Accession of Portugal and Spain in the EU," in The World Bank, (ed), *Making Transition Work for Everyone: Poverty and Inequality in Europe and Central Asia* (Washington D.C. 2000), I-6; WBA General Negotiations, Spain-Leap, 21 September 1984, Roberto Fernandez to Eugenio Lari; Ibid., 16 June 1983, Eugenio Lari to A. W. Clausen.

70. IMF Archives, C/Spain/420.3, Article IV Consultation, 14 January 1987, Secretary to Executive Board; Jimeno, "Integration and Inequality," pp. 6- I-8.

71. Jimeno "Integration and Inequality," I-3, I-4; Sandra Wilson and D. H. Fretwell, *Public Service Employment: A Review of Programs in Selected OECD Countries and Transition Economies* (The World Bank, 1999), pp. 3-5.

72. IMF Archives, C/Spain/420.3, Article IV Consultation, SM/88/69, 9 May 1988, Secretary to Executive Board.

73. IMF Archives, C/Spain/420.3, Article IV Consultation, SM/89/119, 13 July 1989, Secretary to Executive Board; Ibid., SM/91/154, 6 August 1991, Acting Secretary to Executive Board.

74. Keith Salmon, *The Modern Spanish Economy: Transformation and Integration into Europe* (London,1995), 10-23; IMF Archives, C/Spain/420.3, Article IV Consultation, SM/90/114, 12 June 1990, Acting Secretary to Executive Board; WBA, Box 328, Spain-General Negotiations, ES-LEAP, 12 March 1995, Ricardo Soto to Akin Oduolowo.

75. IMF Archives, C/Spain/420.3, Article IV Consultation, SM/93/262, 27 December 1993, Secretary to Executive Board.

76. IMF Archives, C/Spain/420.3, Article IV Consultation, SM/92/145, 24 July 1992, Secretary to Executive Board.

77. Ministerio de la Presidencia y Secreteria General de Portavoz del Gobierno, *Espana en la Union Europea* (Madrid, 1995), 50-59; J. M. De Areilza, Carvajal et al., *Espana y las transformaciones de la Union Europa* (Madrid, 1999); IMF Archives, C/Spain/420.3, Article IV Consultation, SM/93/262, 27 December 1993, Secretary to Executive Board; John Stremlau, "Clinton's Dollar Diplomacy," *Foreign Policy*, no. 97 (1994): 18-35.

78. MF Archives, C/Spain/420.3, Article IV Consultation, 20 January 1995, Massimo Russo and Susan Schadler.

79. IMF Archives, C/Spain/420.3, Article IV Consultation, SM/96/77, 3 April 1996, Acting Secretary to Executive Board.

80. IMF Archives, C/Spain/420.3, Article IV Consultation, SM/95/15, 23 January 1995, Secretary to Executive Board.

81. IMF Archives, C/Spain/420.3, Article IV Consultation, SM/96/77, 3 April 1996, Acting

Secretary to Executive Board; Jimeno, "Integration and Inequality," I-5; P. L. Gomiz Diaz, "Las Nuevas Politicas de empleo y de asuntos sociales en el Tratado de Amsterdam," in Ministerio de Asunto Exteriores de Espana (ed), *Espana y la negociacion del Tratado de Amsterdam* (Madrid, 1998), pp. 120-24.

82. IMF Archives, C/Spain/420.3, Article IV Consultation, SM/96/100, 25 April 1996, Secretary to Executive Board.

83. IMF Archives, C/Spain/420.3, Article IV Consultation, 26 March 1996, Massimo Russo and Susan Schadler.

84. Ibid., SM/96/72, 27 March 1996, Secretary to Executive Board.

Chapter 3

Greece: From U.S. Financial Dependence to EU Integration

Roots of Postwar Economic Dependence: Patron-Client Integration under Americanokratia

The modern history of Greece has been characterized by inordinate dependence on Great Britain from its Independence in 1832 to 1945, and then on the U.S. since the Truman Doctrine in 1947. U.S. aid during the Greek Civil War (1946-1949) was designed to secure Greece along with Turkey as U.S. military satellites, and integrate them into the nascent American sphere of influence. During the 1950s the U.S.-installed regimes in Athens acknowledged that low living standards, high unemployment and underemployment, and low incomes were the core reason for popular sympathy toward Communism, a position with which some U.S. officials concurred. Though the U.S. provided $200 million in balance-of-payments subsidies for Greece in 1951, living poverty levels were comparable with a Third World country. Yet, the IMF recommended a series of austerity measures that would perpetuate immense income gaps.[1]

Acting on the advice of the U.S. and the IFIs, in October 1953 Greece promulgated Law 2687 that encouraged foreign investors to appeal to the government for tax exemptions and other incentives for a period of up to ten years if investment were directed in import-substituting industries like manufacturing and mining. Original investment and reinvested profits were covered under the law, and 10 percent of both could be repatriated one year from commencement of operations. While Greece was a small market with limited raw materials, U.S. and European firms found it far easier to penetrate because of law 2687.[2]

Praising prime minister Alexander Papagos and the minister of the economy Spyros Markezinis, U.S. ambassador John Peurifoy, who enjoyed far greater influence than any Greek official, used U.S. aid to keep Athens in line with U.S. policy. Though U.S. aid covered about half of Greece's balance-of-payments deficits, it was insufficient to cover expenses largely because 51 percent of the $300 million budget for fiscal 1953-54 was devoted to defense. Greece received $25 million in U.S. aid for defense and $16.5 million in NATO assistance. Because it could not secure IBRD and

Eximbank loans, Greece borrowed at unfavorable terms from U.S. companies. Although the State Department supported funding purchases of U.S. equipment, the IBRD and the Eximbank insisted that no credit be extended to companies for non-military Greek projects. As part of a global policy to transition aid recipients from public to private sector capital and to lessen the public sector's role in the economy, in 1954 the U.S. reduced grants to Greece. Adopting the same policy toward the Third World, the U.S. refused to approve IBRD loans for Greece before an agreement to settle prewar foreign debt.[3]

Though by the mid-1950s the patron-client integration model was a resounding success from the U.S. perspective, the government in Athens classified 34 percent of the population as indigent, earning less than $8 per month. More than half of the population lived at or below the poverty line when King Paul appointed Constantine Karamanlis prime minister in October 1955. At the high end of the wage scale, about 160,000 industrial workers earned $500 annually. Despite $1 billion in postwar U.S. aid, unemployment and under-employment were estimated at 1.5 million of a total of 7 million people. Even the IMF acknowledged that economic aid had not benefited the working class, despite propaganda that the U.S. embassy and U.S. missions disseminated through the regime in Athens. Not that political, social, and economic conditions were any better in the Iberian peninsula or the Third World.[4]

The most significant contradiction in U.S. foreign policy was that the U.S., IMF, and World Bank were imposing deflationary policies while at the same time compelling Greece and other underdeveloped countries to maintain liberal trade policies and high defense budgets that caused deficits and inflation without creating jobs, higher incomes, or greater self-reliance. Fixated on stabilization rather than addressing the root causes of endemic poverty, the IMF warned about upward movement in wages, despite the fact that prices had risen substantially from 1953 to 1956. The challenge for Karamanlis's National Radical Union party (ERE) was to stay in office without alienating the working class to the degree that they would back the centrist parties or the leftist United Democratic Left (EDA).[5]

Along with the Portugese and Spaniards, Greeks were at the bottom of the European economic ladder, earning ten times less than the average U.S. per capita income. Whereas northwest Europe spent on average 35 percent of exchange income on foodstuffs, Greece was spending 60 percent, comparable with the Third World. Karamanlis contended that the monetarist and free trade policies were responsible for depleting gold reserves, largely because luxury imports absorbed capital that would otherwise have stimulated domestic production of essentials. The same was true for most underdeveloped countries. With one-quarter of the labor force totally or partially unemployed, one of the highest levels in the world, U.S.-IMF-imposed policies kept half of the people impoverished and seeking to emigrate as their only solution.[6]

In September 1958 the Federal Republic of Germany announced an aid package for

Greece, somewhat comparable to those it offered Turkey, Arab countries, and India. Included were development credits from *Kreditanstalt fur Wiederaufbau* for 200 million marks for a period of 20 years at 6 percent interest. Germany agreed to export financing for 400 million marks over a five year period, with the possibility of providing an additional 250 million marks, after the Bundestag approved the measure. Projects to be financed included export of telecommunications systems, agricultural machinery, funding the Ptolemais power plant, a sugar factory, lignite mines, and hydroelectric plants. Most projects were linked to the Bodosakis-Krupp enterprises whose relationship dated to the inter-war era.[7]

Against the background of the Cuban Revolution and the African decolonization movement, Greeks blamed the U.S. for inordinate national security spending, for demanding repayment of the prewar foreign debt, and for not allowing the IBRD to provide development loans comparable to western Europe's. Just ahead of the IMF-World Bank annual meeting in September 1960, Jose Aragones Vila, IBRD Executive Director, castigated his institution for its inflexible position toward Greece and other debtor countries. Aragones' remarks were made after the World Bank suspended a loan application for the Athens-Thessalonike highway construction, because the State Department linked the loan to debt settlement.[8]

In July 1961 Greece became an associate EEC member, and under special arrangement enjoyed tariff reductions. A major step toward greater western integration, Greece qualified for up to $125 million in EEC loans during the first years of its association. In return, it reduced tariffs on EEC products by 5-10 percent immediately, to be followed by 10-20 percent in 30 months, until completely abolished in 22 years. Though the six EEC members approved $125 million, they warned of no more credits until the prewar debt was settled. Karamanlis promulgated Law 4171 in 1961 and amended it in 1962 by Law 4256 to domestic and foreign investments of up to $2 million. EEC businesses received special custom and tax privileges to invest and to repatriate profits.[9]

Karamanlis claimed that since he took office in 1955 GNP rose 80.7 percent, though the rise was 69.8 percent at most, or about 7 percent annually. While national income rose from $1.9 billion in 1955 to $3.3 billion in 1963, income concentration entailed widespread inequality. Per capita income was about the same as Spain and Portugal, close to the bottom of other EEC associate members. A U.S. senate foreign relations committee revealed that owing to the emphasis on defense rather than economic development, Greece suffered chronic high unemployment and under-employment, and low living standards.[10]

Measured against northwest Europe's economic and social progress during the two decades after the war, Greece did not make much progress. Compared with southern Europe and Third World, Greece was about average in key areas from per capita income to health and education. Between the elections of 1961 and 1963 there was a dramatic rise in agricultural workers' strikes, student protests, and small merchants' grievances, all resolved by force. Although Greece, like Spain and Portugal, experienced relative financial and monetary stability from 1956 to 1963, its economic potential was not realized because of U.S.-mandated defense spending, small productive investment, heavy dependence on foreign capital, and archaic tax system.[11]

Multilateralization of the Patron-Client Model and U.S. Reaction, 1963-1967

When George Papandreou was elected in 1963, the world economy was growing, but Greece was facing high defense costs, owing to the tensions with Turkey over Cyprus. During the campaign the right wing created a panic by announcing that Papandreou's Center Union Party would not defend the currency and it would pursue liberal monetary policies. Consequently, speculators, currency dealers, and investors drained an estimated $100 million, fearing the worst under Papandreou who proved just as loyal to the IMF as his predecessor. Papandreou was the first postwar premier to question the wisdom of the patron-client model and to try to multilateralize Greece's commercial relations and integration.[12]

Despite 315,000 people emigrating from 1959 to 1963, primarily to the U.S., Canada, Australia, and Germany, unemployment and underemployment remained high. Papandreou's critics were concerned that he would jeopardize monetary stability, and the World Bank cautioned about the impact of inflation on direct foreign investment. The fact that Papandreou kept Xenophon Zolotas, the conservative pro-U.S. Bank of Greece governor, was indicative of the administration's commitment to cooperation with the IMF.[13]

Papandreou replaced the one-year pacts with a five year contract with Bulgaria, a three year pact with Czechoslovakia, and multi-year deals with other East Bloc countries. Papandreou was seeking new markets to export tobacco, cotton, citrus fruits, olive oil, and processed foods. Criticism notwithstanding from the IFIs, Washington, and some European conservatives about Papandreou's policies designed to stimulate the economy, material conditions improved for the lower middle classes and even for workers. While GDP rose 6 percent in the 1950s and 8.5 percent in 1960-64, wages were still the lowest in Europe, owing largely to a weak and docile trade union movement that had been coopted by the right wing with U.S. aid.[14]

Although the United States and Britain adopted a hard line toward Papandreou, Germany and France pursued a softer approach on foreign loans in order to secure market share and increase direct investments. After offering a three-year $20 million loan for deliveries of French capital equipment, Pechiney Aluminum company, invested $120 million for an aluminum factory in Greece. Because the French imposed strict conditions on a $25 million OECD consortium loan to help finance capital exports to Greece, Papandreou was anxious to secure foreign investment, partly to validate the government's pro-Western policies.[15]

Rapidly multilateralizing commercial relations and trying to strengthen national capitalism, the Center Union's treatment of foreign firms was generous. Under the Center Union, foreign capital inflow rose 250 percent as did foreign borrowing, while unemployment and underemployment remained at about 300,000 of a total 3.6 million labor force. Considering that most people viewed their economic future with the EEC, Papandreou pledged to develop trade with all countries.[16]

Esso Pappas and Pechiney, the most controversial foreign contracts signed in November 1962, paved the way for French investors, and Greek-American millionaire Tom Pappas to gain access to large scale enterprises, including oil refining, steel, chemical production, among others. Because Pappas' ventures were financed with Greek taxpayers' funds, and because he boasted about his CIA ties, centrist and leftist politicians had reservations about squandering precious resources estimated at $125 million for Pappas enterprises. Although Greece retained liberal foreign investment laws, political instability to which the CIA contributed, greater opportunities in larger markets, and resistance by some local interests to foreign capital, accounted for much smaller foreign investments than Spain's.[17]

Following several months of U.S.-Greece foreign policy disagreements and CIA meddling, in July 1965 the King replaced Papandreou with Stefanos Stefanopoulos. Desperate to meet foreign obligations, strengthen reserves, and restore confidence in the economy and currency by providing massive tax cuts for the wealthy, Stefanopoulos requested a $30 million U.S. loan, $30 million line of credit for earthquake reconstruction, and grants to help with the deficit and higher defense costs for 1965 and 1966. Skeptical of finance minister Constantine Mitsotakis' contention that Greece would be financially sound if more foreign aid were forthcoming, the U.S. and the IMF were pessimistic about the Greek economy and finances. Under pressure from the U.S. and IFIs, Greece reduced spending and increased indirect taxes by 20 percent to curtail consumption. About 70-73 percent of the revenue emanated from indirect taxes that burdened the general population, while about 3000 of the wealthiest families paid a small percentage, and many evaded paying altogether.[18]

Upon publishing a draft of the Five Year Economic Development Plan (1966-1970), the Center of Planning and Economic Research concluded that geographic and income inequality were serious problems. In November 1966 Greece requested IBRD loans for road maintenance and development and other projects ranging from education, agriculture, and industrial financing totaling $60-80 million. The World Bank deemed Greece creditworthy and the EIB agreed to finance 30-40 percent of the total costs for new projects, while considering credits to expand meat production and marketing in northern Greece.[19]

Between 1960 and 1966 the economy had grown at about 7-8 percent annually, slowing in 1966 amid sluggish construction and manufacturing sectors. After 1961 Greece along with Spain and Portugal made a major effort to attract foreign capital. *Aluminum de Grece*, owned by Pechiney and other foreign investors, was the largest foreign manufacturing firm at $135 million, followed by Esso-Pappas at $95 million. Of the $314 million foreign capital invested in manufacturing, $275 million was made in 1966 when the interim pro-U.S. regime offered generous terms to secure U.S. and IFI loans. Between 1962 and 1966 foreign investment in Greece amounted to $2 billion, mostly in mining, shipping, aviation, tourism and manufacturing.[20]

Amid the political turmoil, the economy lapsed into a recession, providing a pretext for a group of ultra-right wing CIA-backed colonels to stage a coup that they had been preparing since 1961. The perennial Cyprus problem, and lack of confidence in the economy and weak finances seemed a tangled web that only the military could solve just as in many Third World countries under the patron-client model. Though Greece was not the Dominican Republic where Johnson could send the marines to topple the regime he disliked, or Sukarno's Indonesia where Communism and non-aligned politics could be used as the reason for backing the coup, the lingering uncertainty that the people would dare elect a centrist regime that would follow a more independent foreign policy and erode the patron-client model was the justification for intervention in the eastern Mediterranean that had become the "other American lake."[21]

The Authoritarian Phase of the Patron-Client Model, 1967-1974

On 21 April 1967 a group of junior military officers took power and imposed a seven-year dictatorship. Colonel George Papadopoulos and general Stylianos Patakos were the Junta's strongmen who vowed to cleanse Greece from anarchism and Communism. Publicly committed to free enterprise, the Junta promised reforms leading toward greater efficiency, productivity and prosperity, while stabilizing the economy and public finances. Espousing a conservative fiscal and monetary policy, the Junta advocated growth by debt under authoritarian capitalism where the state would decide the course of the economy. Besides promising 18.5 percent in private fixed capital formation in manufacturing, a figure never realized, the colonels pledged fair income distribution in an attempt to win over the masses by using populist rhetoric. The irony was that the dictatorship had to lure domestic and foreign private investment with lucrative incentives, while controlling wage and salary raises.[22]

In July 1967 the Junta promulgated Law 89 offering duty and tax privileges to foreign commercial and industrial firms, and to shipping companies. The law was signed two months after an agreement with U.S.-based Litton Benelux, S.A. a subsidiary of Litton Industries which assumed a public and scandalous role in Greece's economy. Under a contract signed on 15 May 1967, Litton Industries was to provide foreign investment at a minimum of $240 million by 1970 and $840 million by 1978, while the government was obligated to commit a minimum of $30 million per year. Litton would receive $1.2 million in 1967, $2.16 in 1968, $3.15 in 1969 and $3.6 thereafter. In addition, the Junta agreed to pay Litton 11 percent of aggregate costs incurred in connection with the projects, and 2.25 percent for equity capital obtained from abroad. Finally, Litton was exempt from duties, corporate income tax and all internal taxes, while the Junta agreed to pay Litton's costs in case of any losses not covered by insurance.[23]

Because the Junta suspended the Constitution, tortured political prisoners, exiled and placed thousands in prison camps, and because of world-wide opposition to the Junta, the EEC suspended relations with the regime. The EIB withheld credits as part of $125 million that it had agreed to make available for development. Refusing to approve more than $12.5 million, the Bank noted that it had to coordinate its lending policy with the EIB, and preferred that Athens continue its relationship with that institution. The Junta relied more on high risk and high interest short-term loans from U.S., Canadian, and European commercial banks. This was a trend that Third World countries followed after 1965, and a root cause of the 1980s debt crisis. The World Bank was concerned that the grim outlook for budget and balance-of-payments deficits had the potential for hyper-inflation.[24]

In January 1968, the Junta promulgated a five-year development plan (1968-1972) predicated on 10 billion drachmas ($300 million) annually of capital inflow. The plan would be carried out with Litton arranging for the foreign investment at 2 percent commission without guaranteeing results. To negotiate loans for an integrated development scheme in Crete under contract with Litton, a Junta delegation met with World Bank chairman Robert McNamara. Considering that Kissinger and vice president Spiro Agnew advocated closer ties with Athens, in March 1968 the World Bank agreed to loans for Greece. The IMF and U.S. urged the Junta and Litton to allow World Bank economists to help with the five year plan that included 316 proposed policy measures and institutional reforms. While the World Bank was skeptical about actual implementation of the Greek plan, the IMF was pleased that the colonels pledged to lift price controls among other liberalization measures.[25]

Like many Third World countries, Greece relied increasingly on short-to-medium commercial bank loans carrying high interest rates from foreign commercial banks. The proportion of public investment financed by domestic sources dropped from 50 percent in 1961 to 16 percent in 1968, and continued dropping under the Junta which relied on foreign loans and direct foreign investment. Foreign debt jumped from $536 in 1966 to $770 million in 1969, with most of the loans contracted at commercial bank rates. While in 1966 the public debt service ratio was 4 percent, it stood at 7 percent in 1969 and expected to rise to 12-15 percent in 1973. Public debt rose 122 percent between 1966 and 1970, while total GNP increased 33 percent, which entailed by the end of 1970 indebtedness amounted to 20 percent of GNP, compared with 12 percent in 1966.[26]

In March 1970 the World Bank approved a $20 loan for Greece, though it characterized the government as a "totalitarian-military regime." Although Papadopoulos had assured the World Bank that he would not exploit the loan for political purposes, the Junta claimed that the loan constituted concrete evidence of international support for its policies. After the Greek consulate in New York published a World Bank memo expressing satisfaction with Greece's economic progress, the World Bank claimed it was misquoted and denied that the loan was a political endorsement. Because Nixon supported the World Bank loan, congressional Republicans admonished the White House not to extend military aid to Greece. Despite European and American critics, Nixon approved large-scale military aid for Greece which he regarded as a significant ally along with the Iberian dictatorships.[27]

Onassis enterprises accounted for $560 million in new investment, and fellow tycoon Stavros Niarchos' projects amounted to $200 million. Both tycoons backed the Junta and both enjoyed influence with the U.S. and international banks. Using their considerable influence to expand their personal fortunes under the colonels, other capitalists included shipping tycoon Stratis Andreadis with investments in banking, hotels, transportation, and manufacturing. Onassis, Niarchos, and Andreadis along with other Greek capitalists had most of their investments overseas. The U.S. supported Eximbank and World Bank loans to finance projects undertaken by Greek shipping tycoons whose fortunes were inexorably linked to U.S. and European corporations. In May 1970 Eximbank approved a $70 million loan to help finance a Bechtel Corporation contract on behalf of Onassis enterprises. This was typical of the nexus between Greek Junta, Washington, the multilateral banks, U.S. capital, and Greek tycoons.[28]

By 1970, direct U.S. investment in Greece was valued at $553 million. Between 1953 and 1971 there were U.S. 94 projects with a minimum investment of $100,000. The largest project was the $132 million Esso-Pappas industrial complex in Thessalonike. Ethyl had $16.5 million invested in an anti-knock compound plant, Goodyear Tire $12.6 million, Coca Cola $8 million in a bottling plant, Parsons and Whitmore $6.3 million in straw pulp and paper mill, Reynolds Metals $4.3 million in a cooperative venture with Pechiney for a smelter, ITT $3.2 million in telephone and telecommunications plant, and American Standard $2 million in a sanitary plant. Investment outside law 2687 included U.S. banks and oil companies with land and off-shore operations. Because World Bank loans instilled confidence, private capital inflows rose. Net public and private inflow of foreign capital was expected to cover $400 million of the deficit in 1970. After committing $150 million in loans, the IBRD planned an additional $155.5 million for 1972-76, although by the end of 1971 the

Bank reduced that figure to $125.4 million.[29]

Foreign borrowing under the dictatorship involved corruption scandals with a number of foreign companies, Greek businesses, and officials. In October 1968 the government signed a contract with the St. Louis-based MacDonald Construction to build a 333-mile highway extending from Igoumenitsa on the Adriatic sea eastward to Alexandroupolis. Estimated at $150 million, in addition to $21 million engineering, construction, and supervision costs to MacDonald, the company was required to provide $105 million in foreign financing guaranteed by the government. Instrumental in helping MacDonald secure the contract, Caterpillar announced that an Italian-Swiss bank signed a contract for $5 million at 7.75 interest, contingent on the company purchasing equipment and securing an Eximbank loan to finance 80 percent of the Caterpillar equipment needed for the project. The French government agency COFACE offered credits to finance the Greek highway, provided that the equipment was purchased from the Creusot-Loire company.[30]

Besides the Litton and McDonald scandals that resulted in the loss of millions of dollars to the Greek taxpayers, the Junta signed a contract with Onassis for an investment of $600 million, of which $560 million would come from foreign sources. In August 1970 Onassis created the Omega Industrial Investment corporation which invited U.S.-based Fluor, Bechtel, Procon, and Foster Wheeler to be in charge of engineering and construction. Although the projects appeared obstacle-free, Onassis tried to change the terms of the contract because of higher oil prices and tanker costs. Premier Papadopoulos sided with Onassis, while Coordination Minister Nikos Makarezos insisted that if the government made the concessions that Onassis demanded Greece would lose hundreds of millions.[31]

After considerable White House lobbying, in April 1971 Eximbank agreed to assist with the financing of Bechtel, Foster Wheeler, Fluor, and Westinghouse contracts with Onassis. For the aluminum smelter, Onassis and the Junta turned to Alcoa Corporation which demanded majority equity in the plant, guaranteed subsidized electric rates, and a guaranteed market for ten years, without providing any of the financing for the company in which it would have majority ownership. Onassis went back to the Soviets and the Hungarians for the aluminum plant, while Niarchos and Kaiser Aluminum were proposing their own deal. More willing to compromise with the colonels, Niarchos was the winner of that contract, while the taxpayers were left with an enormous debt.[32]

From 1967 until the end of 1972, public outstanding floating debt rose 217 percent. Eager to keep the economy stimulated, the government estimated the debt would rise by an additional 15 percent, or 23 percent of GNP in 1973. Public foreign debt service rose from $69 million in 1967 to $171 million in 1972, and it was expected at $204 million in 1973. If the privately-held debt service of $170 million is added to the public debt, the total accounts for 15 percent of current account receipts. In September

1972 the U.S. embassy concluded that the rising external debt and trade deficit posed the most serious threat to the economy. After the Junta devalued the currency, inflationary pressures were exacerbated, forcing the government to raise wages, as prices rose across the board in response to Europe's price hikes in 1972.[33]

Praising the dictatorship for its generosity to U.S. investors, Commerce Secretary Maurice Stans argued that the Junta had drafted very favorable foreign investment laws. Stans had every reason to praise the colonels, considering that Greece had become one of the most attractive countries for foreign investors. Because western Europe was competitive in manufactured exports, the U.S. focused on high tech, medical, telecommunications equipment, aircraft, power generators, and heavy construction equipment.

> In 1972 foreign multinationals were already dominant in several sectors of industry, controlling 96 per cent of production in petroleum products, 60 per cent in transport, 57 per cent in steel, 45 per cent in chemicals, 42 per cent in electrical equipment; the proportion for manufacturing as a whole was 30 per cent.[34]

After Papadopoulos insisted on neutrality during the Yom Kippur War, coinciding with a major student-worker uprising in Athens, the U.S. backed a new Junta in November 1973. A former CIA agent, brigadier-general Dimitris Ioannidis promised to strengthen the economy and increase the minimum wage. Dominated by individuals who lacked in breadth and depth of experience to deal with complex financial and economic problems, the Ioannidis dictatorship pleaded for international aid. Supporting Ioannidis who unlike the deposed Papadopoulos went along with U.S. foreign policy toward Israel, the State Department was losing confidence in the dictatorship which lacked popular support and legitimacy.[35]

U.S. ambassador Henry Tasca noted that the combination of high energy prices, inflation, and lack of an economic program under the Ioannides dictatorship contributed to the general sense of pessimism. Proposing a new U.S. trade, financial, and monetary policy designed to result in greater global integration, Tasca observed that unless such a reexamination took place the U.S. would default its political influence to the rising leftist activity and Soviet influence in the world.[36]

After thousands of people were killed, imprisoned, exiled, and suffering the repression of a pro-U.S. dictatorship, Greeks were left with Turkish military invasion of Cyprus, lack of upward social mobility, lack of opportunities, and more cynical about life and society than ever. The patron-client model had run its course by the summer of 1974 just as it had in Portugal in the spring, to be followed by Spain a year later upon Franco's death. Southern Europe was about to embark on a new course of inter-dependent integration with the EEC.

Foundations for Inter-Dependent Integration, 1974-1981

Former premier Karamanlis returned to Athens to take over the government about the same time that Nixon resigned as a result of the Watergate scandal in August 1974. Greece's economy, finances, and foreign relations had changed dramatically during the dictatorship. As the Vietnam conflict was ending and energy prices skyrocketed, Japan and western Europe had assumed a considerable share of global markets. Whereas in 1950 the U.S. accounted for 50 percent of global defense spending, two-thirds of the world's industrial production, and 50 percent of the financial assets, by the mid-1970s it accounted for 25 percent of the world's defense spending, just one-third of global industrial production, and seven percent of financial assets. Anti-Americanism was on the rise in the world that had grown increasingly skeptical of U.S. moral superiority rhetoric measured against deeds.[37]

The combination of the Cyprus crisis in August 1974, the rise of oil prices, and diplomatic isolation that compelled the Junta to borrow from commercial banks exacerbated the balance-of-payments deficit, forcing the government into even heavier foreign borrowing in the 1970s. In addition, the European recession, global inflation, and the political transition after the Junta contributed to a 4 percent GDP decline in 1974, and an astonishing $1.25 billion in exchange deficit, of which $400 million was oil imports. Karamanlis' regime consulted with the IMF about a wide range of monetary and financial matters, despite reluctance on the part of the civilian authorities in dealing with the multilateral banks and the U.S., especially as long as Kissinger was in the cabinet.[38]

In a candid admission that monetarism had failed to yield the desired results, the IMF noted that western economies were in a recession while simultaneously experiencing inflation. The combination of the high oil prices, global recession, monetarist policies, and the Cyprus crisis precipitated Greece's economic dislocation much deeper than that experienced in the west. Nevertheless, in the second half of the 1970s, labor in Greece, as in Spain and Portugal, benefited from income distribution designed to raise mass consumer demand. When Karamanlis came to power, he relaxed monetary policy, allowed wages to rise after they had been depressed under the Junta, and he pursued a stimulative fiscal policy.[39]

Exceeding EEC's average GNP rise, Greece's economic growth reached 6.1 percent in 1976 and 4.2 in 1977. Because the EEC placed restrictions on Greek textile exports, and rising incomes entailed greater consumer demand for imports, the manufacturing sector was experiencing setbacks, failing to adjust as rapidly as its western competitors. Once France, Italy, Spain, Portugal, and Turkey devalued their currencies, Greece followed suit with exchange depreciation of 12 percent in 1975, 8 percent in 1976, and 3.5 percent in 1977, moves that helped exporters as the IMF recommended. To satisfy capital markets and the IMF, Karamanlis reduced the public debt on which amortization payments amounted to $260 million annually in 1977, and he stabilized the balance-of-payments deficit amounting to $1.4 billion covered largely by capital inflows, while reserves stood at $1 billion.[40]

To facilitate Greece's accession to the EEC as a full member and to stimulate investment, in autumn 1976 Karamanlis agreed to hold down wages, reduce the money supply to 16 percent and credit to 20 percent, and to grant $160 million in tax relief to businesses. These measures went into affect after Washington agreed to provide Greece with a $65 million loan in September 1976 as part of an aid package worth more than $225 million. The loan was made after the press disclosed that a number of U.S.-based multinational corporations had been bribing politicians and military officers in a number of countries where they did business, including Greece under the colonels.[41]

The official transition from the patron-client model to the inter-dependent took place on 28 May 1979 when Greece signed the Treaty of Accession, paving the way for its full membership in January 1981. Once an EEC member, Greece would undergo a transition period to abolish bilateral payment agreements, remove quantitative import restrictions, liberalize capital transactions with the EEC, and customs tariffs would be aligned with the Common External Tariff measures. Athens also pledged to eliminate all export subsidies, though as a result of EEC membership the government expected agricultural prices to rise, as would investment and public consumption.[42]

In May 1980 Karamanlis left the premiership to become president, having accomplished many of his goals, the most important securing Greece's entry into the EEC. The identity of Greece as a European country rather than America's banana republic in the Aegean was made possible by the transition from the patron-client to the inter-dependent integration model. Foreign trade diversification, greater reliance on western Europe, and pluralism took hold across southern Europe. Nevertheless, at the end of the 1970s the oligarchy owned about 35 percent of the wealth, while key industries were foreign-owned. The fundamental structure of dependence based on concentrated domestic and foreign capital had not changed, despite the inter-dependent model. Despite income distribution that no longer resembled the Third World, Greece like its southern European counterparts operated under political patronage, crony capitalists, and large domestic and foreign business dominating the political economy.[43]

Consolidation of the Inter-Dependent Model under PASOK, 1981-1990

In October 1981 the Pan-Hellenic Socialist Movement (PASOK) headed by Andreas Papandreou won the national election, just as the rest of southern Europe along with France experienced a socialist tide during the conservative Reagan-Thatcher decade.

Populist leftist anti-American rhetoric notwithstanding, Papandreou did not deviate from the previous regime's foreign economic policy, though he demanded more concessions as the price for greater integration. Though the inter-dependent model consolidated under Papandreou, he implemented IMF recommendations that compromised the social program promulgated during his inaugural speech. Greece had large public sector expenditures, though its welfare system was vastly inferior to the EEC and closer to Spain's and Portugal's. Nevertheless, during the 1980s, public sector expenditures accounted for 40.6 percent in 1980, rising to 55.5 percent in 1985 when Papandreou was up for reelection. This was largely indicative of a much stronger state structure during the decade when Third World state structures were weakened by the debt crisis.[44]

As was the case with the U.S. bases, Papandreou was simply seeking leverage and greater perks from the EEC, while placating PASOK's left-wing made up of workers and the lower middle class. Unless he appeared anti-west in spirited public speeches, while privately following pro-west policies not very different than other European Socialist regimes of the 1980s, he could not hold on to power.[45]

In addition to steep declines in private investment amid the global recession of 1980-1981, inflation averaged 25 percent, and the pressures on the economy and finances were compounded once the country became an EEC member. Despite $150 million in EEC funds in 1981, and $600 million in 1982, excluding EIB loans, Greece's accession entailed sharp competition in all sectors, especially agriculture. Constantly pressing the EEC to help raise Greece closer to the west European level and not to treat it as a client state, Papandreou wanted to avoid the type of integration of unequal patron-client integration that the G-7 had forged with the Third World.[46]

PASOK invited foreign investment, especially from Greeks in the diaspora, in Greek firms and credit institutions that worked in concert with the government's newly-promulgated five-year plan. Papandreou reassured foreign investors that their money and management skills were needed, as long as they made a contribution to productive enterprises, advanced technology, and obeyed the law. Another area that placated Washington, IMF, and EEC was Papandreou's announcement that he would end credit to debt-ridden enterprises that were of dubious value to the economy. In 1982 PASOK promulgated legislation offering incentives to promote decentralization of production away from Athens and Thessalonike, value-added products and other import substitutes, exports in general, and technological innovation.[47]

Keeping its campaign promise to redistribute income toward the lower classes, PASOK raised wages of the lowest paid workers, while cutting the hours of the work-week. The average earning of non-agricultural real wages rose a modest 5.5 percent in 1982, in comparison with zero the previous year, but unemployment rose from 4 percent in 1981 to 6 percent in 1982. Pleased with the wage/salary raises designed to keep pace with inflation, and higher interest rates intended to curb demand, the IMF was cautiously confident that PASOK's policies were in accord with broad stabilization perimeters. Despite fears that Papandreou's policies would flare hyper-inflation, the CPI decreased from 25 percent in 1980 and 1981 to 21 percent in 1982. In fact, despite the leftist rhetoric, PASOK's policies were more in accord with IMF orthodoxy than the previous regime's.[48]

During PASOK's first three years in power, the economy lagged behind its trading partners, but the same held true for southern Europe. With the exception of Spain, as the figures below indicate, Portugal, Italy and Greece struggled to manage their balance of payments during the early 1980s recession and the second oil crisis.

In Billions of U.S. dollars

Current Account Balance	1981	1982	1983	1984	1985*
Greece	-2.4	-1.9	-1.9	-2.2	-1.7
Italy	-8.2	-5.5	0.8	-2.9	-6.8
Portugal	-2.9	-3.2	-1.7	-0.5	-1.0
Spain	-4.8	-4.3	-2.3	2.0	1.6

(*IMF forecasts)

Source: IMF, C/Greece/420.3 Article IV Consultations 1984/1985, 23 April 1985, L. A. Whittome and J. T. Boorman,

Between 1979 and 1884, total public and private external debt, excluding military debt, doubled. There is a direct correlation between the rise in the balance-of-payments deficit from $2.4 billion in 1981 to $3.288 billion in 1985, and the doubling of the aggregate foreign debt which was $8.5 billion, or 15 percent of GDP in 1980, rising to $16 billion, or 58 percent of GDP in 1985. About 40 percent of the total foreign debt represented public sector borrowing, indicative that deficit financing had become a routine method of capital formation. This was partly because Greece's integration into the EEC anticipated even more capital inflows in the future.

Though the EEC reduced its external imbalances during the first half of the 1980s, Greece had to spend in order to catch up with its west European counterparts. Indicative of Papandreou's pro-business policies, foreign capital was 40.6 percent of investment in the early 1980s, in comparison with 24.8 percent during the 1970s. The modest living standards progress that workers and the lower middle class experienced during the late 1970s and early 1980s, however, would be slowly erased in the late 1980s, just as was the case in southern Europe and to a much greater extent with the debt-ridden Third World.[49]

The Limits of Inter-Dependence: Monetary Stabilization vs. Social Progress

After the parliamentary election of June 1985 in which PASOK won, Papandreou took advice from the more conservative elements of the party, like Costa Simitis who represented Greece on the IMF-World Bank board and who would succeed Papandreou in 1996. Adopting more market-oriented policies, largely owing to domestic and foreign pressures to strengthen the private sector, Papandreou was still trying to balance preponderate influences from big domestic and foreign capital, and his petit bourgeois electoral base, a delicate balance that his European Socialist counterparts also confronted in the 1980s.

The expanding European economy coinciding with a surge of exports, manufacturing, and construction accounted for 2.1 percent GDP growth in 1985. But the combination of higher inflation and higher balance-of-payments and fiscal deficits put greater pressure on PASOK to go along with IMF stabilization measures. Despite Papandreou's toned-down anti-American rhetoric during the campaign, Greece received a great deal of press attention and respect from much of the world for defying the Reagan administration's Cold War policies, and the U.S. campaign against Third World progressive regimes and social movements.[50]

After consulting the IMF and EEC, in October 1985 the government promulgated a two-year stabilization program which the World Bank supported and the EEC was prepared to back with 1.75 billion ECU-loan. The government devalued the currency by 15 percent, modified wage indexation, effectively reducing real wages by 6.5 percent, it reduced public spending, tightened bank liquidity by reducing the money supply growth rate from 27 percent in 1985 to 20 percent in 1986, raised bank reserve requirements, imposed 15 percent on consumer medium- and long-term consumer loans, increased deposit requirements for nonessential imports, and raised gasoline taxes. EEC integration was better than the patron-client, but it did not mean that Greece would become Germany.[51]

As stabilization was in full swing in 1986 and 1987, real wages dropped 10 and 7 percent consecutively. The IMF acknowledged that the new indexation system entailed sacrifices by workers. Because the gap closed modestly between the highest and lowest paid workers under the indexation system in the early 1980s, and GNP share of health, social welfare, and social insurance doubled under the PASOK largely to bring it closer to EEC levels, the government could still claim that it was pursuing income redistribution on an equitable basis. The reality is that the EEC integration model was as significant as Papandreou's policies.[52]

Along with wage cuts, foreign debt contributed to uneven income redistribution as higher taxes were imposed on the lower classes to pay for debt service. During Papandreou's first term in office, the aggregate foreign debt rose from $8.3 billion or 22 percent of GNP in 1981, to $15.6 billion, or 45.2 percent of GNP at the end of

1985. External debt service, excluding short-term commercial debt, rose modestly from $2 billion or 21 percent of receipts in 1984 to 26.1 percent of receipts in 1986. While the U.S. was the largest foreign lender to Greece, German and Japanese loans accounted for 7 and 10 percent respectively by the mid-1980s. A reflection of the chronic current account deficit precipitated by domestic and international economic contraction, deterioration in the terms of trade, higher government expenditures, and a drop in immigrant receipts, Greece's foreign debt was very high for an EEC member, but favorable compared with Latin America or Africa.[53]

Given PASOK's failure to undertake progressive tax reform, it used foreign loans to finance development and current account deficits, a policy no different than southern Europe or the Third World. Since taking office, the Papandreou government had allowed income taxes to drop. In 1986 indirect taxes accounted for 66 percent of revenues, comparable to southern Europe and Third World levels. Nor was Papandreou deterred that the external debt interest payments grew from 2.5 percent of GNP in 1980 to 5.4 percent in 1986, or that debt service absorbed more money than defense and education combined during his second term. In April 1987 the government borrowed $400 million at higher rates than the London Interbank offered from international financial markets. Pursuing a refinancing strategy to reduce amortization payments of $1.9 billion annually in 1988-1990, PASOK tried a variety of diversification instruments.[54]

Instead of addressing structural factors and the growing informal economy that concerned the EEC, the IMF urged the government as the largest employer to set the example by keeping a lid on wages. Like previous regimes, Papandreou used public service jobs to reward his political supporters and to build a patronage network that would assure PASOK's reelection. The total number of employees in public enterprises – Public Power Corporation, Hellenic Telecommunication Organization, Hellenic Railways Organization, Olympic Airways, Urban Transport Organization, Athens Water Supply and Sewage Corporation, Hellenic Aerospace Industry, and Social Insurance Organization – rose from 154,068, or 6.7 percent of the nonagricultural labor force in 1981, to 179,000, or 7.4 percent in 1986, for an annual average increase of 3.5 percent. While the public sector in southern Europe was not much different, higher unemployment was no more a politically-acceptable alternative for Greek Socialists than Spanish or Portugese.[55]

Official corruption remained a fixture at all levels under PASOK, at the same time that Greece was plagued by a thriving contraband trade, especially made easier once the country joined the EEC and there was greater legal and illegal immigration from the Balkans, Asia, and Africa. Estimated at about 30 percent of GDP, the underground economy posed a threat to EEC integration guidelines for Greece. The ubiquitous presence of illegal activities ranged from narcotics traffic, taxis, retail, private tutoring, entertainment, gold and foreign currency transactions, and housing to mention just a few. By far the worst abuses were in the health sector where it was estimated that 51.5 percent of reported activities were part of the underground economy.[56]

During the 1980s, Greece continued to diversify its trade which rose modestly with the Communist bloc, while doubling with the Arab countries, and remaining steady between 60 and 76 percent with the industrialized countries. In terms of geographical distribution, Greece's foreign trade was comparable to southern Europe's, and its fiscal, trade, and monetary policies were also similar under the IMF-EEC watchful eye. Benefiting from a net inflow of EEC subsidies since 1981, Greece experienced the sharpest drop in terms of trade in Europe, lagging behind Italy, Spain, and Portugal. After reaching a peak in 1983, the terms of trade declined sharply, whereas they improved for western Europe. The inter-dependent model did not work equally for all of its members.[57]

From 1980 to 1988, real GDP rose less than one percent per capita, or about half of the EEC average. During the same period, annual inflation averaged 20 percent, the highest in the EEC, except for Portugal, while official unemployment averaged 7 percent annually, much better than Spain's 22 percent. Blaming high government consumption, which rose from 12 percent of GDP in 1960-1973 to 15.4 percent in 1974-1979, and 18.9 percent during the 1980s, the IMF contended that higher wage costs accounted for a drop in profits. Though in 1986 real wages dropped 8.5 percent and in 1987 4.5 percent, the IMF continued to advocate a restrictive wage policy to the exclusion of addressing structural inflationary causes. External debt amounted to $21 billion or 45 percent of GNP, amid growing budgetary and trade deficits and lower living standards.[58]

Following the directive from Brussels in June 1988 to liberalize all short-term capital movements by the end of 1992, Athens lifted travel restriction allowances and securities trades, and completely freed EEC direct investment in Greece. In addition to those measures, the OECD, the IMF, and Washington put enormous pressure on Greece to adopt orthodox monetary and fiscal measures, coupled with deregulation and privatization, just as they did on the rest of the world. Even staunch advocates of integration contended that while there was no credible alternative to the EU, inter-dependent integration entailed a gap between the wealthier and poorer countries, and socioeconomic polarization.[59]

Despite low per capita GDP, proportionally Greece had the highest public sector expenditures in the EEC, rising by 18.5 percent in the 1980s. If the economy had grown at 5 percent annually during the 1980s as it did in the 1970s, PASOK would have been able to better cope with the oil shocks and global competition. Papandreou did not reduce defense or raise revenue needed for the pension program and public firms. While indirect taxes rose from 1.8 percent of GDP in the 1970s to 2.3 percent in the 1980s, direct taxes declined from 1.3 percent to 0.7 percent of GDP. Though revenues represented one-third of GDP by 1989, the revenue ratio was comparable to southern Europe's, but it was very low by EEC standards. In addition to a tax structure that favored the upper income groups, Greece had one of the worst records of tax evasion in the world, largely because of bank record confidentiality, and lack of enforcement mechanisms. On balance, during the 1980s Greece along with southern Europe made significant progress in comparison with the Third World.[60]

Monetarism, Neoliberalism, and Privatization in the Age of Globalization

More inclined to support rapid privatization and globalization than Papandreou, *Nea Demokratia* (New Democracy) premier Constantine Mitsotakis faced serious diplomatic challenges, because his term coincided with a global economic contracting cycle, and the wars in the Balkans and Iraq in which the majority opposed U.S. policy. Because of the need to conform with EU monetary, fiscal, and trade guidelines, in December 1989 Greece raised consumption and utility taxes that the IMF had recommended. The new measure added an estimated 2 percent to GNP. In March 1990 parliament passed legislation to curtail tax evasion, broaden the tax base, and cut expenditures amounting to one percent of GNP.[61]

After 1989 there was political consensus to reduce subsidies to various groups and unprofitable public enterprises, as the IMF and the EU had been recommending, while containing wage costs by capping new government hiring. Though Greece's living standards were among the lowest in the EEC and the average pension was not comparable to those in Europe, both PASOK and *Nea Demokratia* agreed to contain pension costs and went along with the IMF in tightening monetary policy. Insisting on privatization of public enterprises, the IMF noted that since 1983 only 7 enterprises had been sold, 21 operated under the OAE, and 27 deemed non-viable had not been liquidated. Recommending that the solution was to dismiss 26,000 workers, the IMF offered no alternative on how to secure employment for the dismissed public workers. Going along with the multilateral banks, U.S. and EU, in spring 1990 the Greek parliament prepared legislation to deal with non-viable public firms, given that other countries were adopting similar measures on the eve of the demise of the Communist bloc.[62]

The Mitsotakis administration ran on a pro-business and pro-western platform designed to restore confidence in the economy and stabilize public finances. But western pressure to liberalize and privatize entailed conforming to the advice of the IFI's, U.S., and EU which kept Greece from achieving a stronger economic status. Upon announcing a host of stabilization policies on 27 April 1990, the regime stressed fiscal consolidation. This included reducing public sector borrowing under 10 percent of GDP by 1993, privatizing unprofitable public enterprises, offering a host of investment incentives, and "liberalizing" the labor market, which entailed that wages would be determined by free collective and individual bargaining rather than wage indexation. *Nea Demokratia* adopted legislation that placed restrictions on trade unions, including redefining lock-outs and limiting labor strikes, especially in public utilities, measures that some western countries had also implemented.[63]

To support Greece's structural adjustment program, on 4 March 1991 the European Council of Ministers approved 2.2 billion ECU-loan, with the first tranche of one billion ECU disbursed immediately, while the second and third were scheduled for February 1992 and February 1993 respectively. The government would no longer exercise the type of control over the banks that it enjoyed historically, capital movements within the EU were lifted as of May 1991, and many subsidies were eliminated owing to higher interest rate loans.[64]

Of the total 300 public enterprises, Mitsotakis planned to privatize 110, including selling to domestic and foreign investors 49 percent share in some public utilities, the phone company, the electric company, the Public Petroleum Corporation, and Olympic Airlines. To make them more attractive to investors, the government reduced the labor force of public firms, but retained generous unemployment benefits. By far the most controversial and the most egregious scandal of the 1990s was the sale of Iraklis Cement, seven percent of which was traded in the stock market while government agencies owned the remaining stock. While Iraklis' capitalized value was $1 billion, the sale of the company was expected to yield about $600 million. The media alleged that the Iraklis deal involved widespread corruption of top government officials, but it was no different than alleged corrupt privatization deals in England's railway system, Peru's telephone system, Indonesia's banking, or others around the world.[65]

Under the Maastricht treaty, Greece was compelled to reach nominal convergence by 1998 and real convergence by 2000. The EU Economic-Financial Council approved Mitsotakis' stabilization program of June 1993. Questioning the contradiction between Greece's policies and the stabilization's stated objectives to the EU, the IMF doubted that revenues and exports would rise as rapidly as the government estimated for 1994-1999. The stabilization program called for steady reduction in expenditures and public debt, while aiming to reduce unemployment from 10 percent in 1994 to 7.9 percent in 1999. Given the constrictive conditions of the convergence program and Greece's desire to expand by seizing investment opportunities in the former Soviet bloc countries, Mitsotakis' policy mix assumed that Greece would benefit by integrating less developed countries.[66]

Since the mid-1970s the geographical distribution of Greece's foreign trade had been shifting increasingly toward the EU. Japan's share of Greek trade rose in the 1980s and 1990s, while trade with the U.S. remained in the low single digits. Whereas Portugal and Spain adapted much quicker to EU's markets and took advantage of export opportunities, especially in manufacturing, Greek manufacturing export relative to EU trade did not grow. The IMF blamed low productivity and lack of competitiveness on high manufacturing wages, and the surplus labor force in manufacturing. Both Portugal and Spain raised their productivity levels substantially over Greece, reaching approximate parity with the EU average by the late 1980s. Even the IMF acknowledged that since joining the EU, southern Europe's industrial structure remained quite modest, though becoming more specialized in Greece and Portugal, while Spain relied largely on the automotive sector.[67]

Coming to office in October 1993, PASOK did not deviate from privatization, deregulation, and monetarism designed to secure convergence under the Maastricht Treaty. Aging, ailing, and less radical in rhetoric and policy in comparison with his years in the opposition, Papandreou continued the tight monetary and fiscal policies, though he was interested in growing the economy. Applauding PASOK for putting public enterprises on the fast track for privatization and passing a generous foreign investment law, the IMF noted that public spending was still very high, while taxes fell disproportionately on the mass consumer, with widespread tax evasion remaining a problem. The sharp deterioration in public finances, combined with high interest rates owing to drachma devaluation, accounted for lack of investor confidence and relatively low GDP growth in 1993 and 1994 in comparison to the EU.[68]

In January 1996 Papandreou died, leaving PASOK under the leadership of Costa Simitis (1996-2004), former representative on the IMF-World Bank. More moderate than Papandreou, Simitis adopted neo-liberal policies, while insisting he was a Socialist. While in office, Simitis endeavored to legitimize the inter-dependent model and secure as many concessions from the EU as possible. Besides a sharp rise in East European immigration in the 1990s, Greece also experienced a sharp rise in crime, drug traffic, money laundering, and increased subterranean economic activity. Under EU pressure, the Greek parliament passed an anti-money laundering law in May 1993, but it failed to implement specific measures as stipulated by UN and European treaties that the Greek government signed. In fact, with the exception of the Bank of Greece and the Hellenic Banking Association, the government had not taken any serious anti-money-laundering measures during the 1990s, though it fared well in comparison with Cyprus.[69]

In 1998 GDP was $120.5 billion, while annual per capita income was $11,305, rather respectable for the small Balkan country and indicative that it had made enormous progress when compared with Latin America. Greece also made progress on inflation which was a mere 4.7 percent in 1998, dropping to only 2 percent a year later. The price paid for low inflation was unemployment at over 10 percent and aggregate government debt of $119 billion, of which $32 billion was external public debt representing one-fourth of GDP. Though trade with the U.S. dwindled substantially after 1975, U.S. foreign investment remained number one at $1.5 billion by 1994. Because European, Japanese, U.S., and other foreign firms had thoroughly penetrated the economy by the end of the 20th century, Greek firms found opportunities in the former Communist bloc countries where low-cost labor accounted for high profits.[70]

Moving toward greater integration of the regional countries that presented investment opportunities, in 1998 Greece took a lead in establishing Thessaloniki-based Black Sea Trade and Development Bank (BSTDB) initially capitalized at $1.35 billion. A coalition of former Communist countries, Greece, and Turkey, the Black Sea regional trade and investment bloc included Russia, Albania, Armenia, Azerbaijan, Bulgaria, Georgia, Moldova, Romania, and Ukraine where there is a thriving Greek community. As one of the top investors in the Black Sea regional economic bloc based on a variation of the patron-client model, Greece positioned itself for market share in ship-building, telecommunications, computer software, financial services, processed foods, and building materials. Though poverty abounds in the former Communist countries from the Adriatic to the trans-Caspian region, Greek and western capitalists took advantage of low wages, abundance of raw materials, potential markets for consumer products and services, and governments eager for foreign investment in the new frontiers of capitalism.[71]

By 2000 Greece had experienced six years of sustained economic expansion as did much of the western world, and its GDP growth exceeded the EU average by 1999. The price for low inflation, and 2.5-3.5 percent GDP growth in the late 1990s was unemployment hovering at around 10 percent. Recognizing that Greece was under pressure to meet the Maastricht Treaty terms for EMU entry by January 2001, the IMF applauded the Simitis administration's tight monetary policy until Greece adopted the Euro. To ensure price stability and competitive inflation performance within the EMU, the IMF recommended fiscal and wage restraint, combined with vigorous structural policy adjustments to speed up privatization in the new millennium. Under such policies, the result was greater pressure on wages and pensions, lower living standards, and more family members working. Conditions developed very similarly in Spain and Portugal during the 1990s.[72]

Although by the end of the 1990s the average per capita income in Greece was about 60 percent of the EU average, the lower income groups paid an enormous price in terms of low living standards so that their country can fulfill its convergence requirements under Maastricht. Adopting the Euro signaled the official monetary integration into the EMU, but it does not necessarily mean that living standards in Greece will rival those of Germany. Unlike Latin American republics which fell deep into debt and their living standards did not improve appreciably in the last two decades of the 20th century, Greece made some progress, helped in part by integration of the Balkans and the trans-Caspian region that offered low-cost labor and new markets. And unlike NAFTA, which was never designed to engender greater equality within the trading bloc, the EU provided about $7.5 billion in annual subsidies to help lift Greece closer to western Europe. Deregulation, privatization, and stabilization measures, however, resulted in income distribution toward domestic and foreign capitalists.[73]

Greek businesses benefited from the break up of the Soviet bloc, as they moved in the Balkans and took advantage of the cheap labor and new market opportunities. Just as Spain and Portugal have played salient roles in helping to integrate Africa and Latin America into the world economy, Greece has been in the forefront of the Black Sea trading and investment zone designed to integrate its northern and eastern neighbors into the world economy. History, geography, and the evolving world system have determined that Greece's best hope of lifting itself closer to the core of the advanced capitalist countries comes by using its leverage as an EU member to benefit by exploiting the labor of its less developed neighbors.[74]

Notes

1. Archives of the Greek Foreign Ministry (hereafter AHAEG), Box 19, File 2, no. 4145/8, A. G. Politis to Foreign Ministry, 29 August 1950; Ibid., Box 18, File 2, no. 5142/3/US, A. G. Politis to Foreign Ministry, 3 November 1950; Benaki Museum, Plastiras Archives, Box 229, File 6, 5 May 1950; Ibid., 23 September 1950; IMF C/Greece/420-1, Exchange Restrictions Consultations in 1952, Greece: Policy on 1952 Consultations, 23 May 1953; National Archives, CIA Files, RG 263, Box 4, File ORE 4-50, "Current Situation in Greece," 28 February 1950.

2. Giorgos Karagiorgas, *Apo ton IDEA sti Junta* [From *IDEA* to Junta] (Athens, 1975), p. 106; Spyros Markezinis, *Synchroni Politiki Istoria tis Ellados, 1936-1975* [Contemporary History Of Greece, 1936-1975] (Athens, 1994), III, pp. 11-12; Wray Candilis, *The Economy of Greece, 1944-66* (New York, 1968), pp. 91-2; IMF C/Greece/420.1, Exchange Restrictions Consultations 1967/68, Background Material for 1968 Consultation, 21 August 1968; George Coutsoumaris et al., *Analysis and Assessment of the Economic Effects of the U.S. PL 480-Program in Greece* (Athens, 1965), p. 39; A. Gregoroyiannis, *To Xeno Kefalaio stin Ellada* [Foreign Capital in Greece] (Athens, 1980), pp. 25-31; Dimitrios Macheras, *Die Mitgliedschaft Griechenlands in den Europaischen Gemeinschaften* (Frankfurt am Main: Peter Lang, 1988), p. 20.

3. IMF C/Greece/420.1, Exchange Restrictions, J. Pesmazoglou, C. Caranikas, Executive Director of the Fund Team, Greece – 1954 Consultations, 6 May 1954; 23. Ibid., Greece – Indebtedness I, A. S. G. Hoar to Files, 7 December 1954; WBA, Box 4, Mission Diaries, 1953-54, Mission Report No. 1, E. Bachem, 6 August 1954; Ibid., Greece – Indebtedness, II, John Duncan Miller to Martin Rosen, 16 February 1955.

4. SDNA, 881.10/12-2155, No. 579; Konstantinos Karamanlis, *Archeio Gegonota and Keimena* [Archives: Facts and Documents] (Athens, 1996), I, 295; *New York Times*, 1 August 1955; Ibid., 29 September 1957.

5. Karamanlis Archive, I, pp. 294-96; Karamanlis Foundation, Karamanlis Archive, File no. 1-712, 5 March 1956; Ibid., File no. 1-712, 5 March 1956; Ibid., File no. M3 1-484, 15

November 1956; IMF, C/Greece/420.1 Exchange Restrictions, Greece – 1956 Consultations – Briefing Paper Prepared by the European Department & the Exchange Restrictions Department, April 1956; Ibid., Meeting at the Bank of Greece, Merle Cochran et al., 30 May 1956; SDNA 881.10/12-2155, No. 579; P. A. Pavlopoulos, *A Statistical Model for the Greek Economy, 1949-1959* (Amsterdam, 1966), pp. 5-12.

6. IMF, C/Greece/420.1, Exchange Restrictions, SM/58/46, The Secretary to Members of the Executive Board, 1957 Consultations – Greece, 12 June 1958; Yiannis Katris, *E Genesis tou Neofasismou, Ellada, 1960-1974* [Genesis of Neo-Fascism: Greece, 1960-1974] (Athens, 1979), p. 91; Karamanlis Archives, File no. 1.100, M3-38, 1958; Ibid., File no. 1-1094; Ibid., File, no. 1-1097.

7. SDNA, 881.10/11-1258, no. 816; SDNA 881.10/7-2459; SDNA 781.00/5-558, no. 814.

8. SDNA, 881.10/8-2960, No. 206; SDNA 881.10/9-160, No. 217; SDNA FW 781.00/2-2660, No. 2386; SDNA 881.10/8-3160, No. 526; SDNA 881.10/9-2860, No. 304.

9. Karamanlis Foundation, Averoff Archive, File no. A8/33, "Common Market: Trap for Greek Economy," 20 August 1961; S. G. Zambouras, "Continuity and Change in Postwar Greek Foreign Policy" (Ph.D. Dissertation, University of Sheffield, 1993), pp. 186-90; Nikos Psyroukis, *E Neoelliniki Exoteriki Politiki* [Modern Greek Foreign Policy] (Athens, 1981), pp. 273-64; Yiannis Valinakis, *Eisagoge stin Ellinike Exoterike Politike*, 1949-1988 [Introduction to Greek Foreign Policy, 1949-1988] (Thessalonike, 1989), p. 86; Loukas Tsoukalis, "E Ellada kai E Europaike Koinotita" [Greece and the EEC] in D. Konstas and Ch. Tsardanidis (eds), *Synchroni Elliniki Exoteriki Politiki, 1974-1987* [Contemporary Greek Foreign Policy] (Athens, 1989), pp. 200-01; SDNA 881.10/12-2161.

10. SDNA 881.10/1-1563, No. A-615; F.O. 371/169054, CE 1011/1, No. 12, 22 January 1963; WBA, Box 4, Economic Appraisal Meeting, C. H. Thompson to S. R. Cope, 29 December 1964; IMF Exchange Restrictions Consultations 1962/63, Staff Report Recommendations 1963 Consultations, Marcin R. Wyczalkowski to The Managing Director, Preliminary Report on Finding of the Article XIV Mission to Greece, 10 March 1965; Kofas, *Intervention and Underdevelopment*, p. 165.

11. IMF, C/Greece/420.1, Exchange Restrictions Consultations 1962/63, 1963 Article XIV Consultations with Greece, Xenophon Zolotas and Ernest Sturc, 24 June 1963.

12. Jean Meynaud, *Politikes Dynameis stin Ellada* [Political Forces in Greece] part II (Athens, 1974), p. 15; E. K. Stasinopoulos, *Kommata kai Ekloges stin Ellada* [Parties and Elections in Greece] (Athens, 1985),146-47; Markezines, *Politike Istoria*, III, pp. 109-12; Katris, *Genesis tou Neofasismou*, pp. 77-8, 162-69; SDNA POL 2 Greece, 26 November 1963; SDNA POL 2-3 Greece, A-438, 4 December 1964; F.O. 371/169066, CE 103145/2, 18 June 1963; F.O. 371/174806, CE 1011/1, No. 6, 15 January 1964.

13. Maurice Genevoix, *The Greece of Karamanlis* (London, 1973), pp. 144-46, C. P. Danopoulos, *Warriors and Politicians in Modern Greece* (Chapel Hill, 1984), p. 28; Psyroukis, *Istoria*, III, pp. 240-41; Katris, *Genesis tou Neofasismou*, pp. 90-99; Coutsoumaris, *U.S. PL 480-Program*, pp. 150-52, 172-73; SDNA POL 2 Greece, No. A-

369, 30 November 1965.

14. Meynaud, *Politikes Dynameis*, II, p. 25.

15. F.O. 371/174822, CE 1111/64, 5 November 1964; F.O. 371/195671, CE 1151/2, 19 January 1966; SDNA POL 2, Greece, no. A-396, 30 November 1965.

16. WBA, Box 4, Economic Appraisal Mission, C. H. Thompson to S. R. Cope, 29 December 1964; Meynaud, *Politikes Dynamies*, II, pp. 25-6; Christos Jecchines, *Trade Unionism in Greece* (Chicago, 1967), p. 160; Xenophon Zolotas, *International Labor Migration and Economic Development* (Athens, 1966), p. 34; Coutsoumaris, *U.S. PL 480-Program*, p. 27.

17. IMF C/Greece/420.1, Exchange Restrictions Consultation 1967/68, Background Material for 1968 Consultation, 21 August 1968; Candilis, *Economy of Greece*, p. 141; A. Gregoroyiannis, *To Xeno Kefalaio stin Ellada* [Foreign Capital in Greece] (Athens, 1959), p. 95-6, 107-08, 149-50.

18. FN 12 Greece, A-228, 28 September 1965; WBA, Box 4, Economic Mission, Dieter Hartwich to Files, 7 October 1965; FN 15 GREECE No. A-277, 19 October 1965; Zolotas, *International Labor*, p. 38; POL 2 Greece, A-54, 8 February 1966; F.O. 371/185668, CE 1101/9, No. 16E, 5 April 1966; IMF C/Greece/420.1, Exchange Restrictions Consultations 1967/68, Background Material for 1968 Consultation, 21 August 1968; F.O. 371/185671, CE 1151/2, 19 January 1966; Meynaud, *Politikes Dynameis*, II, pp. 100-02; Katris, *Genesis tou Neofasismou*, pp. 92-3.

19. F.O. 371/185668, CE1111/12, No. 30 E, 20 July 1966; WBA, Box 4, Economic Mission, C. H. Thompson, to D.J. Fontein, 23 June 1966; Ibid., C. H. Thompson to Files, 1 November 1966; WBA. Box 11, General Negotiations, Dieter Hartwich to Files, 6 October 1966.

20. SDNA POL 15-1, no. A-498,13 January 1966; SDNA POL 2 Greece, A-54, 8 February 1966; F.O. 371/185670, CE 1113/8, 10 February 1966; SDNA POL Greece A-278, 20 October 1965; WBA, Box 11, General Negotiations II, Nurit Wahl to S. R. Cope, 27 June 1968; Meynaud, Politikes Dynameis, II, pp. 103-14; Pericles Rodakis, *To Xeno Kefalaio sti Chora mas* [Foreign Capital in our Country] (Athens, 1977), pp. 398-99.

21. Kofas, *Under the Eagle's Claw*, pp. 80-85

22. Danopoulos, *Warriors and Politicians*, pp. 76-7; John Pesmazoglou, "The Greek Economy," in Richard Clogg and G. Yiannopoulos (eds), *Greece under Military Rule* (New York, 1972), pp. 80-2.

23. IMF C/Greece/420.1, Exchange Restrictions Consultations 1967/68, Background Material for 1968 Consultation, 21 August 1968; Ibid., Rolf Eversen to the Managing Director, Greece – Article XIV Consultation, 2 July 1968; Ibid., Greece – 1968 Article XIV Consultation, 18 September 1968; Ibid., SM/70/152, Greece – Recent Economic Developments, The Secretary to the Executive Board, 16 July 1970; FN 9 Greece, no. A-234, 20 July 1973.

24. Valinakis, *Eisagoge stin Ellinike Exoterike Politike*, p. 110; WBA, Box 11, General Negotiations II, Bruce Cheek to Files, 26 September 1967; Ibid., Richard Westebbe to Ernst

Schaad, 1 November 1967; Ibid., John H. Adler to Douglas Fontein, 2 November 1967 IMF C/Greece/420.1 Exchange Restrictions Consultations, Background Material for 1968 Consultation, 21 August 1968; Van Coufoudakis, "The EEC and the Freezing of the Greek Association, 1967-1974," *Journal of Common Market Studies* (1977): 114-31; Pesmazoglou, "Greek Economy," p. 76; FN 15 GREECE A-236, 2 November 1967; Greek Ministry of Finance, *Greek Public Finance, Three Years Report, April 1967-April 1970* (Athens, 1970), pp. 27-30; FN Greece, no. A187, 15 May 1971.

25. IMF C/Greece/420.1, Exchange Restrictions Consultations 1967/68, 1968 Article XIV Consultation with Greece, C. A. Thanos et al., 17 June 1968; Ibid., Greece, Part II, Background Material for 1968 Consultation, 21 August 1968; WBA, Box 11, General Negotiations II, Nurit Wahl to S. R. Cope, 27 June 1968; Ibid., General Negotiations, 1969 I, No. EC/0/69-48/1, C. F. Owen to McNamara et al., 24 April 1969.

26. FN 15, Greece, no. A-473, 25 November 1969; FN 15 Greece, no. A-537, 18 December 1969; FN 14 Greece, no. A-229, 9 June 1970; WBA, Box 11, General Negotiations II, Nurit Wahl to M. P. Benjenk, 9 February 1970; Ibid., Country Program Paper Greece, 25 March 1971; IMF C/Greece/420.1 Article XIV Consultations 1971, SM/72/7, Greece – Recent Economic Developments, The Acting Secretary to Members of the Executive Board, 19 January 1972. Nixon Project, Box 593, George Anastaplo, "Swan Song of an Eagle," 12 March 1970.

27. WBA, General Negotiations II, article by Evans and Novak, May 1970; Kofas, *Under the Eagle's Claw*, p. 108.

28. FN 9 Greece, no. A-118, 28 March 1970; FN 9 Greece, no. A-312, 12 August 1970; FN 6-1 Greece, no. 107, 12 November 1970; Katris, *Genesis tou Neofasismou*, pp. 313-14

29. FN 9, Greece, no. A-328, 30 August 1971; WBA Box 11, Indebtedness III, Country Program Paper Greece, 25 March 1971; Ibid., Guy de Lusignan to Benjenk, 1 December 1971; FN 12 Greece, no. A-153, 14 April 1971; FN 12, Greece, no. 2676, 16 June 1971.

30. WBA, Box 11, General Negotiations II, Benjenck to Lusignan, 1 December 1971; SDNA FN 12, Greece, no. A-153, 14 April 1971; FN 14 Greece, no. A-229, 9 June 1970; FN 6-1 Greece, no. A-157, 23 April 1971; Pesmazoglou, "The Greek Economy," pp. 85-7; 99-103; WBA, Box 11, General Negotiations II, No. EC/0/71-188, J. Chaffey, 22 December 1971; FN 6-1 Greece, no. A-50, 14 February 1972; Gregoroyiannis, *Xeno Kefalaio*, pp. 109-10.

31. IMF C/Greece/420.1 Exchange Restrictions Article XIV Consultations, 1969/70, Article XIV Consultation Discussions - Greece, Rolf Eversen to the Managing Director, 18 May 1970; SDNA FN 8 Greece, no. A-200, 20 May 1971.

32. FN 8 Greece, no. A-200, 20 May 1971.

33. FN 14 Greece, no. A-161, 17 May 1973; IMF C/Greece/420.1, SM/73/184, Greece - Recent Economic Developments, The Secretary to Members of the Executive Board, 31 July 1973; FN 12 Greece, no. A-329, 21 November 1972; IMF C/Greece/810, Mission G. Tyler, "Greece," L. A. Whittome to Files, 26 August 1971.

34. FN 12 Greece, no. A-140, 27 April 1973; IMF C/Greece/420.1, Article XIV Consultations

1972-73, Greece - 1973 Article XIV Consultation Discussions, Geofrrey Tyler to The Managing Director, 15 May 1973; Nicos D. Kritsantonis, "Greece: From State Authoritarianism to Modernization" in Anthony Richard (ed), *Industrial Relations in the New Europe* (Cambridge, 1992), p. 605.

35. FN 12 Greece, no. A-290, 4 October 1973.

36. IMF C/Greece/810, Mission Tyler & Staff, April-May 1976, Geoffrey Tyler to Managing Director, 17 May 1976; IMF C/Greece/420.1 Article XIV Consultations, 1977/78, EMB/78/70, 8 May 1978 Nixon Project, no. 903, Embassy/Athens to Secretary of State, 24 January 1974; Ibid., no. 812, Embassy/Athens to Secretary of State, 2 January 1974.

37. Valinakis, *Eisagoge*, p. 267; C. W. Maynez and H. Ulman, "Ten Years of Foreign Policy," *Foreign Policy* (1980): 5-6.

38. IMF C/Greece/420.1, Article XIV Consultations 1974/75, Staff Report for the 1975 Article XIV Consultation, A. Pfeifer and Ernest Sturc, 30 April 1975; Ibid., Greece - 1975 Article XIV Consultation Discussions, Geoffrey Tyler to the Managing Director, 24 February 1975; Karamanlis Archive, VIII, p. 279.

39. IMF C/Greece/810, Mission, Tyler & Staff, April-May 1976, Geoffrey Tyler to Managing Director, 17 May 1976.

40. Karamanlis Archives, File no. 41-2338, April 1976; IMF C/Greece/420.1 Article XIV 1976, EMB/76/134, 8 September 1976; IMF C/Greece/810 Mohammed and Staff, February 1978, A. F. Mohammed to Managing Director, 28 February 1978.

41. N. B. Charissopoulos, *Committee on the Working of the Greek Financial System* (Athens, 1980); IMF C/Greece/420.1 Article XIV Consultations 1977/78, EBM/78/70, 8 May 1978; Ford Library, WHCF Box 4, FO2/00-54, 20 September 1976, Clift to Scowcroft; Kostas Vergopoulos, "Oikonomike krisi kai eksynchronismos sten Ellada kai ston Europaiko noto" [Economic Crisis and Modernization in Greece and Southern Europe] in A. Manesis and K. Vergopoulos (eds), *E Ellada se Exelixe* [Developing Greece] (Athens, 1986), p. 77; Macheras, *Griechenlands in den Europaischen Gemeinschaften*, pp. 90-115.

42. Karamanlis Archive, X, p. 370; Jean Catsiapis, *La Grece: dixieme membre des Communautes europeennes.* (Paris, 1980), pp. 128-31; Valinakis, *Eisagoge*, pp. 249-52; IMF C/Greece/420.1 Article IV Consultations-1979, L. A. Whittome and Ernst Sturc, August 1979; Andreas Koutris, "To Exoteriko Eborio tis Elladas, 1975-1985," in Konstas and Tsardanidis, op. cit., p. 83.

43. IMF C/Greece/420.3 Article IV Consultations 1980, A. Mountford, R. Kincaid, E. Kintzmantel, and J. Wein, 13 August 1980; Ibid., Article IV Consultations, SM/84/21, Secretary to Members of the Executive Board, 18 January 1984; Yiannis Katris, *E Aletheia einai to Fos pou Kaiei* [Truth is the Light the Burns] (Athens, 1983), pp. 66-7; Koutris, "Exoteriko Emborio", p. 83; Tsoukalis, "E Ellada kai e Europaike Koinotita," p. 208; Katris, *Prodomenos Laos*, I, p. 203.

44. Kritsantonis, "State Authoritarianism to Modernization," p. 622.

45. *Greek Government Programme*, pp. 16-7; Konstas, "Oi Stochoi," p. 27.

46. IMF C/Greece/420.3, Article IV, Consultations, 1981/1982, L. A. Whittome and Subimal Mookerjee, 22 February 1983.

47. *Greek Government Programme*, pp. 36-43; IMF C/Greece 420.3, Article IV Consultations 1986 Acting Secretary to Members of the Executive Board, 15 August 1986.

48. IMF C/Greece/420.3 Article IV Consultations 1981/82, Brian Rose and Subimal Mookerjee, 18 March 1983; Ibid., L. A. Whittome and Subimal Mookerjee, 22 February 1983; Ibid., The Secretary to Executive Board, 7 March 1983; Koutris, "Exoteriko Eborio," p. 93.

49. Sakis Karagiorgas and Theofanis Pakos, "Koinonikes kai Oikonomikes Anisotises," in Manesis and Vergopoulos, op. cit. pp. 274-75; Konstas, "Oi Stochoi," pp. 43-4; IMF C/Greece/420.3 Article IV Consultations 1984/1985, Whittome and Boorman, 23 April 1985; Ibid., Article IV Consultations 1988/1989, Acting Secretary to Members of the Executive Board, 29 March 1989; Ibid., Consultations 1987, SM/87/185, Secretary to Members of the Executive Board, 21 September 1987; Ibid., Consultations, 1988/1989, Acting Secretary to Members of Executive Board, 22 March 1989; Kritsantonis, "Authoritarianism," p. 405.

50. *New York Times*, 9 August 1985.

51. Tsoukalis, "E Ellada kai e Europaiki Koinotita," pp. 213-15.

52. IMF C/Greece/420.3, SM/87/185, Secretary to Members of the Executive Board, 21 September 1987; Ibid., SM/87/228, Secretary to Members of the Executive Board, 28 September 1987; Macedonian Press Agency, Simitis-Evert Debate, 13 September 1996.

53. IMF C/Greece/420.3 Article IV Consultations 1986, SM/86/186, Secretary to Members of the Executive Board, 31 July 1986.

54. IMF C/Greece/420.3 Article IV Consultations 1983, Secretary to Members of the Executive Board, 28 August 1987; J. Siotis, "La situation internationale de la Grece et la demande hellenique d' adhesion aux Communautes," in Institut d' Etudes Europeennes, *La Grece et la Communaute* (Buxelles, 1978), p. 54.

55. IMF C/Greece/420.3 Article IV, Consultations 1987, SM/87/185, Secretary to Members of the Executive Board, 30 July 1987; IMF C/Greece/420.3 SM/87/228, Secretary to Members of the Executive Board, 28 August 1987; Kritsantonis, "State Authoritarianism to Modernization," p. 622.

56. IMF C/Greece/420.3 Article IV Consultations 1987, Secretary to Members of the Executive Board, 28 August 1987; Valinakis, *Eisagoge*, pp. 240-41.

57. IMF C/Greece/420.3 Article IV Consultations 1987 SM/87/228, Secretary to Members of the Executive Board, 28 August 1987.

58. IMF C/Greece/420.3, Article IV Consultations 1988/1989, Acting Secretary to Members of the Executive Board, 29 March 1989.

59. IMF C/Greece/420.3 SM/89/58, Acting Secretary to Members of the Executive Board, 22 March 1989; Byron Theordoropoulos, "Public Management Forum," *SIGMA*, 3/6 (1997).

60. IMF C/Greece/420.3 Article IV Consultations 1990, Secretary to Members of the Executive Board, 25 May 1990.

61. Tasos Yiannitsis, "Ellada: E Ekviomechanise se Krisi" [Greece: Industrial Crisis] in A. Manesis and K. Vergopoulos (eds), *E Ellada se Exelixi* [Evolving Greece] (Athens, 1986), pp. 247-48.

62. IMF C/Greece/420.3 Article IV Consultations 1990, P. de Fontenay and J. T. Boorman, 26 April 1990; Secretary to Members of the Executive Board, 25 May 1990.

63. IMF C/Greece/420.3 Article IV Consultations 1990, Massimo Russo and J. T. Boorman, 13 June 1990; Ibid., Article IV Consultations 1991, Secretary to Executive Board, 6 June 1991.

64. IMF C/Greece/420.3 Article IV Consultations, 1990, SM/91/85, Secretary to Members of the Executive Board, 6 June 1991; Ibid., Consultations 1994, Dimitri Demekas and Sunil Sharma, 1 July 1994.

65. IMF C/Greece/420.3 Article IV Consultations 1992/1993, J. R. Artus and S. Kanesa-Thasan, 7 July 1992; Ibid., Secretary to Members of the Executive Board, 12 May 1993.

66. OECD, *Managing Across Levels of Government. Greece* (Paris, 1997); IMF C/Greece/420.3 Article IV Consultations 1994, Dimitri G. Demekas and Sunil Sharma, 1 July 1994.

67. Ibid., SM/94/151, Acting Secretary to Members of the Executive Board, 13 July 1994.

68. *Macedonian Press Agency*, 22 August 2000.

69. IMF C/Greece/4203. Article IV Consultations 1994, Desmond Lachman and Mark Allen, 16 June 1994; OECD, *Recent Public Management Initiatives in Greece* (Paris, 2001); OECD, *Financial Action Task Force on Money Laundering. Annual Report, 1993-1994* (Paris, 1994), p. 39.

70. IMF Greece PIN no. 99/102, IMF Concludes Article IV Consultations with Greece, 8 November 1999; Ibid., PIN no. 98/56, IMF Concludes Consultation with Greece, 10 August 1998; OECD, Economic Survey of Greece (Paris, December 1998).

71. IMF Greece – 1999 Article IV Consultation Discussions, Preliminary Conclusions, 28 June 1999.

72. IMF Greece PIN No. 99/102, IMF Concludes Article IV with Greece, 8 November 1999; Athens News Agency, 17 April 2000.

73. IMF C/Greece/420.3 Article IV Consultations 1994, SM/94/151, Acting Secretary to Members of the Executive Board, 13 July 1994; OECD, "Economic Survey of Greece."

74. Chrysanthe Frantzeskaki, "Evangelos Mitelineos: The Balkans are not for Games and Laughter," *Oikonomike Biomechanike Epitheorise*, (September 2000): 56-9; *Athens News Agency*, 17 April 2000.

Chapter 4

Portugal: From Corporatist State to Interdependence under the EU

Introduction

In 1960 Portugal's population was about 9 million, rising to 10 million by the 1980s, or about the same as Greece. Predominantly agricultural, Portugal does not have much fertile land and historically the concentration of land ownership, low rainfall, and summer droughts have made food imports necessary. At $235 in per capita annual income in 1960 and about $2000 in the mid-1980s, Portugal had the lowest living standards in non-Communist Europe and spent the lowest per capita GNP on education. Illness rates, lack of proper medical facilities, and per capita GNP incomes were comparable to Third World averages from the 1940 to the 1970s. Struggling to keep pace with Spain, Portugal suffered low productivity and relied heavily on tourism and emigration for income and to raise living standards during the three decades after the war.[1]

Coming to office in 1932, Antonio de Oliveira Salazar remained dictator until he died in 1968. He forged a patronage network that included the Church, the armed forces, police and the paramilitary Legion, and a few families that owned most of the wealth in the metropolitan area and the colonies. Besides the armed forces and secret police as the backbone of Salazar's power structure, the employers' guilds and the employees' associations were represented in the Corporative Assembly. Because the ruling party *Uniao Nacional* (National Union) published the list of the proposed candidates in advance of the elections, the winners were known. Despite futile attempts by opposition candidates, Salazar crushed all efforts that would threaten his monopoly in every sector of society from the military to labor unions.[2]

Concentrated in Lisbon, Oporto, and the northern areas, the political opposition, which included a segment of the working and middle class and an estimated 4000 members of the outlawed Communist party, hardly posed a threat to Salazar. Despite periodic labor and student protests, the International Police never allowed popular protests to go unpunished and the government-controlled press presented the official version of events. Salazar's western backing afforded him international legitimacy, though the Catholic Church also helped in that regard. Britain retained very close ties with Portugal, but strongest relations with Spain and NATO provided the appropriate political cover amid the Cold War and deflected attention from the authoritarian state.[3]

Without permitting free and legal opposition to challenge the authoritarian state, Salazar projected a facade of tolerating political opposition. Concerned about the colonies of Goa, Timor, Macau, San Tome, Cape Verde, Guinea, Angola, and Mozambique, he kept the armed forces strong. Meanwhile, there was widespread poverty and economic backwardness, not just in the colonies where apartheid prevailed, but at home as well. Besides Portugese companies and individuals who owned assets in the metropolitan area and colonies and were in Salazar's political inner circle, European and U.S. corporations played a major role in the integration process. Not only was Portugal integrated under the patron-client model, it was a U.S.-European conduit for integrating its colonies.[4]

National Development Plans and Global Integration, 1950-1961

As the government in Lisbon was drafting a Six-Year Development Plan (1953-1958), in June 1951 the State Department lobbied to have Portugal join the IMF and IBRD. The development plan revealed that the regime was prepared to adopt limited steps toward greater western integration. The most controversial issue was the level of foreign financing for various programs designed to expand the infrastructure, electricity, irrigation works, and steel and iron. In short, the U.S. determined to finance the same sectors in Portugal as in Brazil or underdeveloped countries.[5]

In November 1957 Washington and Lisbon signed a 5-year agreement for the Azores base with an aid package attached. Without the benefit of large foreign loans, the second Six-Year Plan (1959-1964) was making slow progress confined to development of roads and railways, and steel financed by German and Belgian investors. Like all underdeveloped countries that relied inordinately on raw materials exports for foreign exchange, Portugal suffered from deteriorating terms of trade and deficits that contributed to low living standards.[6]

Paranoid about mounting domestic opposition and Afro-Asian demands to end colonial rule, in 1958 the government raised defense spending from 28.8 percent to 30.8 percent of the budget. Economic development funding received no increase. As was the case in Greece and Turkey, Portugal considered NATO-related projects like roads and buildings part of economic development. Largely because of the bloated defense budget and NATO obligations, Portugal's finances continued to deteriorate and the trade deficit widened. The burden of taxation in Portugal fell on the mass consumer, direct taxes were low, and tax evasion was pervasive. Hence the need to borrow from abroad to finance development and greater integration with the west.[7]

The cost of the second Six-Year Plan promulgated in 1958 was estimated at 30 billion. Continuing the export-oriented growth strategy that Peru and other Latin American countries had adopted, the second Six-Year Plan provided incentives for export industries. Indicative of a commitment to the primary sector, only 13 percent of the entire budget was devoted to manufacturing and a tiny percentage for technical education and basic research. The highest percentage of funds were destined for Lisbon and Oporto, for the benefit of large landowners in the south as opposed to the small farmers in the north, and for exporters at home and in the colonies. The entire development plan operated under crony capitalism, as Salazar personally designated the individuals and companies to benefit from the programs and loans.[8]

In 1959 Portugal joined the IMF and the World Bank, and in 1960 it established the Bank for Economic Development and committed to EFTA, and two years later to GATT. Like Franco's Spain, Salazar's Portugal pursued monetarist policies resulting in high exchange and gold reserves, although growth did not translate into higher living standards for rural and urban workers as he had promised. Rising from $500 million in 1950, Portugal's reserves were above $700 million from 1954 to 1959, translating into a relatively strong currency backed by gold and foreign exchange. The IMF, the World Bank, and Washington were pressuring Portugal, Spain, and Greece to liberalize their economies and open them more to foreign investors.[9]

In February 1960 the Minister of the Economy J. N. Ferreira Dias praised the Stockholm Agreement that Portugal had signed in 1959 to join EFTA. Supporting the U.S. and Canada in their bid for OECD membership, he was cautious about free trade, noting that open market economies suffer disequilibrium which can be rectified by capturing new foreign markets. Because Portugal's entry into EFTA entailed a 20 percent drop in custom duties as of July 1960, Ferreira Dias urged reorganization of agriculture, communications, and industry. To better compete with foreign competition, Portugese commerce minister Fernando Correia de Oliveira announced the *Fundo de Fomento de Exportacao* that would assist export industries in the mainland and the territories. Coordinating its activities with the European Production Agency, the Fundo was responsible for the Six-Year Plan and awarding contracts to foreign companies whose projects contributed capital to domestic firms.[10]

In an official state visit to Lisbon in March 1960, Eisenhower reiterated U.S. policy of strengthening relations with Salazar. A NATO member, host to U.S. military bases, and supporter of U.S. foreign policy and economic goals, Portugal was increasingly concerned about western pressures to decolonize Africa, especially after Nigerian independence in 1960 and after de Gaulle decided to negotiate Algeria's independence. Salazar expected Eisenhower to reciprocate with financial assistance and greater understanding on Angola and Mozambique, especially after Portugal awarded the contract for the Lisbon bridge to U.S. Steel, instead of choosing British, German, or French firms. Using the Cold War as pretext, Salazar linked Communism with the Afro-Asian decolonization forces, and dismissed all freedom fighters as terrorists. Salazar's rhetoric aside, Portugal as a country operating under the patron-client model did not have the means to remain a colonial power. Therefore, the question was under what conditions it would yield to a U.S.-western European neo-colonial patron-client model for Africa.[11]

Defense spending was inexorably linked to Portugal's need for greater western integration. Accepting the advice of the World Bank and EEC, Portugal liberalized payments transfers between regions. As the most important advocate of liberalization, Correa de Oliveira pressed ahead with IMF, World Bank, and EEC recommendations for greater integration in the world economy. Aware that foreign competition would impact the domestic industries like textiles, the government tried unsuccessfully to concentrate and consolidate Portuguese industries and to borrow from IFIs. While Portugal had a balanced budget and exchange surplus, the World Bank did not approve a loan because of Salazar's refusal to disclose details about financial and economic affairs, or to go along with proposed World Bank reforms.[12]

Portugese Colonial Policy, U.S. Reaction, and IFI Policy, 1961-1968

The loss of Goa to India in 1961 made the dictatorship even more determined to hold on to its African colonies. For the U.S. and UK to offer financial and diplomatic assistance for the formation of a Lusitanian community that included Brazil, foreign secretary the Earl of Home and U.S. secretary of state Dean Rusk insisted that Portugal must accept the principle of self-determination for Angola. After Kennedy came to office, the U.S. and western Europe were pressuring Lisbon to make some symbolic movement toward greater African self-determination, largely because Moscow and Beijing exploited the issue for propaganda. Immersed in the illusion of imperial grandeur, the elites failed to accept the fact that the escudo regional integration plan would not have mitigated the patron-client model in which the U.S. dominated.[13]

Because of its NATO and colonial military commitments, the IMF argued that defense was cutting deeply into the civilian economy. On 29 March 1961 Portugal became a member of the IMF with an initial $60 million quota subscription. As it had prior to 1961, the IMF recommended pursuing monetary and fiscal discipline, eliminating exchange and trade restrictions, and ending bilateral payments agreements with other IMF members. Above all, the IMF and U.S. wanted Portugal to open its doors to foreign investment, and to pursue rapid integration with the EEC and North America along the lines of Greece and Spain.[14]

Despite high levels of imports and low exports, shortage of private investment capital, and depressed agriculture, Portugal was enjoying faster industrial production than western Europe in the early 1960s. In November 1961 it obtained a $13 million U.S. loan to purchase wheat and barley, and an additional $20 million for infrastructural and agricultural development, to which west Germany contributed 150 million marks. Foreign loans were also intended to slow down the emigration to France, and high unemployment and underemployment, especially in upper and lower Alentejo districts. Taking advantage of cheap labor and friendly government to capital, General Motors, Mercedes-Benz, and Citroen announced plans for manufacturing plants in Portugal.[15]

In February 1962, Dr. Franco Nogueira, foreign minister and one of the largest sugar plantation owners in Angola, announced that without its colonies Portugal would be reduced to Spain's province, or an insignificant member of the European federation. Salazar argued that the U.S. criticized Portugal's colonial policy only because it was interested in capturing Africa's raw materials and markets. Because of Angola and Mozambique, Portugal enjoyed a trade surplus and kept the escudo stable. Spending $70 million on defense, primarily because of the colonies, the Salazar regime lacked public support for sustained colonial control amid rising internal unrest and global political opposition. Reflecting the views of some capitalists, the Portuguese Steel Company stressed that the country's future rested with EEC integration, not Africa. Just as de Gaulle realized that France was paying the price of colonization in Algeria while western corporations were deriving the benefits, some Portuguese came to the same conclusion about Angola and Mozambique.[16]

After an uprising by the 3rd Infantry regiment in January 1962, rumors spread quickly about Salazar's imminent fall. Many officers were disgruntled that no NATO power sided with Lisbon after Goa reverted to India. Facing problems at home and in Angola, in July 1962 Lisbon signed an IMF agreement that coincided with Rusk's talks about global opposition to Portugal's colonial policy, the U.S. military bases, and U.S. foreign aid cuts. In an interview with an American magazine, Salazar noted that Washington preferred Angolan independence rather than supporting a loyal ally fighting international Communism. Considering Portugal's foreign aid requirements, Nogueira agreed that Lisbon had no choice but to cooperate with Washington which privately assured the Portuguese of support on the colonies.[17]

After de Gaulle withdrew his forces from NATO's Atlantic fleet and restricted U.S. take-over of French firms, Washington began constructing a NATO air force training base and radar station at Beja, thus providing Portugal with geopolitical leverage for economic assistance. Germany agreed to 200 million Deutschmarks for construction costs at the base, and an additional 300-400 million for its operations. This commitment coincided with lease negotiations for the base in the Azores in 1963, and with Algeria's, Ethiopia's, Cameroons', and Egypt's severance of diplomatic relations with Lisbon over the colonial issue. Though Portuguese trade with Africa was about one percent of the total, free African states demanded that the world condemn Portugal for having a very poor human rights record at home and abroad. Both Washington and London were facing a terrible dilemma by privately supporting Portugal, yet publicly paying lip service to decolonization. Nor was EEC integration a solution as long as the Council of Europe objected to Salazar's colonial regime.[18]

Behind the veneer of the colonial struggle was the deeper issue affecting the manner by which Africa would be integrated. Refusing to allow more than six percent of foreign capital in Portuguese enterprises, Salazar backed the ruling families that held tight control of industries at home and in the colonies, and which borrowed from abroad to finance expansion rather than issuing shares on the domestic market. Conceding that Portugal was in a transition from a semi-isolated position to western integration, the IMF could not press for liberalization against the background of overriding NATO considerations, complicated by Angola's and Mozambique's anti-colonial resistance movements. The IMF noted that defense was absorbing a disproportionate percentage of liquidity from the economy, and that Salazar subordinated economic growth to maintain monetary and financial stability.[19]

In June 1963 Salazar appointed Luis Maria Teixeira Pinto to head the ministry of the economy, who acknowledged the limitations of economic nationalism amid the regionalization of the European and world economy. He added:

> In the context of the world today it would be less than realistic to think that the national factor is shortly to be abandoned and it will therefore be in the light of each country's own necessities, exigencies and advantages that we must view the tendency to great multi-national economic areas. That is to say, the degree and speed of the sinking of the Portugese economy exists in the world economy is a variable which must be handled in the light of the demands of the economic policy of the Portuguese Economic Area and be evaluated in the light of advantages and disadvantages under varying heads, that is to say the economic, the social, the political, and even the cultural.[20]

Only half of the population was engaged in the agricultural sector that produced 25 percent of the national income and remained primitive by western standards, a situation comparable to Greece and other Third World countries. Struggling to elevate themselves above subsistence, peasants and small farmers had no hope for their children. Nor did the periodic arrests of alleged Communists and other repressive measures, or the labor exchanges with Spain's trade unions appear to distract peasants and workers from demanding improved living conditions.[21]

Teixeira Pinto's commitment to building the infrastructure stemmed partly from the World Bank's offer for $20 million for the *Hidro-Electrica do Douro* and $5 million for *Empresa Termoelectrica*. After 1961 Portugal borrowed $55 million from the Eximbank to finance the Tagus bridge project, $13 million in PL 180 wheat surplus aid, and $21 million from eleven U.S. banks. While the U.S. and the World Bank were the most significant sources for foreign loans, Germany, France, Holland, and Sweden provided some credits for Portugal, just as they did for Spain and Greece in consortium packages. In July 1963 the government drafted a three-year investment plan predicated on import-substitution industrialization, quite similar to plans in the rest of southern Europe and the larger Latin American countries. Though the development plan assumed that 25 percent of investment would emanate from foreign loans, Lisbon planned to borrow at much higher levels.[22]

Partly because of several anti-inflationary programs in continental Europe, the Iberian economies were weak. Unemployment continued to rise and more peasants were leaving their villages for overcrowded cities which needed labor. Acknowledging chronic unemployment and underemployment as major problems, the IMF argued that labor shortages in western Europe would likely absorb southern Europe's surplus labor force. But Portugal's best hope, contended the IMF, was foreign capital investment.[23]

Though Salazar remained skeptical about the U.S. African policy, in 1964 the Johnson administration and most of its NATO allies were losing interest in decolonization amid the escalating Vietnam conflict, Nasser's popularity, and the radicalization of Angola, Mozambique, and Guinea Bissau. Because Mao Tse-tung, Nikita Khrushchev, and Nasser supported African liberation movements, because of common western economic interests, and partly because Lisbon threatened to leave NATO if pressed on decolonization, the U.S. and UK eased pressure on Salazar, focusing instead on Portugal's integration and loyalty to the western bloc.[24]

The IMF reiterated that since 1950 Portugal's reliance on its colonies to cover balance-of-payments deficits had actually prevented greater integration with the west. Backed by the OECD and U.S., the IMF proposed that Portugal include Angola and Mozambique in the policies that pertained to the metropolitan region, but Salazar refused to have the colonies subjected to GATT and IMF policies. Portugese nationalists resented that the process of African integration entailed greater direct western access of the colonial market. Realizing that foreign businesses benefited from Portugal's colonial economy, and altering colonial policy would have far reaching implications for the domestic economy and politics, Salazar refused to go along with the U.S.-OECD-IMF proposal.[25]

Deflecting focus from domestic issues, in January 1965 Nogueira told the press that Egypt and Algeria were encouraging anti-colonialism in Africa. Accusing the world press of anti-Portugal bias, he added that the west wanted direct access to Africa's natural resources. Having lost over 5000 people in the Angolan insurrection, he dismissed freedom fighters as terrorists and contended that Communists had been active in Africa, a position that the Johnson administration shared. Stressing Lisbon's strong U.S. ties, Nogueira noted that Johnson unlike Kennedy had a moderate position on the colonies. Despite increasing U.S. military and economic aid to Portugal, the State Department denied any policy change. The stated U.S. goal was to persuade Lisbon to accept the principle of self-determination, and to work with Zambia, Tanzania, and Congo for the future decolonization of Angola and Mozambique. At the same time, the State Department informed the Foreign Office that U.S. would not veto German military sales to Portugal.[26]

Whereas Spain's economy was moving at a much healthier pace, Portugal along with Greece lagged behind. In late October 1966, IMF officials assessed Portugal's economy and finances, urging further liberalization of trade and transportation, and an end to bilateral trade agreements with IMF members. Greater integration was proceeding rapidly, as the government allowed banks to borrow from abroad on behalf of their domestic and foreign clients. Interest rates were lower than in western countries, benefiting large borrowers. Blaming excess liquidity, the IMF advised the Portuguese to redirect capital toward investment in industry and agriculture. Industrial output was expected to grow faster in the next five year plan (1968-1973) which called for 5.8 billion escudos, or 2 billion less than originally estimated after the IMF warned about pouring too much money into the public sector.[27]

After a spike in insurgency in the summer of 1965, international pressure mounted against Portugal's colonial regime. In 1966 and 1967 the U.S. voted against African-sponsored UN resolutions condemning Portugal's colonial policy, and U.S. support for South Africa and its overseas investment policy. The armed forces and Salazar's inner circle contended that the west wanted to substitute Portuguese colonization with neo-colonization. Considering America's historic racial problems, Salazar did not believe that Washington had the moral authority to preach to others on race matters. When Nogueira confronted State Department officials about U.S. economic and political preponderate influence if not control of the Congo, he was told that American businesses are simply competitive.[28]

Until such time as the government adopted policies based on IMF and U.S. policy recommendations, the World Bank repeated that it would not provide loans, thereby serving the UN agenda of punishing Lisbon for its refusal to make any concessions on colonial policy. Appreciative of Portugal's geopolitical significance to NATO, the Johnson administration reassured Lisbon that Eximbank and USAID would extend loans for projects in the metropolitan area and the colonies. Viewed from the prism of the East-West conflict and justified on the basis of defending against Communist rebels, U.S. African policy was designed to perpetuate a variation of the patron-client integration model for Portugal and its colonies. After all, not only did a substantial percentage of Angola's and Mozambique's exports go to the U.S., but Texaco, Standard Oil, Union Carbide, Mobil, Diversa of Texas, Tenneco, and GE, to mention some of the companies operating in Portugal's colonies were beholden to Salazar.[29]

Against the background of student and labor unrest in major cities after 1967, Salazar critics contended that Spain adamantly opposed change in Portugal. Viewing the colonies as essential for economic and geopolitical reasons, the government recognized that it would have to decide whether it wanted to be a European country and embrace full-fledged western integration, or opt for apartheid like South Africa and risk isolation and lack of access to foreign capital. Despite the internal report, the regime accused the EEC and the U.S. of betraying an ally over the colonies.[30]

Caetano's Dictatorship, 1968-1974

After four decades of tyrannical rule Salazar died in September 1968, leaving Marcello Caetano to take the oath of office as premier and foreign minister. Caetano warned about the dangers of Communism, stressing the importance of domestic and national security, and reassuring continuity in domestic and foreign policy. A principal architect of the corporate state, Caetano favored greater liberalization and western integration, but less of a monetarist orientation and more stimulus. With the exception of the leftists, anti-Salazar groups were willing to give Caetano a chance. Washington's private assessment was that the new regime was authoritarian, but one that would ease police state tactics, thus worthy of support. Nor was the U.S. interested in openly pressuring Caetano on decolonization, given the significance of the military bases, and the world-wide publicity that UN sanctions had received.[31]

In October 1968, the Caetano administration notified its allies that it would uphold all international financial obligations and commitments to NATO, ETFA, OECD, and UN. Insisting that there would be no change in its colonial policy, Lisbon urged Washington and London to vote against a UN resolution condemning apartheid and Portugal's colonial policy, otherwise African liberation fighters would be encouraged at the expense of a loyal NATO ally. Washington appreciated Portugal's support of U.S. foreign policy, cooperation with the IMF, and favorable treatment of foreign capital. More significant, the outgoing Johnson administration was not about to support sanctions as some in the UN advocated, considering that would harm U.S. political and economic interests in Africa.[32]

Beyond the colonial issue, in the second half of the 1960s inflation was a problem for Portugal, as for the rest of the world. Caetano came to office at the same time that student and worker demonstrations were on the rise throughout the western world, including Portugal. From 1967 to 1970 demonstrators and labor strikers targeted GM and Ford assembly plants, Firestone, and other large domestic and foreign enterprises. After reducing the industrial tax rate in 1971 to stimulate growth, the government intended to stimulate investment by offering fiscal incentives and increased spending.[33]

Though UN resolutions 2105 and 2107 called on IFIs to withhold aid to Portugal and South Africa, U.S. opposition provided the cover that the World Bank and IMF required to continue doing business as usual. After Robert McNamara became World Bank president, the State Department accused him of acquiescing to non-aligned bloc pressure on Portugal. While Kissinger used the World Bank to deflect Portugal's criticism away from the administration which needed the Azores bases, he made it clear that African freedom fighters were not part of the East-West conflict as Lisbon had been insisting. Just as the U.S. used linkage in foreign aid policy, Portugal argued that its military bases negotiations and IMF compliance depended on whether Washington would back Portugal's application for a World Bank loan.[34]

Arguing that countries much poorer than Portugal deserved aid, McNamara noted that if Lisbon did not spend 40 percent of its budget on defense, it would not need to borrow. Moreover, the proposed loan would benefit mainly large landowners linked to the regime. To join the EEC, Portugal was asking for modest protection of its industries like tomato paste, canned fish, and wines. Though textiles constituted a major export to EFTA, finance minister Jose da Silva Lopes did not think that industry had a future owing to Third World competition. Under a 1964 agreement, the U.S. was purchasing Portuguese cotton yarn, but American cotton producers lobbied to reduce such imports.[35]

Besides the challenge of a shrinking U.S. market, Portugal along with other countries paid the price for the U.S. balance-of-payments deficit and weak dollar. In April 1972 the IMF recommended that the escudo (27 per dollar) must appreciate at the same rate as other European currencies, otherwise there was an unfair advantage to Portuguese exporters. To minimize the state's role in the economy, the IMF objected to the *Secretaria de Estado do Comercio* determining product quality guidelines, distribution, prices, and marketing. Along with a number of Third World countries, Portugal demanded that the U.S. provide better terms for textile exports in order to integrate the garment and chemical industries in which there was foreign investment. Both Lisbon and Singapore demanded that GATT, which safeguarded the interests of the developed countries, demonstrate greater understanding of underdeveloped economies.[36]

Trade and loans were inexorably linked to foreign policy, especially after Portugal had privately backed the U.S. during the Yom Kippur War by permitting use of its bases despite serious reservations about offending friendly Arab countries. In return for backing the U.S., Caetano expected aid and diplomatic support on the colonies. Agreeing with him that African leaders, including U.S.-backed dictators like Congo's president J. D. Mobutu, were hardly capable of governing effectively, Kissinger told Caetano that decolonization was inevitable. Some domestic businesses and western companies doing business in Africa wanted this matter settled to end the political stigma, lessen the burden on the budget, and raise foreign capital investment.[37]

Decolonization became increasingly a perceptible reality as it was intertwined with the end of dictatorship in Portugal. On 13 March 1974 the security forces arrested dozens of government opponents, including members of the Espiritu Santos Banking group and Jorge de Melo, the richest man in the country. A few weeks prior to the mass arrests, Caetano dismissed general Antonio de Spinola, former governor of Guinea and deputy chief of the armed forces, for advocating decolonization through political means. Junior officers rallied behind Spinola, but the military regime announced that it would outlaw some parties and would not hand over power to civilians. On 25 April 1974 the opposition finally exploded and a revolutionary movement swept away the dictatorship. Under the label *Movimento das Forcas Armadas*, a Spinola-backed group began paving the way for an open westernized society.[38]

After decades of authoritarian rule, the majority of the population saw the country's future resting with pluralistic institutions similar to western Europe's with which they identified. By the mid-1970s Portugal had a sufficiently large lower middle class that demanded a representative government and which hoped to be a candidate for full EEC membership. Lamenting the twilight of the old regime, banking-oil tycoon Manuel Boullosa stated that Portugal lost talented and wealthy people to Brazil, adding: "But there was reason to make changes. A country cannot belong to a half a dozen people."[39] Pursuing integration with the EEC and close ties with the U.S. to retain the status quo and its regional role, the Portuguese dictatorship allowed western influences to shape society in the age of mass politics and mass communication.

By helping to westernize the country and advocating decolonization, the IFIs inadvertently contributed to the dictatorship's demise. In so far as the penetration of public and private foreign capital entailed that capitalist integration must operate under a regime responsive to the mass consumer, Portugal along with Spain and Greece were headed for an irreversible course as EEC members operating under similar institutions and a new model of interdependent integration. The advanced capitalist countries had demonstrated that capital operated more efficiently in the bourgeois liberal state, while the authoritarian state was obsolete and a hindrance to liberal capitalism for semi-developed European countries.

The Road to EU Membership: Portugal's Road to EU Membership

Radicalized by the mass popular uprising, *Movimento das Forcas Armadas* called for immediate liberalization of colonial policy, restoration of civil liberties, and democratic institutions. A new progressive constitution laid the foundations for the country's future, though all parties except the Communists would endeavor to undo the charter within months after it was promulgated. Kissinger wrote to Nixon that despite the Portugese oligarchy's inordinate influence and divisions within the armed forces, the country was ready for transition toward an EEC-style regime. While the U.S. embassy urged backing the new government, neither Kissinger nor the CIA backed the idea. Because of the Azores bases, U.S. private investments, and fearful that Portugal would set a precedent for other countries, the CIA tried to destabilize the Revolutionary government just as it had Salvador Allende's Chile. Though

Washington imposed an arms embargo on Portugal and blocked its access to NATO briefings, the realization that Europe supported it and there was an opportunity to integrate Angola's and Mozambique's markets more closely entailed that Nixon and Kissinger would have to embrace Lisbon's new regime.[40]

Socialist Party leader Mario Soares who lived in Paris from 1970 to 1974, and Communist party leader Alvaro Cunhal who lived in Prague, returned to Lisbon. They were permitted to broadcast their views on television and to take part in the new government. Foreign investors were skeptical about the new regime, because the Revolutionary government allowed free trade unions, offered the ministry of labor to the Communists, and nationalized some enterprises. Initially, a number of wealthy people fled with their liquid assets. Nor did it help matters that the economy had been weak since the oil crisis of 1973, world trade was soft, the Nixon administration was not approving loans for the Revolutionary regime, and the CIA in collaboration with old regime officials were covertly undermining the government.[41]

In December 1974 the IMF told finance minister Silva Lopes of the need for monetarist policies, and IMF's involvement in Portugal's colonies after independence. Warning that the Revolution had precipitated a sharp rise in prices and wages, the IMF did not take into account that wage-price hikes occurred in all industrialized countries after the oil crisis. Because of high energy and imports, prices rose 27 percent, while minimum wages went up to $130 per month or 35 percent higher, meager in comparison with western Europe.[42]

Competing for control of the trade unions, the Communists vehemently opposed the economic program that did not dismantle monopolies linked to the dictatorship. Shortly after the Communist critique of economic and labor policies, tens of thousands of people poured into the streets of Lisbon protesting unemployment at 7 percent, and the antiquated economy benefiting large domestic and foreign companies. Because of tense relations between the Communist party and the Social Democratic Center, which was affiliated with the European Christian Democrats, the Socialists threatened to withdraw from the coalition in January 1975. The presence of 11,000 NATO troops in Lisbon for naval exercises prompted protesters to decry U.S. pressures on Portugal to follow pro-U.S. policies. Amid political and social turmoil, the World Bank began providing policy advice and approving loans to stabilize the pro-west political parties.[43]

On 20 February 1975 the government announced that it was breaking up large land holdings and taking over key industries like banks and insurance companies. Rather than confiscating investors' deposits or interfering with foreign investment, premier Vasco dos Santos Goncalves insisted that reforms were necessary. Given that a few banks dominated the economy while small businesses were hurting, most people accepted reformism. While reaffirming his commitment to NATO and honoring the U.S. military agreement, he repeated that the Azores would not be used in future wars against Arab countries.[44]

The Constituent Assembly elections proved that the Socialist Party was the clear winner in April 1975, followed by the Popular Democratic Party, with the Communists receiving about 13 percent of the vote. *Movimento das Forcas Armadas* leader Admiral Antonio Rosa Coutinho, former governor-general of Angola and member of the High Council of the Revolution, reassured a group of U.S. businessmen that the government would promulgate a very liberal investment policy, though Socialism was the future of the world.[45]

Considering the U.S. had just committed $13.2 million aid and $20 million guaranteed loan for low-cost housing, the new regime's foreign policy and its measures toward foreign investment were not nearly as ominous as they appeared. Because the government raised transport fares and prices on essentials, while unemployment was in double-digits, there were mass demonstrations in July and August 1975. Though the Portuguese would learn eventually that Socialism in southern Europe was not the same as in Scandinavian countries, it was responsible for strengthening the state, providing more social safety nets, and securing the transition from the patron-client to inter-dependent integration model.[46]

After domestic businessmen and western governments had accused the regime of steering Portugal toward Communism, in August 1975 Vasco dos Santos Goncalves was ousted. Promising to restore confidence in the private sector, attract foreign capital, and pursue market-oriented policies, admiral Jose Pinhiero de Azevedo headed the new coalition that included Socialists backed by Germany's Social Democrats, and the Popular Democratic Party that Washington supported. Convinced that Portugal must accept IMF-World Bank advice, prime minister Pinhiero de Azevedo urged the country to curb consumption and prepare for austerity that would impact living standards.[47]

Pressured by the traditional elites, U.S., IFIs, and EEC, the government launched a campaign to limit the influence of the Communist party in all aspects of society, especially after the wealthiest families had transferred most of their liquid assets out of Portugal. On 25 November 1975 the military with the collaboration of the non-Communist parties eliminated the Communists and revolutionary left from all positions of power, and prepared to go along with IFI policies. Western countries applauded Lisbon's decision to adopt austerity, welcomed foreign capital, and collaborated with NATO.[48]

Though Lisbon's center-left coalition agreed to IMF austerity and a pro-western orientation, it also acknowledged that it must lessen its preponderate dependence on the west by diversifying commercial relations with Eastern Europe and the Third World. This was the same policy that Spain and Greece had adopted, and it signaled the gradual transition from the patron-client model to the EEC.[49]

The transition from the dictatorship to parliamentarism and conformity with EEC institutions entailed a stronger state structure and more social safety nets but not the end of socioeconomic polarization. From November 1975 to February 1976 the government imposed a freeze on new wage contracts, and even after lifting it, wage increases were very modest. The government pledged to forge a new foreign investment code designed to provide incentives and guarantees for foreign capital. Satisfied with Lisbon's direction, USAID approved $20 million in government-guaranteed loan provided by a commercial bank in Boston for low-cost housing. In January 1976 labor unions, farmers, and neighborhood committees announced mass rallies against IMF austerity measures that resulted in sharp price increases and cuts in wages.[50]

To lift the economy from current difficulties, prime minister Jose Pinheiro de Alzevedo reiterated that Portugal needed foreign loans and speedy integration into the EEC, the same position that Greece and Spain adopted. The EIB approved emergency loans of $150 million, of which $100 million was through EFTA for industrial development. Sweden and Switzerland were the largest contributors with 30 percent and 25.5 percent respectively. Besides high unemployment, inflation, balance of payments deficits, and social unrest, the issue was whether the Socialists were in a strong position to secure EEC aid. Ambassador Frank Carlucci urged Carter to support the Socialists instead of the Social Democrats. Presenting themselves along the lines of Willy Brandt, and Olaf Palme, Soares Socialists won 107 of 262 Assembly seats against the Social Democrats, Popular Democrats, Communists, and a host of smaller parties.[51]

In June 1976 Carlos Saldanha do Valle, governor of the Banco de Portugal, finance minister Jose da Silva Lopes, and other officials met with an IMF mission to discuss the drop in production and trade, and 4 percent GNP decline in 1975. Though financial and economic policy was in a transitional phase, officials agreed with the IMF on the need to make state-owned enterprises profitable as a precondition to qualifying for foreign loans. From 1976 to 1980 the public investment program was estimated at $4 billion, to be financed in part by foreign loans, and with World Bank and OECD technical assistance. Foreign loans and technical advice on planning and investment focused on large-scale, capital-intensive projects where multinational corporations would secure contracts, instead of smaller labor-intensive works that would have sustainable benefits for the majority.[52]

The independence of Portugal's African colonies added 8-9 percent to total population, or 600,000 people who returned home seeking employment amid unofficial reports that unemployment was 15 percent. Though the multilateral banks insisted that the Socialists must strengthen the private sector, Banco de Fomento explained that Portugal's economy was more stable than Italy's, Spain's, or Greece's, all of which pursued similar fiscal and monetary policies. Losing Angola and Mozambique while experiencing deteriorating terms of trade were salient factors in Portugal's economic downturn. Nevertheless, the World Bank and IMF blamed inflation on budgetary deficits and rapid wage increases in the second half of the

1970s. Higher energy costs, global inflation, and decapitalization by the oligarchy accounted for Portugal's economic and financial problems, not wages which along with subsidies were reduced in 1976.[53]

Portugal's per capita GNP was about $1,000 less than Spain, Greece, and Ireland, and about the same as Argentina and Yugoslavia. Soares' policies made it difficult for the per capita GNP to rise closer to the EEC average. To close the gap on the $1 billion balance-of-payments deficit and qualify for foreign loans, Soares went along with pro-business policies that the domestic elites, U.S., IFIs, and EEC advocated. As expected, the IMF and businesses applauded the new measures, while the labor unions and Communists called on the Socialists to reject western style capitalism. Soares stated that he did not wish to meet with the same fate as Allende in 1973.[54]

A few weeks after opening the stock exchange in January 1977, Portugal formally adopted an IMF stabilization program and three months later received a $42.4 million stabilization loan. Because stabilization coincided with the global recession and energy crisis, costs associated with the independence of its African colonies, and barriers erected against Portuguese products in certain countries, unemployment reached double digits, deteriorating terms of trade exacerbated existing inflationary pressures and caused the current account deficit to balloon to $1.5 billion in 1977, or 9 percent of GNP.[55]

After the IMF announced a loan for Portugal and president Carter asked western Europe to aid Lisbon, EEC politicians criticized Washington for pursuing a unilateral approach to Portugal's balance-of-payments problems. The Germans, French, and Belgians argued that Carter's unilateral approach was designed to undercut EEC multilateral efforts. This was a significant challenge to the patron-client model as it applied to southern Europe which was rapidly becoming an integral part of the EEC interdependent bloc. While the World Bank and EIB approved development loans, and the European central banks provided short-term aid, the U.S. offered Portugal a medium-term loan of $550 million for 1978-81. Bonn agreed to offer bilateral aid linked to German companies' contracts, while France, Belgium, and Japan were satisfied with multilateral consortium assistance. The total package of the U.S.-led consortium amounted to $750 million, or half of what Carter had proposed. Despite foreign loans, inflation and social unrest persisted, as unemployment was at 17 percent.[56]

At of the end of 1977, Portugal's medium and long-term debt was $1.9 billion, private non-guaranteed debt amounted to $1.7 billion, and total outstanding debt was $4.8 billion or 50 percent higher than the previous year. Though Portugal's foreign debt level was not as alarming as the Third World's, Soares was seeking new foreign loans for various projects to compete with the rest of Europe. In February 1978, just a few weeks after Soares formed a coalition cabinet with the Center Democratic Socialist Party, a Portuguese mission conveyed to the IMF, World Bank, OECD, and

U.S. that the new regime wanted to lower inflation from 28 percent in 1977 to 20 percent in 1978. The EIB committed $150 million for three years, largely as part of the ongoing program to rapidly integrate Portugal into the EEC. In March 1978 the World Bank encouraged finance minister Victor Constancio to implement the monetary, fiscal, trade, and labor reforms that the IMF recommended.[57]

On 14 September 1978, about a month after Antonio Ramalho Eanes dismissed Soares as premier, the Socialist and Center Democratic Socialists parties voted against the government of Alfredo Nobre da Costa, bringing its downfall. Lisbon received World Bank assistance to invest in the Alqueva Dam for power and agricultural development, the Moncorvo Iron works, Lisbon-Oporto highway, synthetic fibers plant in Oporto, Lisbon metro, national sewage systems, and construction of university buildings. In November 1978 an IMF mission met with finance minister Jose da Silva Lopes and others to discuss the negotiations of new Paris Club credits, after USAID approved $300 million in PL480 commodities.[58]

A volatile executive branch resembling Italy's revolving door premiership, in 1979 Portugal had its tenth government since the revolution. Prime Minister Carlos Mota Pinto appointed Manuel Jacinto Nunes, former president of the largest savings bank and former Banco de Portugal governor, to serve both as finance minister and vice premier for economic affairs. Because the cabinet was pro-business, political problems with the opposition were inevitable. By 1979 the wealthiest families that had pulled their money out during the revolution were back in the country, but merged their capital with large foreign companies. In February 1979 the new government requested an IMF stand-by arrangement and assistance to reform the fiscal structure amid large deficits. Besides devaluing the currency, Lisbon agreed to cut interest rates, set strict limits on wage increases, limit public borrowing and imports, remove some subsidies to public corporations, and raise their prices.[59]

In January 1979 the *New York Times* commented that the IMF dictated Portugal's economic policy, a statement that could be made about any country operating under the patron-client model. After 1975 IFI policy toward southern Europe was largely a function of the EEC's preparation to absorb these countries into the interdependent system in which the private sector was strengthened but balanced with a stronger social policy. In view of women's rights, civil rights, and freedoms never before experienced, Portugal's middle class naturally believed that joining the EEC and following IFI policies was part of what it meant to be in western civilization and under a democracy.[60]

Headed by conservative law professor Carlos Mota Pinto, the new government strengthened both the private sector and the state by resorting to more foreign borrowing from commercial banks. On 2 August 1979 Lisbon borrowed $300 million from a group of banks led by Bankers' Trust, in addition to $100 million that the State Savings Bank (Caixo Geral) borrowed. The following day, premier Mota Pinto, finance minister Jacinto Nunez, and the governor of Banco de Portugal Silva Lopes asked the IMF to negotiate a stand-by arrangement. Amenable to raising utility rates eventually, the premier stated that IMF recommendations would embolden the left. He threatened to resign, but the IMF asked him to make sure a stand-by arrangement was signed before the October 1980 elections. The IMF once again noted that the government had broken its pledge not to raise wages above 20 percent, after offering railroad workers and civil servants 30 percent increases.[61]

In December 1979 the right-wing *Alianca Democratica* (AD) won parliamentary elections with 45 percent of the vote. Portugal's election coincided with a rightist turn in U.S. foreign policy after the Iranian and Nicaraguan revolutions, questions about the Kremlin's role in Afghanistan, and a widespread belief among U.S. conservatives that defense and intelligence spending must increase sharply to restore Pax Americana in its pre-Vietnam war glory. Though U.S. geopolitical concerns entailed that Portugal had bargaining leverage with the military bases to secure more aid, Washington expected compliance with the IFIs.[62]

At the IMF's and World Bank's urging as it was preparing for full EEC membership, Portugal remained committed to deregulation, and subsidized interest rates and other incentives for businesses. Anti-inflation policies were especially essential amid negotiations for new IBRD loans. After the revolution, the IBRD had extended 12 loans amounting to $518 million. To counter the internal and external causes of economic sluggishness, the government directed foreign loans toward capital goods and resource-based basic industries in the private sector. World Bank lending had been geared toward commercial agriculture and manufactured export industries with emphasis on foreign contracts.[63]

Despite numerous problems associated with the transition from the dictatorship to representative government, in the second half of the 1970s Portugal gradually lifted itself from the patron-client model and laid the foundations for EEC membership that would strengthen the country's sovereignty and lessen dependence on the U.S. That the benefits of EEC integration were not evenly distributed was to be expected. But unlike Third World countries that were about to sink deeper into external dependence and suffer lower living standards in the 1980s, Portugal's socioeconomic and political status were lifted.

Deregulation, Privatization, and Integration

The 1980s were characterized by a shift toward a rightist ideological orientation in the UK and U.S., while in Spain, Greece, Portugal, Italy, and France Socialist regimes vowed to work within the EEC and NATO. Southern Europe's technocratic socialism appeared to further the interests of labor and the petit bourgeoisie, but the focus was on rapid development and integration that favored large domestic and foreign enterprises. As they had in the past, the IFIs played a pivotal role in Portugal's integration and income redistribution that favored the domestic and foreign business community. In November 1980 the EEC approved $275 million in aid of which $150 million was in EIB loans, $100 million in grants, and $25 million in interest-subsidy on the loans. Working closely with the IMF and World Bank, the EIB was involved in modernizing various sectors of Portugese society.[64]

In January 1981 prime minister Francisco Pinto Balsemao, a 43 year old former newspaper editor, headed the Democratic Alliance coalition of Social Democrats, Christian Democrats, and monarchists who won parliament's vote of confidence to change the constitution and modernize the economy. The World Bank and EEC immediately conveyed to the new regime that because Portugal was relatively underdeveloped in comparison with Spain and Greece, it was not ready for accession in January 1983. Despite reservations about Portugal's policies and administrative ability to carry out development projects, in July 1981 the World Bank approved an additional $100 million and it was studying two more loans for $65 million. Of the $518 million IBRD loans approved from 1975 to 1980, only $97.5 million had been disbursed. The EEC supported the loan, as did the Reagan administration which needed Portugal's military and diplomatic cooperation during the second Cold War, and promulgation of the Reagan Doctrine.[65]

By mid-1981 Portugal suffered 25 percent inflation, budgetary deficit at 5 percent of GNP, current account deficit at 14.5 percent of GNP, the highest in Europe, and foreign debt at $10 billion. Backed by the World Bank and the EIB, the IMF advised Lisbon to curb public spending, wages, and credit. Having failed to silence critics of the ruling Social Democratic party, on 10 August 1981 Pinto Balsemao threatened to resign unless he received a unanimous mandate. A political bluff just before he introduced a new 3-year stabilization program in mid-September, the ultimatum worked. Pledging to reduce the 17.8 percent inflation rate, cut the $2.6 billion budgetary deficit, raise taxes, and modernize Portugal before it joined the EEC, the premier saw no way out of fully cooperating with western Europe and the U.S.[66]

Protesting the austerity policies, thousands of people participated in national demonstrations on 6 March 1982. Given that inflation was at 24 percent, trade union leaders called upon the government to allow for raises of more than 17 percent. A World Bank study concluded that per capita GNP was actually $2,300 and the population was 9.771 million, whereas the government claimed that GNP was at $2,625 and the population at 9.338 million. The average person, therefore, was much poorer than official statistics indicated.[67]

As Portugal prepared for EEC accession, the IMF, World Bank, EIB, and OECD were advising massive restructuring affecting public finances, banking, industry, and agriculture. To make certain that U.S. investment continued to remain competitive after accession, in 1982 USAID contracted Price Waterhouse to survey opportunities for American capital in Portugal's nine largest industries. To secure IMF Stand-by credits, and medium term commercial bank loans for $1.5 billion, premier Pinto Balsemao and finance minister Joao Salgueiro visited Washington in mid-December 1982, presenting an austerity budget for 1983. On 20 December 1982 the prime minister resigned, amid bitter disputes over the extent of austerity and after the Socialists scored major victories in municipal elections a week earlier. The austerity program withdrawn, the government could not borrow $650 million to cover part of the $3 billion balance-of-payments deficit.[68]

The election of April 1983 returned to power Soares' Socialists who formed a coalition with Social Democrats just as the world economy was improving. Facing high unemployment and underemployment, 23 percent inflation, and $3 billion current account deficit, Soares promised 100 measures in 100 days. Initially reluctant to go along with the IMF, he capitulated to secure new loans and foreign investment, to appease Portugal's business community, and to remain competitive within the EEC. The IMF approved $445 million, after Lisbon agreed to public spending cuts, tax adjustment, higher prices for administrative costs, including sharply lower subsidies to publicly-owned firms, and reduction in public employment.[69]

Disposal income dropped 5 percent, and official unemployment rose to 10.5 percent where it hovered for most of the decade as it did in Greece. Unofficially, unemployment and underemployment was much higher, but there were more women who entered the labor force after 1974. The government pledged to restructure public enterprises based on the Reagan-Thatcher model, internationalize the economy, and continue with austerity, including fiscal and credit restraints, and more caps on wage increases. Because of tight monetary policy, inflation dropped from 34 percent in December 1983 to 30 percent in May 1984, but foreign debt rose.[70]

Foreign debt climbed from $11 billion in 1981 to $14 billion in 1983, and the IMF estimated that it would reach at least $20 billion by 1990, but that was not as serious as Brazil or other Latin American republics. As foreign debt-service ratio reached 36 percent of foreign exchange earnings in 1984, the government pledged to reduce short-term debt that was most serious. To encourage foreign investment and avoid large public spending as a means of stimulating the economy, the IMF urged the government to provide incentives for capital markets, and "labor reform" which meant fewer legal protections for workers and wage cuts. Remaining the poorest European country with $2,300 per capita GNP in 1983, Portugal lagged behind Greece by 50 percent and was just above Turkey's level.[71]

Just before becoming a full EEC member in January 1986, the IFIs, OECD, and U.S. advised Lisbon to strengthen its finances and economy. The World Bank had been engaged in negotiations for over a year to provide a restructuring loan for money-losing public enterprises. Proposing that public companies must operate on the private sector model, the Bank discovered that the government was reluctant to make drastic changes. Though the IFIs and the Paris Club promoted all types of government incentives to the private sector, the World Bank and IMF argued against public sector subsidies if Portugal hoped to secure more loans. The traditional elites and nouveau riches backed the U.S.-UK privatization trend, but labor, professionals, and small merchants feared that large foreign enterprises would take a commanding role in the political economy.[72]

Upon EEC accession in January 1986, Portugal qualified for $300 million that was coordinated by the World Bank, EIB, and EEC for the first five years, and an additional $23.5 billion through 1996. The massive influx of EEC funds designed to modernize Portugal's roads, railroads, agriculture, education, and other programs elevated the country's economy and accounted for modest social mobility in the next two decades. Though per capita income was about $2800 and a quarter of the people were engaged in agriculture which produced just 10 percent of GNP in 1986, the future looked much brighter. EEC funds were the catalyst to Portugal's new role in the semi-periphery, especially considering the absence of sectoral restrictions on EIB funds. Though steel, textiles, and shipbuilding were areas that the EIB did not want to fund, the influx of other EEC funds allowed Portugal to borrow from other sources.[73]

Diogo Freitas do Amaral, Christian Democrat candidate for the presidency, won 46.6 percent of the vote, forcing a runoff election against Soares in February 1986. Widely seen as a victory for Anibal Cavaco Silva's conservative policies, Freitas do Amaral benefited from the fractionalism among the leftists who had been bitterly divided over Soares' pro-U.S. and market-oriented policies under the cloak of Socialism. Though Soares had managed to deradicalize labor and a segment of the lower middle class while placing Portugal on the path toward inter-dependent EEC integration, the Communists and Socialists came together in the runoff election to hand Soares a surprise victory.[74]

Following the Thatcher-Reagan privatization model, the IFIs, EEC, and U.S. expected Portugal and the rest of the world to fall in line. Portugal's first year as a full EEC member was characterized by a 4.25 percent GNP growth, 10.5 percent inflation, and 4 percent of GNP in current account surplus. Even after the passage of legislation making it easier for employers to dismiss workers, the IFIs advised Lisbon to remain vigilant in creating a mobile labor force by lifting employer restrictions. Hence, unemployment was expected to rise by another 3-4 percent, although $700 million EEC aid for rural development served as a safety net that Third World countries did not have at a time they were making immense debt service payments to the G-7.[75]

In October 1986 an EEC report revealed that Portugal's economy had failed to develop domestic industrial capacity, and was too dependent on external factors. Announcing $1.05 billion in new loans, the EEC's goal was to modernize Portugal's economy and raise living standards closer to the other members. To improve inter-

Iberian commercial relations, Lisbon and Madrid vowed to cooperate on many fronts. As inflation dropped from 19 percent in 1986 to 12 percent in spring 1987 amid a global recession, real income rose along with productivity. Despite modest progress, the Communists and Socialists joined the Democratic Renewal party to censure Silva's regime for failing to energize the economy.[76]

After winning 148 of the 250 parliamentary seats in the election of July 1987, Cavaco Silva's Social Democrats insisted that the election was a mandate to pursue a centrist course. The Social Democrats contended that the majority favored free-enterprise, deregulated the economy, and change in labor laws that protected jobs. With the strong encouragement of the IFIs, U.S., and EEC, the government adopted a law to privatize 49 percent of public enterprises which were a major source of political patronage.[77]

Foreign investment rose from $200 million in 1986 to $920 million in 1988, thus stimulating the economy in the late 1980s. Emboldened by the modest economic progress, the premier proposed strengthening relations with Washington by offering Portugal as an alternative site to Spain for the U.S. air force. Within weeks after that enthusiastic proposal, Silva threatened to scrap the treaty for the U.S. base unless the terms were more attractive. Not only had the Reagan administration cut aid from $205 million to $117 million annually, but U.S.-Portugal trade had dropped sharply since 1985. Despite the booming economy, U.S. aid reduction left a gap in the budget and soured otherwise excellent relations between Lisbon and Washington. Spain and Greece made similar threats over the issue of aid in connection with the U.S. bases, and always linked economic aid and trade to defense. In July 1989, the IMF urged monetary and fiscal tightening, cutting labor costs, liberalizing trade, and adjusting interest rates to reflect comparable costs between the public and private sectors.[78]

In a showdown between trade unions and the government's attempt to hold down wages and lessening job security, Portugal experienced a wave of labor strikes sporadically in 1988 and 1989. From dock workers to doctors, most professions experienced slowdowns or work stoppages, and took part in mass demonstrations against the government's policies. Partly because of EEC capital investment, official unemployment declined from around 10-11 percent in the early 1980s to 7 percent in 1987. Justifying its labor and economic policy as necessary to achieve successful integration, Silva's Social Democrats insisted that Portugal had to remain competitive.[79]

As an EEC member Portugal along with Spain and Greece had to increase spending on health and education which lagged far behind western European standards. Thus, the caps on wages to pay for the welfare system. State-owned firms had dropped from 6 percent of GNP in 1985 to 1.5 percent in 1987, with the goal of reducing it to less than 1 percent by 1990. That was largely because the government was selling 49 percent of the state firms to private investors, including the largest commercial bank. The IMF contended that the steel company *Siderurgia Nacional*, chemical company Quimigal, petrochemical company CNP-EPSI, railroad and electric companies needed to cut jobs and reduce labor costs. Although the European Social Fund was seeking to moderate the growth of labor through various EEC-subsidized programs, the IMF insisted that the state must curtail wage hikes. Free market laws applied selectively to certain countries, certain sectors, and invariably excluded wages.[80]

In December 1989 the Socialists won key local elections, including Lisbon under Jorge Sampaio as mayor. Voter retaliation discontent with the Social Democrats' pro-business-anti-labor policies amid 12 percent inflation, rapid privatization, and massive foreign capital take-over of key industries accounted for the resurgence of Socialists. The decade had proved that regardless of which party or coalition was in power anywhere in southern Europe, EEC, U.S., and IFI constraints limited the government's ability to pursue policies that differed very much. The price of integration meant conformity to certain policies impacting the economy, finances, and division of labor.[81]

EEC grants to Portugal rose from $1 billion in 1988 to $1.6 billion in 1990, new foreign investment in 1989 amounted to $1.5 billion, GNP growth averaged 5.5 percent from 1989 to 1992, inflation was below 10 percent, wages were barely catching up with the losses sustained during the stabilization of the 1980s, and per capita income was 55 percent of the EEC average, or slightly below the rest of southern Europe's. Although studies projected that living standards would not be at par with the rest of the community until 2050, that was much better than any projection for the Third World operating under the patron-client model. Nevertheless, the government was not comfortable that integration entailed increased foreign domination, though it had to compete for foreign investment with southern and Eastern Europe. As liberalization measures and deregulation measures affecting labor and capital took hold, foreign investment jumped from $900 million in 1988 to $2.4 billion at the end of 1989.[82]

Upon EEC accession, Lisbon introduced a value-added tax, augmenting it in 1989 by an income tax as part of a broader effort to strengthen the fiscal structure to remain competitive with northwest Europe and to be in compliance with IMF-World Bank recommendations regarding privatization of public enterprises. To stimulate the economy, the government raised spending by 8 percent comparable to EEC levels and broadened the tax base. Indirect taxes rose 14 percent from 1985 to 1987, while direct taxes rose from 31.9 percent of the total revenue in 1988 to 41 percent in 1991. Starting in 1989, privatization, especially in banking and insurance, compelled the government to raise public spending, because jobs and wage/salary income were declining. Privatizing 27 firms for 704 billion escudos, or 1.7 percent of GNP, the government sold publicly-owned assets to domestic and foreign investors.[83]

Maastricht, the EU, and Globalization

During the last decade of the 20th century, Portugal along with its southern European counterparts pursued monetary convergence, in accordance with Maastricht Treaty provisions. Successfully achieving convergence by the end of the 1990s, Portugal experienced further income redistribution toward the upper income groups, under an increasingly conservative political orientation that resulted in policies reflecting more of Washington's and western Europe's interests. Though 20 percent of the population was engaged in agriculture in the early 1990s, the country imported half of its foodstuffs. Decades of World Bank agricultural policy advice had made western multinationals richer, but it had not resulted in self-sufficiency for Portugal or any other country operating on the patron-client model.[84]

Overshadowed by the Persian Gulf crisis, in January 1991 Soares was reelected to a five-year term as president, and in October Silva's Social Democrats won a parliamentary majority. Benefiting from $5 billion in EEC assistance since 1986, living standards had risen significantly, especially in comparison with Third World countries under the patron-client model. The U.S., UK, and the IFIs continued to advise privatization, a process that many capitalists supported. Privatized enterprises did not prove to be universally more efficient or any more responsive to consumers than public entities, to say nothing of how they treated workers. In addition to privatization, the government shifted public debt-deficit management from the central bank and EEC and U.S.-based multilateral banks to private financial firms. Shifting from public to market-based debt instruments entailed much higher interest and fees that benefited domestic and foreign institutional investors at the expense of the taxpayer.[85]

At a meeting in Lisbon in July 1993, the IMF applauded Portugal's progress in achieving convergence under Maastricht rules, lowering inflation, and deregulation. Nevertheless, the IMF urged greater fiscal discipline, an exchange and monetary rate policy, and "a more incentive-oriented tax system" that would attract private capital investment. Oblivious to popular protests in 1992, and violent clashes by *Air Portugal* workers in 1993, the government remained loyal to deregulations and privatization. As unemployment increased and wage earners' income declined in relation to the upper classes during the recession of the early 1990s, foreign direct investment skyrocketed. OECD investment rose from $1.5 billion for 1989 to $2.4 billion in 1993. Because of a net transfer of EU funds amounting to 3.5 percent of GDP in 1992, the Portuguese economy was cushioned from the combination of several blows ranging from privatization, deregulation, and greater competition.[86]

Whereas in Italy, Greece, and to some degree Spain, investment and exports were catalysts for growth in the 1990s, Portugal lagged behind. Portugal's GNP dropped from 5.4 percent in 1988 and 1989 to -1 percent in 1993, reflecting a drop in EU GNP.

Nevertheless, per capita GNP rose from 51.4 percent in 1985 to 64.4 percent in 1994, closing the gap to a substantial degree under the Socialist regime, a trend prevalent throughout southern Europe, but notably absent in the Third World. Unlike Italy's, Spain's, and Greece's disinflation programs of the 1980s under IMF auspices which resulted in much higher unemployment without having a great impact on lowering prices, Portugal sustained lower rates of inflation, and lower unemployment.[87]

Maastricht-mandated convergence programs compelled all southern Europe to curb consumption by following rigid fiscal and monetary policies that resulted in income redistribution from labor to investment. Real wages and social security benefits fell in the early 1990s, resulting in a drop of disposal income for the lower classes. But the upward social mobility realized in the expansion of the lower middle class accounted for the rise in per capita GNP. The IMF confirmed that labor's share of GNP in southern Europe declined in the first half of the 1990s, while productivity and investment rose.[88]

As was the case in Greece and to a lesser extent in Spain, Portugal's large deficits entailed high interest rates and weak currency. The IMF blamed liberal fiscal and monetary policy, but the recession was deeper and longer in the semi-periphery and the periphery than in the G-7, and the recovery after 1994 was not as robust as in the U.S. and western Europe. Nevertheless, Portuguese authorities pursued convergence and rapid integration regardless of the pain that would cause to the general population, especially in view of sharp cuts in real wages and the government's policy that future productivity increases would be used to enhance profitability that encouraged investment, rather than raising wage rates.[89]

In July 1995, shortly after Washington signed an agreement renewing the Azores pact in exchange for aid, an IMF mission, Portugal's governor of the central bank, and the minister of finance discussed employment and social security policies and fiscal future strategies. Both the ruling Social Democratic party and the opposition Socialist party affirmed their commitment to Maastricht and to monetarist policies. Pleased that Portugal had opened the gates to foreign investment, liberalized, and deregulated the economy to the degree that the state had a minimal role, the IMF was especially gratified with the stabilization programs of the past two decades. Inflation was the lowest since the early 1970s and per capita income levels for Portugal rose closer to the European average in the 1990s. However, unemployment had been rising especially among the young, and wage earners had not benefited from the mid-1990s expansion nearly as much as the middle and upper classes.[90]

The sluggish economy, rampant corruption of the center-right Social-Democrat party that had been in office since 1985, and anxiety over EU convergence resulted in a parliamentary victory for the Socialists led by Antonio Guterrez in 1995. In January 1996 Socialist candidate Jorge Sampaio won a decisive victory over Silva for the presidency. Not much different than Spanish, Greek or French Socialists, the

Portuguese were as loyal to the EU and NATO as the conservatives. Despite the close and cordial Iberian relationship, and concern about western European dominance in the EU in the post-Cold War era, Portugal remained focused on its sovereignty and its special relationship with Africa and Latin America.[91]

Owing to consumer demand and construction that helped lift all related sectors, the Socialists benefited from rising domestic economic activity in the second half of 1996. As unemployment declined, GNP growth for the year was around 2.3-2.8 percent. Cutting interest rates to stimulate demand, the Bank of Portugal was following the Bank of Spain's lead to remain competitive. Because of higher revenues in 1996 and a commitment to early EMU participation, the budget deficit target was 2.9 percent of GNP or about half as much as 1995.

While pursuing corporate welfare, Portugal was trying to cut "fraud and waste" in unemployment and sickness benefits. After privatizing *Telecom, Banco de Fomento*, and the state-owned power company, the cement company *Cimpor* was offered for sale as was 65 percent of the tobacco company *Tabaqueira*. The privatization process in Portugal was no different than in Greece, Spain, Peru, or other countries amid the euphoria of transferring public assets to private domestic and foreign ownership, some under a cloud of corruption. Reflecting the views of Wall Street and neo-liberal ideology, the IMF contended that privatization increases efficiency, strengthened markets, and reduces costs. While privatization resulted in higher profits for a few investors, it also meant a rise in alleged corruption, lower wages, and higher costs for consumers.[92]

Following the EU lead, Portugal's central bank cut interest rates in the hope that growth could be maintained on the eve of the single currency era. With a 5 percent unemployment rate, per capita income three times higher in 1998 than in 1975, Portugal was ready to adopt the euro, despite concerns about sluggish growth. In late May-early June 2000, president Clinton met with president Sampaio, prime minister Antonio Guterrez, and European Commission president Romano Prodi to discuss EU restrictions on U.S. exports of genetically modified foods, beef, and bananas. For its part, the EU continued to protest the tax breaks that U.S. provided for corporations, especially those with offshore offices. Portugal was as concerned as the rest of Europe that Clinton's pursuit with the development of the space-based missile defense system would undermine EU security and force more defense spending among western countries, thereby diverting resources from the civilian economies. To retain economic leverage, Portugal remained loyal to U.S. foreign policy, but it had the luxury of having the EU cover.[93]

Like its southern European counterparts, Portugal used its NATO role to secure optimal foreign aid. Though the Portuguese people identified with the EU and were increasingly critical of U.S. foreign policy toward the Middle East, skeptical of U.S.-based globalization and Clinton's dollar diplomacy, and skeptical of U.S. failure to engage in multilateral cooperation ranging from environmental conventions to undercutting the UN, all non-Communist political parties were anxious to deal with Washington and the IFIs in return for any real or symbolic benefits. In short, the weaker EU members used the U.S. and IFIs as leverage within the bloc to counterpoise France and Germany. In many respects, inter-dependent integration represented more constrictive conditions on Portugal's financial, trade, labor, environmental, and social policies, but it also meant greater sovereignty that would only rise with the EU's growing global influence.

Notes

1. SDNA 853.00/1-560, No. 271; F.O. 371/169451, No. CP 1102/7, 8 August 1963; A. Seda Nunes, *Sociologia e ideologia do desenvolvimento* (Lisbon, 1969), pp. 195-200; F. Madeiros, *A Sociodade e a economia portugesas nas origems do salarismo* (Lisbon, 1978), pp. 18-30; H. Blasco Fernandes, *Portugal atraves de algunas numeros* (Lisbon, 1976), pp. 78-82.
2. F.O. 371/136537, No. 10, 11 January 1958; J. Plonchard D'Assac, *Dictionario Politico de Salazar* (Lisbon: SNI, 1964); D. P. Machado, *The Structure of Portugese Society* (Westport, CT, 1991), pp. 41-72.
3. F.O. 371/117860, RP 1011/1, No. 1, 5 January 1955; A. G. Duarte, *A Resistencia em Portugal* (Sao Paolo, 1962), pp. 50-59; Antonio Marques and Mario Bairrada, "As Classes sociais na populacao ativa portugesa," *Analise Social*, 17/72-74 (1982): 1279-97; J. A. Silva Marques, *Relatorios da clandestinidade: O PCP Visto por dentro* (Lisbon, 1977).
4. William Minter, *Portuguese Africa and the West* (New York, 1972), pp. 32-3.
5. IMF Archives C/Portugal/810, Visit A. N. Oberby, 1951; 19 June 1951, Acting Managing Director to Secretary; Ibid, 20 June 1951; F.O. 371/115927, No. E186, 27 September 1952.
6. F.O. 371/124059, No. 10, 12 June 1956; F.O. 371/130252, No. 115, 20 May 1957; F.O. 371/136537, No. 10, 11 January 1958.
7. F.O. 371/ 136544, No. 18E, 17 January 1958; Ibid., No. E25, 22 January 1958; Ibid., No. 8E, 15 April 1958.
8. F.O. 371/136543, No. E 99, 14 May 1958; F.O. 371/144816, No. 220, 31 December 1958.
9. F.O. 371/163785, 12 October 1962; SDNA 853.00/1-560, No. 271.
10. F.O. 371/153116, No. E 31, 19 February 1960; F.O. 371/153116, No. E 36, 14 March 1960; F.O. 371/153118, No. RP1112/4, 5 July 1960; SDNA 853.00/4-2861, No. G-160.
11. F.O. 371/153107, RP10345/1, 17 March 1960; Ibid., No. 66 28 May 1960; SDNA 853.00/12-2860, No. 224; F.O. 371/153098, No. 3, 5 January 1960.
12. F.O. 371/169440, No. 8, 11 January 1963.
13. F.O. 371/163774, 29 April 1962, "Record of Conversation between Foreign Secretary and Rusk."

14. IMF Archives, C/Portugal/420.1 Exchange Restrictions, Consultation Article XIV, 17 April 1965, Whittome to Sturc; IMF Archives, C/Portugal/420.1 Exchange Restrictions, Consultation Article XIV, 23 May 1962, Irving Friedman to Executive Board; F.O. 371/163783, No. 15, 19 February 1962.

15. F.O. 371/105784, No. 44, 27 April 1962; F.O. 371/169783, No. 15, 19 February 1962; SDNA 853.00/7-2162, No. A-34; SDNA 853.00/7-2162, No. A-37; SDNA 853.00/8-462, No. A-60; SDNA 853.00/8/1862, No. 82.

16. F.O. 371/163774, No. 1016/22/62, 24 August 1962; *The Guardian*, 7 February 1962; F.O. 371/163784, No. CP1102/2, 3 April 1962.

17. F.O. 371/153771, No. 4, 2 January 1962; Ibid., No. 1011/62, 11 January 1962; Ibid., No. 18, 23 February 1962; Ibid., No. 1011/36/62, 1 May 1962; D. L. Raby, "Portugal," in Joan Campbell (ed), *European Labor Unions* (Westport, CT., 1992), p. 361; *New York Times*, 12 May 1962; F.O. 371/153780, No. 66, 3 July 1962; Ibid., No. 1035/62, 10 July 1962; Ibid., No. 17, 20 July 1962; Minter, *Portuguese Africa*, p. 91.

18. Alfred Grosser, *French Foreign Policy under de Gaulle* (Boston, 1967); FCO 9/382, CP 1018, 1 December 1967; Ibid., 25 November 1967; Ibid., 18 February 1967; F.O. 371/169443, No. 14 18 July 1963; Ibid., No. 1011/63, 4 October 1963; Ibid., CP 1022/10, 3 December 1963.

19. IMF Archives, C/Portugal/420.1 Exchange Restrictions, Consultation Article XIV, SM/62/92, No. 2, 24 April 1963; Ibid., 29 April 1964, H. Ponsen to R. de Faria Blanc; F.O. 371/174921, CP 1111/2, No. 49E, 27 April 1964.

20. F.O. 371/169451, No. 1106/63, 2 July 1963.

21. SDNA LAB 2 PORT, A-389, 5 March 1964.

22. Ibid. F.O. 371/169451, No. 1106/63, 2 July 1963; F.O. 371/169451, No. CP 1102/7, 8 August 1963.

23. IMF Archives, C/Portugal/420.1 Exchange Restrictions Article XIV Consultation, 17 April 1965, Whittome to Sturc; Ibid., 6 July 1964, A. Pfeifer to Frank A. Southard; F.O. 371/174921, CP 1111/2, No. 49E, 27 April 1964; F.O. 371/174921, CP 1111/2, No. 49E, 27 April 1964.

24. F.O. 371/174915, CP103145/1, No. 2222/64, 4 February 1964; Ibid., No. 1, 19 March 1964; F.O. 371/174909, No. 30 July 1964; Ibid., No. 1016/64, 4 November 1964.

25. IMF Archives, C/Portugal/420.1, Consultation Article XIV, 27 April 1965, Ponsen to Whittome; Ibid., 30 June 1965, Ponsen to Whittome.

26. F.O. 371/180079, No. CP1021/1, 6 January 1965; Ibid., CP1021/2, 1 March 1965; F.O. 371/180084, No. 1038/65, 6 April 1965; Ibid., No. 11974, 27 May 1965; Ibid., No. 15112, 6 October 1965.

27. IMF Archives, C/Portugal/810, Visit Ponsen, January 1966, H. Ponsen to L. A. Whittome; Ibid., C/Portugal/420.1 Article XIV Consultation, No. 2, 24 October 1966; Ibid., No 3, 25 October 1966; Ibid., No 5, 26 October 1966; Ibid., No. 6, 27 October 1966.

28. SDNA, POL 15-1 No. A-386, 24 May 1967; Ibid., A-476, 24 July 1968.

29. SDNA POL- 2 Portugal, No. A-197, 16 January 1967; Ibid., POL 15-1 Portugal, No. A-247, 17 February 1967; Nixon Project, WHCF, Box 62, CO-122, 19 November 1969; WBA, Box 3 Portugal-General Negotiations Vol. III, EM/M/68-23, 21 May 1968, C. F. Owen to Distribution; Minter, *Portuguese Africa*, pp. 120-23.

30. SDNA POL 18 Port., A-20, 28 February 1967; FCO9/359, 17 July 1968; FCO 9/382, No. CP1018, 7 March 1968.

31. SDNA POL 1 Portugal, 27 November 1968; Ibid., 17 September 1968; FCO9/354, No. CP 1/4, 3 October 1968; R. Blake, *A History of Rhodesia* (New York, 1978).

32. Nixon Project, WHCF, Box 62, CO-122, 19 November 1969; UN General Assembly, "Resolution Adopted by the General Assembly," 4 December 1968; F.C.O.9/359, 9 October 1968; SDNA, POL 1 PORT-US, A-326, 3 April 1968; SDNA POL 2 Portugal, No. A-91, 21 March 1969; Ibid., No. A-78, 21 March 1969.

33. IMF Archives, C/Portugal/420.1 Article XIV Consultation, SM/71/27, 4 February 1971, Secretary to Executive Board; Nixon Project, NSC, Box 760, Caetano to Nixon, 13 April 1971; Ibid., Nixon to Caetano, 29 April 1971; Ibid., Box 62, CO-122, M. Wright to Kissinger, 8 December 1970.

34. Nixon Project, NSC, Box 701, R. V. Allen to R. M. Flanigan, 29 September 1971; Ibid., Flanigan to Kissinger, 6 October 1971.

35. SDNA, EUR-18, No. 3573, 2 October 1971; Nixon Project NSC, Box 62, State Department to Senator Sam Erving, 1 December 1971; IMF Archives, C/Portugal/420.1 Article XIV Consultation, No. 13, 12 April 1972.

36. SDNA FN 17, No. 498, 23 February 1972; IMF Archives, C/Portugal/420.1 Article XIV Consultation, No. 12, 12 April 1972; Ibid., No. 26 18 April 1972; Nixon Project, NSC, Box 701, 10 November 1972.

37. Nixon Project, NSC Box 701, 9, December 1973; Ibid., 17 December 1973; Ibid., 26 November 1973; Ibid., 15 October 1973; IMF Archives, 810, Mission Van Houtven, 5 December 1975, Leovan Houtven to Managing Director; IMF Archives, C/Portugal/420.1 Exchange Restrictions Article XIV Consultations, 19 August 1976, Brian Rose and C. David Finch.

38. Antonio de Spinola, *Portugal e o futuro* (Lisbon, 1974); Ben Pimlot, "Were the Soldiers Revolutionary? The Armed Forces Movement in Portugal," *Iberian Studies* 7(1) (1978): 13-22; Ford Library, WHCF, Box 46, Folder CO-139, 13 March 1975; New York Times, 14 August 1996.

39. *New York Times*, 9 December 1979.

40. Nixon Project, NSC Box 701, Kissinger to Nixon, 29 April 1974; Ibid., A. D. Clift to Kissinger, 26 April 1974; Anderson, *Portugal*, pp. 173-74.

41. James Anderson, *A History of Portugal* (Westport, CT, 2000), pp. 166, 175; Raby, "Portugal," p. 363; Machado, *Portuguese Society*, pp. 169-75.

42. IMF Archives, 810, Mission Rose, 18 December 1974; Ibid., 18 December 1974 Rose to Managing Director.

43. Bill Lomax, "Ideology and Illusion in the Portugese Revolution: The Role of the Left" in L.
S. Graham and D.L. Wheeler (eds), *In Search of Modern Portugal* (Madison: WI, 1983),
pp. 110-20; *New York Times*, 27 January 1975; Ibid., 8 February 1975; WBA, General
Negotiations, Box 3, 3 April 1981, Lucien E. Moreau to M. Sriram Aiyer.

44. *New York Times*, 21 February 1975; Ibid., 15 March 1975; Ibid., 9 April 1975; Ibid., 17
April 1975; WBA General Negotiations, Box 3, 20 October 1978, Portugal.

45. WBA General Negotiations, Box 3, 6 May 1975, Guy de Lusignan to Distribution; Ibid., 30
June 1975, Memorandum on Developments in Portugal and Relations with the Bank.

46. WBA General Negotiations, Box 3, 22 March 1977, Mate Durdag to Benjamin King;
Ibid.,19 June 1975, M. P. Benjenk to Robert McNamara; *New York Times*, 30 June 19⁷5;
Ibid., 5 July 1975; Ibid., 8 July 1975.

47. Machado, *Portuguese Society*, pp. 180-82; WBA General Negotiations Box 3, Portugal-
General, 13 August 1975, M.J.W M. Paijmans to Files; Ibid., Portugal-National
Development Bank, 8 October 1975, Paul E. Smith to G. de Lusignan; *New York Times*, 11
September 1975; Ibid., 29 August 1975; Ibid., 20 September 1975; Ibid., 4 October 1975;
Ibid., 4 November 1975.

48. IMF Archives, C/Portugal/420.1 Article XIV Consultation, 1974/75/76, No. 9, 14 June
1976; *New York Times*, 17 December 1975; Raby, "Portugal," p. 364.

49. IMF Archives, C/Portugal/420.1 Article XIV Consultation, 1974/75/76, No. 8, 11 June
1976; Ibid., 19 August 1976, Brian Rose and David Finch; *New York Times*, 21 December
1975; Ibid., 9 January 1976; Ibid., 11 January 1976; Anderson, *Portugal*, p. 173.

50. WBA General Negotiations, Box 3, 23 April 1981, Sriram Aiyer to Attila Karaosmanoglou;
Ibid., 28 January 1976, Paul E. Smith to Files; Ibid., 8 October 1975, Paul E. Smith to G.
de Lusignan; *New York Times*, 2 January 1976; Ibid., 14 March 1976; Ibid., 16 March
1976; Ibid., 12 April 1976; Ibid., 21 April 1976; Ibid., 15 February 1988.

51. Anderson, *Portugal*, pp. 173-74; Machado, *Portuguese Society*, pp. 191-92.

52. IMF Archives, C/Portugal/420.1 Exchange Restrictions Article XIV Consultation, No. 1, 1
June 1976; New York Times, 15 August 1976.

53. IMF Archives, C/Portugal/420.1 Exchange Restrictions Article XIV Consultation, No. 3, 3
June 1976; Bela Balassa, *Economic Policies in Portugal* (Washington, D.C., 1983), pp.
111-12; IMF Archives, C/Portugal/420.1 Exchange Restrictions Article XIV Consultations,
19 August 1976, Brian Rose and C. David Finch; WBA General Negotiations, Alan Roe to
Witteveen, 9 May 1978.

54. WBA General Negotiations, Box 3, 15 December 1976, J. Burke Knapp to Robert
McNamara; World Bank, *World Development: Report 1978* (Washington, D.C., 1978);
New York Times, 2 October 1976; Ibid., 17 October 1976; Ibid., 14 November 1976.

55. IMF, C/Portugal/1760, Stand-by Arrangements, Press Release No. 77/31, 25 April 1977;
New York Times, 15 January 1977; Ibid., 31 January 1977; Ibid., 26 February 1977.

56. IMF, C/Portugal/1760, Stand-by Arrangements, 18 May 1977, Hans Schmitt to the Acting
Managing Director; WBA General Negotiations, Box 3, 9 May 1978, Alan Roe to

Whittome; Ibid., 12 November 1982, Jane Loos to Files; *New York Times*, 11 July 1977; Ibid., 23 February 1977; Ibid., 20 November 1977; Ibid., 21 March 1984; Anderson, *Portugal*, p. 175.

57. IMF Archives, C/Portugal/1760, Stand-by Arrangement, 10 February 1978, L. A. Whittome to Acting Managing Director; Ford Library, Arthur Burns Papers, B61, International Economic Developments, 6 January 1978, Irene Cavanagh to Siegman; *New York Times*, 27 January 1978; WBA General Negotiations, Box 3, Malvina Pollock to Helen Hughes, 29 March 1978; Ibid., Malvina Pollock to Victor Constancio, 21 April 1978; WBA, General Negotiations, Box 3, Sriram Aiyer to M. J. W. M. Paijans, 4 October 1978.

58. IMF Archives, C/Portugal/420.3, Article IV Consultation, 20 November 1978; IMF Archives, C/Portugal/810 Mission Schmitt, 24 November 1978, Hans Schmitt to Managing Director; WBA, General Negotiations, Box 3, 21 December 1982 Jane Loos to Files.

59. IMF Archives, C/Portugal/1760, Stand-by Arrangement, EBS/78/107, 24 January 1979, Secretary to the Treasurer; WBA General Negotiations, Box 3, Shalid A. Chaudry to Files, 1 February 1979.

60. *New York Times*, 21 January 1979; Ibid., 26 February 1979.

61. IMF Archives, C/Portugal/810, Mission Schmitt, 13 August 1979, L. A. Whittome to Managing Director; Ibid., 3 August 1979, L. A. Whittome to Managing Director; Ibid., 3 August 1979, P. de Fontenay to Whittome.

62. WBA, General Negotiations, Box 3, 28 March 1980, M. Sriram Aiyer to Attila Karaosmanoglu; Carter Library, Box 192, Office of Staff Secretary, File 6/18/80, 18 June 1980, Jody Powell & Al Friendly to the President.

63. IMF Archives, C/Portugal/420.3 Article IV Consultation, 1979-80, EBM/80/100, 30 June 1980, Portugal - Article IV Consultation; WBA General Negotiations, Alan Roe to Lucien Moreau, 24 July 1980; Ibid., "Country Brief- Portugal," 16 December 1980.

64. *New York Times*, 20 November 1980; WBA, General Negotiations, Box 3, Sriram Aiyer to Attila Karaomanoglou, 23 April 1981.

65. *New York Times*, 23 January 1981; Ibid., WBA, General Negotiations, Box 3, Sriram Aiyer to Joao Morais Leitao, 12 February 1981; WBA, General Negotiations, Box 3, Sriram Aiyer to Joao Morais Leitao, 6 March 1981; Ibid., Lucien Moreau to M. Sriram Aiyer, 3 April 1981.

66. IMF Archives, C/Portugal/420.3, Article IV Consultation, SM/82/87, 30 April 1982; WBA, Box 3, 18 June 1981, M. Sriram Aiyer to Alan Roe; Ibid., 1 September 1981, M. Sriram Aiyer to Roger Chaufournier; *New York Times*, 10 August 1981; Ibid., 28 November 1981.

67. WBA, General Negotiations Vol. III, Sriram Aiyer to Helen Hughes, 19 June 1981; *New York Times*, 7 March 1982.

68. WBA Box 3, Portugal-General Negotiations Vol. III, 23 September 1982, Portugal, Country Program Paper; Ibid., 15 September 1982, Price Waterhouse to World Bank; *New York Times*, 5 January 1983; Ibid., 23 January 1983; Ibid., 24 January 1983.

69. IMF Archives, C/Portugal/420.3, Article IV Consultation, 17 May 1983, L. A. Whittome

and S. Mookejee; Ibid., SM/93/224, 22 October 1993, Secretary to Executive Board; WBA, General Negotiations, Box 3, V. N. Rajagopalan to E. F. Lari, 22 May 1984; *New York Times*, 26 April 1983; Ibid., 28 April 1983; IMF C/Portugal/1760, Stand-by Arrangement, 10 December 1984, L. A. Whittome and E. Brau.

70. WBA, General Negotiations, Box 3, V. N. Rajagopalan to E. F. Lari, 22 May 1984; *New York Times*, 21 May 1984; Ibid., 21 March 1984.

71. IMF Archives, C/Portugal/420.3 Article IV Consultation, EBS/84/1432 July 1984; Joao Cravinho, "The Portugese Economy: Constraints and Opportunities," in K. Maxwell (ed), *Portugal in the 1980s* (Westport, CT., 1986), pp. 111-14.

72. IMF C/Portugal/1760, Stand-by Arrangement, 8 May 1985, L. A. Whittome and J. T. Boorman; IMF, C/Portugal/420.3, Article IV Consultations, 16 August 1985, L. A. Whittome and J. T. Boorman.

73. WBA, General Negotiations, Box 3, PO-Leap, Philippe Nouvel to Eugenio F. Lari, 13 September 1985, Ibid., "Country Brief-Portugal," 5 January 1990, Barber Conable to Eugenio Lari; Ibid., 27 August 1982, Jane Loos to Files.

74. *New York Times*, 27 January 1986; Ibid., 17 February.

75. IMF C/Portugal/420.3 Article IV Consultations, 16 August 1986, L. A. Whitome and J. T. Boorman; Ibid., 8 July 1988, Massimo Russo and S. Kanesa-Thasan; *New York Times*, 4 May 1986.

76. *New York Times*, 16 October 1986; Ibid., 16 March 1987; 4 April 1987.

77. WBA, General Negotiations, Box 3, PO-Leap, 22 July 1988, Ken Kwaku to Jane Loos.

78. *New York Times*, 19 May 1987; Ibid., 21 August 1988; IMF Archives, C/Portugal/420.3, Article IV Consultation, SM/89/150, 27 July 1989, Secretary to Executive Board; Anderson, *Portugal*, 174.

79. *New York Times*, 6 March 1988; Ibid., 24 July 1988; WBA General Negotiations, Box 3, PO-Leap, May 1988, "Portugal"; Ibid., 15 June 1988, Ken Kwaku to Files.

80. *New York Times*, 24 July 1989; WBA, General Negotiations, Box 3, PO-Leap, 12 August 1988, Philippe Nouvel to Rua da Alfandega; IMF Archives, C/Portugal/420.3, Article IV Consultation, SM/89/150, 27 July 1989, Secretary to Executive Board.

81. WBA, General Negotiations, Box 3, PO-Leap, 5 January 1990, Philippe Nouvel to Distribution; Anderson, *Portugal*, pp. 179-80.

82. *New York Times*, 29 April 1990; Ibid., 7 May 1990.

83. IMF Archives, C/Portugal/420.3, Article IV Consultation, SM/90/179, 7 September 1990, Secretary to Executive Board; *New York Times*, 22 January 1990.

84. *New York Times*, 12 March 1992; Ibid., 7 October 1991.

85. IMF Archives, C/Portugal/420.3, Article IV Consultation, SM/93/224, 22 October 1993, Secretary to Executive Board.

86. Ibid., SM /94/212, 8 August 1994, Secretary to Executive Board; Ibid., SM/95/269, 13 October 1995, Secretary to Executive Board; *New York Times*, 12 March 1992; Anderson, *Portugal*, p. 179.

87. IMF Archives, C/Portugal/420.3, Article IV Consultation, SM/95/269, 13 October 1995, Secretary to Executive Board.

88. IMF Archives, C/Portugal/420.3, Article IV Consultation, 28 September 1995, Acting Secretary to Executive Board.

89. IMF Archives, C/Portugal/420.3, Article IV Consultation, SM/94/212, 8 August 1994, Secretary to Executive Board.

90. *New York Times*, 2 June 1995; IMF Archives, C/Portugal/420.3, Article IV Consultation, 26 September 1995, Michael Deppler and Susan Schadler.

91. Joao Marques de Almeida, *Portugese Security Policy* (Lisbon, 1995); *New York Times*, 3 October 1995; Ibid., 15 January 1996.

92. IMF Archives, C/Portugal/420.3, Article IV Consultation, 17 October 1996 Jacques R. Artus and Susan Schadler.

93. Roy and Kanner, "Spain and Portugal," 253; *New York Times*, 4 November 1998; Ibid., 10 May 1997; *New York Times*, 31 May 2000.

Chapter 5

The Third World under the Patron-Client Model: Indonesia, Nigeria, and Peru

Sukarno's Non-Aligned, Quasi-Statist Experiment

Composed of 14,000 islands, Indonesia has the largest Muslim population in the world, and it is ethnically and culturally diverse. To explain chronically low living standards, social scientists who embrace the Malthusian theory ignore grossly uneven income distribution and the manner by which Holland as the colonial master drained Indonesia's wealth and relegated it to the periphery as an exporter of raw materials and importer of manufactured goods. Despite its rich natural resources, under the patron-client model Indonesia has suffered chronic low living standards in the second half of the 20th century, especially after 1966 when the Suharto dictatorship allowed a small clique linked to the regime and foreign capitalists to pillage the nation's wealth and profit from cheap labor.[1]

In 1966 the annual per capita income was $41, the lowest in the world outside of sub-Sahara Africa. Indonesia was integrated under the patron-client model by Holland, western Europe, the U.S. and Japan. The winds of decolonization swept Indonesia during Japanese occupation in WWII from which Achmed Sukarno emerged as the first president. After independence in 1949, Indonesia was settled with immense debt repayment to the Netherlands whose companies remained dominant in the islands. Neo-colonial control made it impossible for Sukarno's government to function in the absence of becoming financially dependent on the west and Japan, or escaping the patron-client model. With a foreign debt of $2.5 billion in 1966 when the New Order established under general T. N. J. Suharto's pro-west regime, Indonesia averaged about 5 percent growth rate until the global debt crisis and recessionary decade of the 1980s. By the time that Suharto was forced from office in 1998, Indonesia had gone through a turbulent period of cyclical growth and recessions, but remained chained to the patron-client model in the periphery.[2]

To preserve Indonesia's sovereignty in a bipolar world order, Sukarno was not as successful as Yugoslavia's Marshall Tito in using the superpowers to succeed with the non-aligned quasi-statist experiment. Because greater integration into the capitalist world system appeared inescapable for former colonies in the early 1950s, Indonesia joined GATT. In August 1952 it became an IMF/IBRD member, and secured a loan after agreeing to an austerity program, liberal trade, exchange rate reform, and foreign investment policies conducive to attracting capital. However, Sukarno rejected U.S. Mutual Security Act assistance conditioned on military and diplomatic backing of U.S. foreign policy.[3]

In the first half of the 1950s, Indonesia signed a number of trade pacts with the Communist bloc, while rejecting repeated appeals for a commercial treaty with some European countries. Because Indonesia's trade deficit with Japan was 160 million pounds sterling, Sukarno tried to diversify trade while cutting some Japanese imports in an attempt to avoid falling into the patron-client model with any one country. Comparing Indonesian nationalism to Iran under Muhammad Mossadiq, the Foreign Office argued that from 1945 to 1951 western oil companies paid 145 million pounds sterling to Jakarta, a sum that Indonesians considered tiny in comparison with the oil companies' profits.[4]

European and U.S.-owned oil and mining companies refused to raise production until they secured favorable concessions. Jakarta demanded that Dutch banks finance export-import trade with government guaranteed loans, and that foreign banks employ more Indonesians and provide more credit to Indonesian businesses. The Dutch Borneo Sumatra Trading company dispensed with five of its industrial units, Procter and Gamble ceased its margarine operations in Sumatra, while Unilever and Goodyear were as uncertain about the future as other foreign firms. After foreign banks and companies lobbied their governments to protest anti-western policies, in November 1954 Sukarno made cabinet changes as a precondition to securing foreign loans and investment.[5]

Amid a Third World recession, owing to depressed commodity prices and rising manufacturing prices in the mid-to-late-1950s, a year after the Bandung conference Indonesia announced that Dutch debts would not be repaid and two years later the government nationalized Dutch firms. After 1956 Sukarno emerged as the chief foreign policy spokesman, nationalizing Dutch property and trying to become increasingly independent of the west by forging new ties with Communist and non-aligned countries. Though he did not sever economic ties with the capitalist countries, Sukarno redefined the patron-client model by relying more on Japan, and focusing on economic nationalism and socioeconomic reform. In January 1958 Japan agreed to war reparations of $223 million, $177 million waived in commercial debts, and $400 million in commercial credits. In return, Sukarno permitted large scale Japanese investments, including North Sumatra petroleum concessions, timber, and nickel mines.[6]

Pursuing "Guided Democracy," political economy focused on greater self-reliance, diversified foreign trade, land reform, and support for peasant and trade unions, Sukarno endeavored realignment of the patron-client model. On 28 September 1959 Nasser and Sukarno signed MFN trade and payments agreements, though this was a political statement of non-aligned solidarity and rejection of the patron-client model rather than a substantive trade deal. Announcing a foreign economic policy that was neither pro-west nor pro-East, Sukarno knew that the economy was dependent heavily on the western bloc. According to the 8-year plan promulgated in 1960, Indonesia aimed for self-sufficiency in consumer necessities within three years, and steady growth throughout the 1960s. The combination of declining terms of trade and an average annual inflation rate of 22 percent from 1952 to 1960 challenged the regime's plans and revealed that it operated within the context of the patron-client model despite Sukarno's realignment efforts.[7]

In April 1961 Sukarno visited Bolivia and spoke of the need for Third World development based on cooperation between mineral producing countries to stabilize prices. On 15 June 1961 the government charged that foreign companies had failed to advance the national economy by investing in new oil reserves, expanding the domestic market, assisting the government solve the foreign exchange problem, or employing Indonesians in management positions. Oil companies had been granted special rights, but the new policy focused on meeting domestic consumer demand and optimal use of reserves. The U.S. charged that Mao proposed that Sukarno nationalize the oil industry and sell oil to China, a claim repeated by India embroiled in a tense relationship with China over the Himalayan conflict. The Rubber Growers' Association asked that British and Dutch governments intervene to secure compensation from Indonesia which was nationalizing the plantations, buildings, and other foreign-owned property. The seizure of foreign firms and mass anti-west riots alarmed Europe and the U.S. which blamed Sukarno's pro-Communist regime.[8]

In February 1963 Sukarno asked for IMF, U.S., EEC and Japan financial assistance. An IMF mission concluded that Indonesia's finances had deteriorated, mostly because of a 50 percent increase in government wages, and state compensation for ending the rice subsidy. Opposed to subsidies for essentials like rice, the IMF advised Indonesian officials to remove price controls and to allow public enterprises to operate like private companies. Under the IMF program, the central bank could not extend any credit to the state in 1963, and credit expansion to the private sector was under 6 percent.[9]

Jakarta devalued the rupiah from 45 to the dollar to 300, and 500 rupiah for all imports, except rice, government debt, military supplies, and government services. The government allowed prices to rise, it cut credit and public spending, but pursued development projects to keep employment. Besides providing Indonesia with a $17 million loan for U.S. imports, the Kennedy administration arranged for a PL480 agreement to transfer cotton to reward Jakarta for its cooperation with the IMF, the west, and for restoring cordial relations with Holland. The IMF and western creditors warned that instead of counting on foreign aid to stimulate the economy, Jakarta should cut spending and monetary expansion, stimulate exports, liberalize imports, and offer incentives to foreign capital.[10]

After adopting stabilization on 23 May 1963, Indonesia continued to suffer high price inflation, budgetary and balance-of-payments deficits. To stimulate the economy and reduce unemployment, the government embarked on new industrial projects, before repairing the poorly-run sugar mills. Investing in hotels, airport, and public buildings, Sukarno failed to control costs at the level that the IMF and western creditors demanded. Although Jakarta had rescheduled $100 million in debt, it was negotiating to rollover $411 million. In September 1963 Washington accused Jakarta of violating the IMF stabilization agreement. The real motive behind U.S. charges was Sukarno's reliance on the Communist bloc for military aid.[11]

In September 1963 Tokyo approved $12 million emergency export credits for Indonesia to reduce its debt service obligation. Provided by Japan's Export-Import Bank and commercial banks, the new credits were announced just before an Indonesian trade mission departed for Tokyo and right after Mitsui Mining won the Caram oil concession. Under a 1958 agreement, Japan had paid $101 million in reparations, $82 million in Export-Import Bank commodity loans, and over $182 million was invested by Japanese companies in Indonesia's economy. Japan's new credits to Indonesia coincided with the Indonesian nationalization of British-owned firms, after Britain announced that it backed a federation of Malaysia. The U.S. and IMF informed Jakarta that they were canceling $400 million in consortium aid, after Sukarno failed to accept a U.S. ultimatum on his foreign policy.[12]

Coinciding with labor-management problems involving U.S. and European companies laying off workers and confronting trade unions, in the second half of 1963 U.S.-Indonesian relations deteriorated. After the Johnson administration adopted an aggressive stance toward Sukarno, Japan was contemplating a $300 million development loan for numerous projects in Indonesia suffering from high inflation, thriving black market, and foreign exchange shortage. The announcement was surprising in April 1964, because Tokyo had just cut exports credits to Jakarta, using as a pretext Indonesia's failure to repay its debts amounting to $85 million. While Japan curbed exports credits to Brazil, Argentina, India, and Pakistan for failing to pay on time, commercial opportunities with Indonesia were very attractive.[13]

The U.S. charged that by using trade, diplomacy, and international labor relations, Sukarno was strengthening the Afro-Asian non-aligned bloc and trade unions as a counterweight to western capitalism. During Sukarno's visit to Tokyo seeking financial assistance in June 1964, Washington and London were pressuring Japan to demand substantial political and commercial concessions. After numerous U.S.-Indonesian disputes, including Sukarno's refusal to sign an investment guarantee accord, Dean Rusk threatened to cut off aid, demanding that all allies follow suit. West Germany and Australia ended aid to Indonesia, arguing that Sukarno would claim it was a political endorsement. Defending Indonesia's withdrawal from the UN, China castigated the U.S. for manipulating the UN and attacking Jakarta. Prime minister Ikeda Hayato

(1960-1964) argued that the only way to influence Indonesia's policies was through economic integration, otherwise the Communist bloc would benefit from its isolation. Ikeda warned Sukarno that no new aid was possible, though Tokyo would honor commercial agreements and development projects already in the pipeline. Besides China's political support for Sukarno, Japanese oil and manufacturing companies were pressuring Ikeda not to follow Washington's lead.[14]

Preferring Japanese firms like Nippon Electric, which sold microwave equipment to Indonesia, Sukarno expropriated U.S. subsidiaries, partly to retaliate against the U.S.-led aid blockade. By rejecting the U.S. as Indonesia's patron, Sukarno was dismissed as promoting Communism in Asia. This is not to excuse the reality of inflation rising from 20 percent in 1960 to 594 percent in 1965, or the decline in exports as the money supply rose 37 percent in 1960 to 302 percent in 1965. Nor is there much doubt about the power struggles between various political factions that accounted for a chaotic and unstable climate.[15]

Many factors contributed to Sukarno's downfall, including inept policies that yielded hyper inflation without the kind of tangible for the economy that Japan was experiencing. Faced with Vietnam, the Johnson administration undermined Sukarno's regime that was not cooperating with Washington. Besides securing the support of all of the industrialized countries to severely curtail trade and loans to Indonesia, the U.S. was also engaged in covert activity. In March 1965 the U.S. ordered all non-essential personnel out of the country. Anticipating major turmoil after repeated U.S. denunciations of the regime and its policies, only foreign non-petroleum companies were carrying normal operations. With three million members, Indonesia's Communist Party was the third largest in the world at a time that the Johnson administration was escalating the war against Vietnam, landing troops in the Dominican Republic to install a pro-U.S. regime, and blatantly spying on Latin American governments.[16]

Besides CIA covert operations since the 1950s, along with the U.S. military and political role in undermining Sukarno, the U.S. and its allies helped undermine Indonesia's economy by withholding aid. Moreover, the price of rubber dropped by 33 percent between 1960 and 1965, while prices of manufactured products rose during the same period. Sukarno's solution was to borrow heavily from abroad, amid a climate of triple-digit inflation. While population pressures, mounting foreign debt, and inflation weighed heavily on the economy, such conditions existed for many Third World countries. The difference in Indonesia was the U.S.-led campaign against the Sukarno regime and the decision to use Indonesia and the Philippines in forging a regional patron-client model for future political and economic considerations.[17]

From the U.S. perspective, Sukarno's foreign policy and economic measures reflected a pro-Communist bias that had to be crushed to stop the dominoes from falling, to allow IFI policies to prevail, and to give western corporations the opportunity to exploit Indonesia's resources and labor at the lowest possible cost.

Establishing contacts inside the Indonesian military, the U.S. was able to undermine Sukarno and help in his ouster. On 1 October 1965, the military staged a coup d'etat in which 500,000 to 1,000,000 people were killed. The U.S. embassy and CIA provided names of political opponents targeted for execution. In March 1966 Sukarno signed power over to the New Order of pro-U.S. general T. N. J. Suharto. By helping to remove Sukarno, the U.S. put an end to the Bandung system and reinforced the patron-client model under its hegemony.[18]

Suharto: Dependence and Integration under the Patron-Client Model

From 22 February to 12 March 1966 there were mass demonstrations in Jakarta and raids on the U.S. embassy. With the army's backing, Suharto assumed executive authority in March 1966 and created a brutal and corrupt pro-west dictatorship. Suharto suppressed trade union and peasant organizations, invited foreign capital, and accepted IMF-World Bank economic, fiscal, trade, and labor policies. Indonesia's fate was no longer with the non-aligned bloc or dedicated to greater self-sufficiency. Rather the strategy was to put all its faith with the advanced capitalist countries, especially the U.S. and Japan. This entailed revising all policies, ranging from labor-management laws and foreign investment to dealing ruthlessly with the opposition. According to the British embassy in Jakarta, the Suharto government was responsible for the slaughter of many Communists as part of a purge campaign to demonstrate the resolve of the new authoritarian regime.[19]

Within months after Suharto took power hundreds of U.S., European, and Japanese firms signed multi-million dollar contracts in everything from manufacturing to petroleum. Because a small group of people controlled public institutions and benefited from the new economic policies, the Suharto regime was no different than any other Third World dictatorship from the Philippines under president Ferdinand Marcos to the Shah of Iran. To camouflage its pro-business pro-U.S. policy, the new regime employed the same rhetoric as Sukarno about African-Asian solidarity, opposition to imperialism, self-reliance, and pursuing an independent foreign policy. By the summer of 1966, however, it was obvious to the world that the New Order had lined behind Washington, while distancing itself from the previous regime whose followers it persecuted.[20]

In September 1966, after consulting with Washington and western creditors, Indonesia rescheduled her Communist bloc debts, which amounted to $1.2 billion. The Johnson administration took the lead in backing Suharto and urged the consortium members to assist under the leadership of the Asian Development Bank (ADB), which played a key role in the policies that Suharto followed. Besides a general economic liberalization, freeing of prices, cutting subsidies, the new right wing regime tried to balance the budget and control inflation in accordance with the IMF mission that completed its task in November 1966.[21]

In October 1966 the government announced a series of stabilization measures, including cutting public spending and tightening the money supply. At the same time, restrictions were lifted on trade and foreign capital allowing for the Indonesian economy's foreign domination. On 20 December 1966 the Paris Club, which included the OECD, IMF, World Bank, U.S., UK, France, Japan, Australia, West Germany, Netherlands, and Italy, decided to reschedule $357 million of debt, and to have payments begin after 1971 at a reduced interest rate. The deal that finally emerged was the result of very close collaboration between creditor governments, corporations doing business in or with Indonesia, commercial banks, and the multilateral institutions.[22]

After the creation of the Inter-Governmental Group for Indonesia (IGGI), Suharto established the Aid Indonesia Task Force open to all foreign governments and companies interested in investing in Indonesia. Promoted as a plan to foster housing construction, schools, hospitals, roads, and businesses in general, the Aid Indonesia Task Force, which was a scheme driven by the U.S. and EEC, asserted that foreign companies were free to propose their own plans.[23]

"Operation Hope," a rehabilitation program for Sumatra, was part of the larger national scheme in which foreign companies would exploit the raw materials, cheap labor, and domestic market. Despite Asian competition, western countries saw great opportunities in Indonesia. On the basis of advice from the multilateral banks, the consortium, and large domestic companies, Suharto approved a new investment law that provided generous terms for foreign capitalists. Meanwhile, he crushed opposition trade unions and coopted those loyal to his regime.[24]

After considerable U.S. and European pressure on Tokyo, in January 1967 Japan proposed $50 million in new loans linking them to market share. Under Suharto, Japan became Indonesia's second most significant financial and economic partner, largely with the encouragement of the U.S. which maintained a dominant voice in the consortium. In February 1967 an IMF mission's recommendation resulted in radical policy shifts toward austerity and devaluation of the rupiah. Recommending the adoption of an open market system, the World Bank proposed that public enterprises must become self-financed which entailed slashing jobs and raising prices. After studying Indonesia's agriculture, transportation, and manufacturing sector, the World Bank recommended that Indonesia import more seeds and fertilizers from the advanced capitalist countries.[25]

Suffering the worst balance-of-payments deficit in the world, Indonesia went along with consortium recommendations. Donor governments were well aware of massive official corruption, ruthless persecution of opposition labor and political leaders, and the use of rewards to coopt trade union and political leaders. The U.S. embassy noted that the ministry of labor interpreted labor law and regulations any manner it saw fit. The U.S., which led Amsterdam-based Consortium, encouraged all members to contribute 2/3 of $600 million in loans needed for 1967, while Washington would contribute $200 million.[26]

After a banking crisis in August 1967 and serious rice shortages in September, Indonesia was confronting social and political problems that the new regime had promised to alleviate. Pledging favorable treatment of foreign investment, finance minister F. X. Seda requested a new aid package to continue making payments on $2.5 billion in debt obligations. The U.S.-led consultative group met to discuss Indonesia's debt and new loan requirements amid 15 percent unemployment that would only rise under Suharto. At the Amsterdam meeting in November 1967, the creditors agreed to an aid package of $325 million, and loans due for payment in 1968 would be postponed until 1972-1979. The U.S. once again volunteered to provide up to one-third of Indonesia's loan needs, provided the other members agreed to the balance. The World Bank noted that Indonesia needed to develop her infrastructure that required foreign contacts. There was no mention of Amnesty International's report that Suharto used foreign aid to hold over 50,000 political prisoners and to engage in mass killings.[27]

Despite Japanese criticism of Suharto's policies, the IMF, the World Bank, and the U.S. defended the dictatorship. The AFL-CIO was collaborating with the State Department and International Labor Office (ILO) to foster a pro-business trade union movement, despite continued government persecution of opposition leaders. Washington contended that despite setbacks and high unemployment, Indonesia's economy was improving. Massive U.S. and multilateral aid notwithstanding, agriculture was depressed and the country needed to import 600,000 tons of rice to meet domestic demand. All aid was linked to trade and contracts awarded to the donor countries' corporations.[28]

In September 1969 World Bank officials met with the consultative group for the Third World to refine the rules of operations amid rising pressures to provide more loans to Africa, Asia, and Latin America. The IFIs and Suharto claimed that stabilization had been successful. Despite manageable inflation, controlled credit expansion, and lower public spending, no one could claim that the Indonesian people were better off at the end of the decade than they were at the beginning, nor that the country as a whole was not more self sufficient. Nor did endemic official corruption have any effect on the consultative group. General Leo Lopulisa proudly told the U.S. ambassador in Jakarta that he appropriated 650 hectares from poor peasants and ordered 1200 of his own men to work the land.[29]

A Paris Club agreement obliged Indonesia to adopt non-discriminatory measures toward the U.S.-led Consultative group members. In return, Paris Club members urged commercial creditors to accept the terms agreed with Jakarta, the most lenient ever offered to a Third World country, largely because of the Nixon administration's efforts. The Paris Club capitulated to U.S. pressure on debt rescheduling, but in return Suharto yielded to Washington on foreign investment. Despite U.S., Paris Club, and the multilateral banks' support of the Suharto regime, European governments wanted Indonesia to repay its debts in full, while European exporters and bankers remained very apprehensive about another debt crisis.[30]

Japan committed $155 million, $90 million of which was devoted for project aid linked to contracts offered to Japanese companies, and $65 million in commodity aid, including $20 million for rice exports. Indonesia and the rest of Japan's neighbors feared Japan's commodity dumping in the form of aid. Latin America had similar fears about the U.S., and to a lesser extent the Middle East and Africa about European and U.S. commodity dumping. Foreign investment rose in all sectors, especially from U.S. firms and their subsidiaries registered in Australia and Philippines. By 1971 U.S. earnings from investments in Indonesia amounted to about 30 percent of the total capital, while reinvestment amounted to less than one percent.[31]

Because of the government's hard line on labor and leftist opposition, high unemployment and underemployment, and relative price stability, social unrest was not as widespread as many feared. The International Confederation of Free Trade Unions (ICFTU), AFL-CIO, ILO, and West German trade unions continued to provide financing, training, and guidance for the Indonesian labor force which was about 48 million by 1970, rising by 1.5 million annually. In February 1972 labor minister Mohammad Sadli insisted that freedom of assembly and the right to strike inhibited economic development. The government was pressuring all employees wishing to keep their jobs to join Suharto's Sekber Golkar-affiliated organizations like IKAR, and to campaign for the ticket. As the authoritarian state assumed tight control of the labor movement, it became skeptical about the CIA-AFL-CIO's efforts to influence it through the Asian-American Free Labor Institute.[32]

Despite $500 million of public and private capital inflow in 1970, and $600 million in foreign assistance in 1971, Indonesia needed an annual average of $600 million for the first half of the 1970s to achieve 7 percent GDP growth rate that the government projected for the 1970s. Given that in 1970 debt-service to GNP ratio was 6 percent, the IMF and World Bank projected 15 percent debt-service to GNP ratio by the end of the decade, and that assumed a sharp rise in the volume and price of exports. Because oil production as a percentage of GNP rose from 5.2 in 1970 to a high of 22.2 in 1974, Indonesia escaped the stagflation fate of the Third World non-oil producers. The economy stayed afloat largely because of foreign loans. With $1.5 billion the U.S. was the largest foreign investor, followed by Japan with $350 million, making the country an economic satellite of the two largest economies in the world.[33]

On 17 August 1971, Indonesia's Independence Day, Suharto declared that the economy could not possibly improve under the five year plans and that the gap between poor and rich would not close any time soon. Arguing that it would take more than a generation for the economy to improve dramatically and to grow out of exporting raw materials to develop a viable manufacturing and financial services sector, he noted that the second five-year plan would emphasize processing raw materials, while the third five-year plan would be a transition toward finished products.[34]

Unconcerned with unemployment, labor unrest, reduced representation of the political parties, Suharto accepted the western advisers' argument that overpopulation was jeopardizing the development program drafted in Washington at a time that the Nixon administration was considering aid cuts. In September 1971 he made cabinet changes to reflect his goal of strengthening the economy in accordance with U.S.-IMF-World Bank policy guidelines. To deflect attention from the foreign-dominated development program, Suharto ousted a number of high ranking military officers who owned businesses through corruption and extortion. Because the police kept files on Suharto's corrupt associates, he cut ties with them to demonstrate that he was above suspicion. The World Bank advised restructuring Indonesia's development bank that was a source of national and international corruption.[35]

Denying there were strings attached to foreign aid or that Indonesia had become an economic colony of the advanced capitalist countries, Suharto defended foreign capital and technology as essential. Because foreign investment laws afforded new guarantees, the government approved 522 projects totaling just under $2 billion, of which $444 million emanated from the U.S. directly, $284 million from mostly U.S. subsidiaries in the Philippines, and $383 million from Japan. Suharto promised that the second five-year plan would address unemployment, technology, and industrial expansion.[36]

There were almost 43,000 political prisoners, but on New Year's Eve 1972 Suharto announced that he would release 11,000. Suharto's message was designed to assuage the public, when the government did not in fact release nearly as many as promised. A few days after the amnesty announcement, Suharto lashed out at critics during a ceremony for the opening of a hospital. Warning that he would suppress all critics and that the armed forces would remain the pillar of his regime, he denied there was corruption involved in development projects, especially with the construction of the hospital. Suharto's threats toward his critics and corruption denials notwithstanding, the U.S. embassy remained concerned about widening corruption. To deflect focus from the regime's decadence, interior minister general Amir Mahmud charged that universities were subversion centers and legitimate targets for government surveillance.[37]

Both the British and Australian embassies in Jakarta noted that Indonesia's political, social, and economic situation was much more dire than the U.S. and the multilateral banks portrayed it. Political opposition was growing, there was rising nationalism, xenophobia, Javanism in sharp conflict with Islam, all in reaction to deteriorating socioeconomic conditions and rampant corruption by a regime widely perceived as a puppet of the advanced capitalist countries. Kissinger and Nixon sent general William Westmoreland to convey to Suharto that the U.S. needed him to contain Communism and curtail China's and Russia's influence, exactly the international legitimacy that the regime needed to continue its authoritarian rule.[38]

On the 27th independence anniversary in August 1972, Suharto told parliament that his government had brought inflation down from 600 percent in 1966 to 2.47 in 1971. He added that detente between the U.S., China, and the USSR were positive developments, and all of East Asia looked forward to avoiding future conflicts. As a member of ASEAN, Indonesia was concerned about the international monetary crisis of 1971 which had adverse effects on global trade. Requesting $670 million for the period from April 1972 to March 1973, of which 20 percent was expected from the U.S., Jakarta was mostly concerned about continued foodstuff shortages amounting to $110 million annually. Subservient to the creditor countries, ASEAN was an efficacious instrument of the patron-client model, rather than a means to achieve self-reliance.[39]

A report by critics noted that the government was militaristic and unaccountable for disastrous policies for which the U.S., western governments, and the multilateral banks were partly responsible. At the same time that Muslim voices were becoming increasingly prominent in the opposition, there was more mainstream criticism of dependence on the west. General Besar Nasution was very critical of the Suharto regime and its policies amid severe shortages of rice, prolonged electricity stoppages, rampant corruption, and political repression. In a sea of corruption, the budgetary process was meaningless, while Suharto and his henchmen were prospering.[40]

Largely because of the U.S.-Japan-European competition in a predominantly Muslin country, Suharto's Indonesia had a unique patron-client relationship, especially in the context of ASEAN's regional role. In February 1972 Fuji Bank sent a large delegation to Jakarta to determine how Japan could raise its investments in the country. While Indonesians welcomed Japan's investment mission, many were concerned that Japan along with the U.S. were well on their way to dominating the national economy. While it had established nine of its largest banks in Indonesia and the largest multinational corporations, in 1972 and 1973 the U.S. was raising questions about the pervasive corrupt practices involving Japanese companies and Indonesian officials in every sector from oil to processed foods. Japanese businessmen and some politicians believed that Indonesians and the rest of their fellow-Asians favored U.S. companies and products, while squeezing Japan for aid and loans. The World Bank tried to play honest broker by insisting on the consortium model as the best option.[41]

To secure more foreign loans and investment, in 1972 Indonesia cut taxes on foreign loans by half, over and above cuts made in corporate tax cuts in 1970. New tax cuts were approved after Eximbank and World Bank loans to the state petroleum agency PETRAMINA designed to finalize private investment from a consortium led by US Steel and Newmont Mining companies. Just as Japan used private banks, trading companies, the Overseas Economic Cooperation Fund, and Japan-Eximbank, the U.S. used World Bank and Eximbank loans, and direct private investment as a means of securing Jakarta's compliance with the IMF. Because Kissinger wanted PETRAMINA's compliance with the U.S. as tensions were rising in the Middle East ahead of the Yom Kippur War, Jakarta was able to borrow freely without strictly observing IMF conditions. The U.S.-dominated consortium agreed in May 1973 to move ahead with more assistance for Indonesia, despite U.S. and other government reports that mismanagement and corruption were so pervasive that they affected foreign aid. Market share was paramount in U.S.-Japan competition in Indonesia, especially given the decline of the dollar and the global struggle for minerals and energy.[42]

Like Nigeria, Indonesia was a net gainer from the oil spike in the 1970s, reversing the current account deficit into a surplus and enjoying a rise in capital inflow from new domestic and foreign investments. Australia, Japan, and the U.S. were close to Suharto, but foreign investors and the IFIs were also comfortable with his regime. However, corruption was so pervasive that in 1977 the Securities and Exchange Commission accused the Indonesian government of demanding pay offs from foreign companies. To deflect attention from rampant corruption, the government crushed student protests, ordered an end to free press, and suppressed the few political freedoms left. Though some of the 100,000 political prisoners were released, most were under house arrest or sent to remote islands.[43]

Far from improving its balance of payments deficit and becoming less debt-ridden as the multilateral banks and the consortium members had publicly stated, by 1982 Indonesia's balance-of-payments deficit amounted to $2.5 billion, and its foreign debt was about ten times that amount. As the economy based on oil-financed growth ended in 1982, the 1980s was characterized by mounting foreign debt and economic contraction throughout the Third World. By the end of the decade Indonesia was the second largest debtor in the Third World, carrying official foreign debt of $100 billion and debt-service ratio of about 35 percent. Because private sector borrowing was inexorably linked to the public sector, the debt burden to the taxpayers was actually far greater than the official record indicated. Though real GDP rose at an annual average of 7.7 percent from 1971 to 1981, and per capita GDP rose 230 percent in 1982 as compared with 1969, those gains were wiped out during the decade. In 1992 per capita GDP was below the 1976 level and corruption had reached new heights.[44]

The debt-and-oil-financed vertical growth on the 1970s ended in 1982, and the new reality of sluggish economic activity coincided with maturing of loan payments and a drop in foreign investment, owing to the global recession. Making matters worse for labor, the government accepted IMF stabilization that included slashing public works programs and devaluing the rupiah in April 1983. While fiscal austerity coupled with a liberalization program made it easier for foreign investors to own more of Indonesia's assets, and the country experienced 3.3 percent GNP growth from 1980 to 1990, the vast majority of Indonesians experienced a drop in living standards.[45]

As the wave of privatization of public assets swept across the west in the 1980s, the IFIs encouraged cash-strapped Indonesia to follow the U.S.-EU lead of allowing more foreign ownership of its economy. In August 1989 Suharto permitted foreign companies to own up to 49 percent of Indonesia's publicly-traded companies. Symptomatic of the exodus of manufacturing from the advanced capitalist countries to the Third World, Indonesia offered cheap labor and a large domestic market. Non-fuel exports and manufactures rose steadily in the 1980s, doubling during the second half of the decade, as oil and gas revenues dropped by 50 percent. But the economy remained structurally weak because of foreign dependence, an archaic fiscal structure, and a corrupt regime favoring a few thousand families and foreign companies. In April 1992 Suharto allowed 100 percent foreign ownership in some cases.[46]

There was a broad popular outcry for the government to raise the minimum wage, increase employment opportunities in the rural sectors, and foster greater social justice, just as political and business corruption scandals were revealing the extent of crony capitalism and foreign ownership of the national economy. In 1998, more than three decades after ruling the country as a fiefdom for the domestic elites and foreign investors, Suharto was forced out of power under one of the biggest corruption scandals in history of any country.[47]

Neo-colonial under the Patron-Client Model in Nigeria: 1960-2000

As was the case with the rest of Africa, Nigeria suffered the legacy of colonialism, tribal and regional divisions that continued to plague contemporary society whose economy has remained outward-oriented and designed to serve the needs of the core rather than its own people. Living under the gun and commerce of the British empire, Nigeria, a country of 357,000 square miles with a population of 55 million in 1970 and equal to Japan's in 2004, could not transform itself overnight into a society where social justice would prevail. It was hardly surprising, therefore, that the armed forces would play a significant role in politics under a neo-colonial structure.[48]

Nor did the end of colonialism entail the end of economic imperialism for Nigeria any more than for the rest of the Third World operating under the patron-client model. Great Britain remained the conduit to Nigeria's integration into the U.S.-centered global economy. Like other client states, Nigeria was rewarded on the basis of what it could offer geopolitically and economically to the western bloc. Despite high hopes and enthusiasm that Africa under indigenous rule would mirror western institutions, the reality was rampant corruption, military dominance in society, greater foreign dependence and underdevelopment, widespread endemic poverty, and local conflict that precluded all of sub-Sahara Africa from making material and social progress.[49]

The developed countries used loans and grants as a means of integrating post-colonial Nigeria and Africa into the capitalist world system, influencing their policies from monetary to labor, and decapitalizing the poorest countries on the planet by keeping them perpetually in debt and dependent. Nigeria offers an excellent case study of decapitalization that reflects the Third World's financial dependence. To attract foreign investment, Nigeria, like other Third World countries, followed the multilateral banks' advice on liberalizing the economy under export-led models, building pro-business, pro-west trade unions, and providing incentives to foreign investors, including building the infrastructure designed around the needs of foreign companies.[50] As Barbara Callaway noted, the connection between foreign firms, local capital, and the state are very significant in the decapitalization process.

> The promotional activities of German, Italian, and Israeli machinery merchants obtained over 30 million [pounds sterling] in public investment from 1962-1966 in support of largely uneconomic privately operated projects [in Nigeria].... None of these firms produced a profit for the Nigerian investors, but the repayment of the loans plus interest guaranteed profits to the creditors. In this way foreign firms were able to use local capital to finance their operations because very little cash outlay was required from the foreign investors, whose loans were generally guaranteed by their governments.[51]

Because the government was the largest employer, the public bureaucracy was an important political instrument as part of the patronage network that politicians at the local and regional level, or military dictators at the central level used to retain power.

Foreign loans and foreign capital filled the gap left by the domestic elites which invested abroad. Like other monocultural economies where workers and peasants are perpetually near or below poverty level, Nigeria was no exception. Though Nigeria gained its independence in October 1960, British officials remained in key government positions, especially the ministry of finance. Nnamdi Azikiwe, former commander-in-chief and governor-general under British rule, became Nigeria's first president until he was forced out in 1966. American-educated and solidly pro-west, Azikiwe and prime minister Abubakar Tafewa Balewa followed London, Washington, and IFI advice on a wide range of matters from foreign affairs to the economy. In 1963 Nigeria became a republic, though its policies remained essentially the same and the country was highly centralized from Lagos.[52]

Given the considerable pressure by the UK, Nigeria formally joined the IMF-World Bank on 30 March 1961. British nationals were running not only Nigeria's central bank, but also the ministry of finance, while London enjoyed preeminent influence in the former colony's policies at all levels. A U.S.-led economic mission to

Lagos in June 1960 concluded that the west African country had one of the best development plans and prospects in the Third World, even better than India's. Especially pleased with Nigeria's commitment to strengthen the private sector and invite foreign investment, the commission went so far as to conclude that Nigeria was well on its way to becoming a western style democracy. After choosing Nigeria as the model state that the other African countries would emulate, the U.S. provided more aid to that country than any other on the continent.[53]

In March 1961 Kennedy announced a U.S. mission to Nigeria would help draft a five-year development plan, and explore the role that the U.S. government and business could play. Congress debated foreign aid legislation, but Wall Street protested that it was not sufficiently consulted before Kennedy sent the mission. The Nigerian government was very vague on how to proceed with development, while western governments, IFIs, and foreign companies were interested in the primary sector. To promote the plan and secure financial assistance, finance minister Festus S. Okotie-Eboh visited western capitals to solicit aid. Given Okotie-Eboh's interest in promoting trade and financial arrangements between the U.S. and Nigeria, the State and Commerce Departments arranged for the mission to meet with bankers and business leaders.[54]

In August 1961 an IMF mission cautioned Lagos not to run down reserves under the six-year development plan (1962-1968). Warning against exchange controls and restrictions, while favoring free flow of capital, the IMF coordinated its work with the State Department which had already struck a deal with Nigeria to form a World Bank-led aid consortium to provide assistance and secure contracts for western businesses. Lagos initially resisted the idea, but the U.S. insisted that Nigeria must accept the consortium and the inclusion of the World Bank's considerable role in shaping the development plan, otherwise there would be no aid.[55]

Hoping that the IBRD would provide 18 million pounds sterling for the railroad and 40 million pounds for steel works, British firms encountered opposition from Washington which wanted U.S. companies to secure contracts for World Bank-funded projects. In December 1961 the DLF was considering an additional $10 million and the Eximbank $9.2 million for Nigeria for the purchase of telecommunications equipment from U.S. companies. The Kennedy administration announced that it would contributed $225 million to fund Nigeria's development plan, of which $145 million would be devoted to the Volta project and contracts would be awarded to U.S. companies. Just as eager to sell equipment and secure Nigerian service contracts, British telecommunications company Marconi strongly objected to U.S. dominance of the Nigerian market and the use of multilateral banks to achieve that goal.[56]

The World Bank hosted a consortium meeting for Nigeria to determine how much each country contributes in aid and which contracts to allocate. The UK demanded assurances from the World Bank and indirectly from the U.S. that British projects would not be impacted regardless of what the World Bank report recommended. France accused the consortium of lacking any interest in aiding Nigeria per se, but in using aid as a means to secure control of its economy. Small countries outside the consortium were precluded from competing owing to the monopolistic practices of the advanced countries. Ignoring France, the U.S. and the other consortium representatives praised the World Bank's work in Nigeria.[57]

In cooperation with the IBRD, Cooper Brothers consultants examined all aspects of Nigeria's economy, ranging from ports and roads, to the Niger Dam, and a host of other possible projects falling under the 6-year development plan. Having earmarked $225 million for Nigeria's development plan, the U.S. expected to have most of the contracts awarded to U.S. firms. As Europeans scrambled to make sure that their firms were not excluded, bribery became a way of doing business, thus undermining the development plan and fostering a corrosive political climate in Nigeria from the local to the federal level.[58]

Throughout spring and summer 1962, the World Bank-led consortium for Nigeria placed most emphasis on the Niger Dam. All loans were spent in the creditor countries for the purchase of equipment and services. Japan was equally interested, but it was seeking unique opportunities that would not confront other bidders. Nigerian officials reminded the consortium that the development plan goal was not to reward foreign companies, but for Nigeria to reach 4 percent annual growth by investing 15 percent of GDP. In the absence of a strong domestic private sector, the Nigerian government insisted that the state would have to lead economic modernization. Washington advised Lagos to seek "soft" loans for development, which would allow U.S. companies to secure the contracts.[59]

In September 1962 the consortium members met in Washington under the World Bank's and USAID's auspices to coordinate Nigeria's financial and development needs. Because the IFIs and the consortium viewed Nigeria as a model for Africa, it was essential for all parties concerned to set a sound foundation. Concerned about Nigeria's low exchange reserves, in November 1962 the World Bank signed an agreement for $13.5 million for the Apapa wharf extension.[60]

The Kennedy administration used the World Bank and the consortium to foster the idea that all developed countries must share in the foreign aid burden, if they wanted to derive commercial benefits from the aid recipients. Coordinating its policies with the IMF and OECD, the World Bank led discussions on the consequences of Nigeria's debt service once it started borrowing heavily for the development plan. At the 7th annual IMF-IBRD meeting the consensus was that Nigeria's development plan would require 300 million pounds sterling in external assistance. The U.S. pledged 80 million pounds, west Germany provided 9 million, and the UK committed just 15 million, instead of 50 million the Nigerians had requested. Meanwhile, the World Bank began making loans to Nigeria on a large scale, given the U.S. policy toward Lagos and the prospects for oil revenues.[61]

The World Bank consultative group helped draft the six-year plan estimated at 1.25 billion pounds sterling, of which 400 million would emanate from foreign public loans, 400 million from foreign private firms, and 450 million from Nigeria's domestic sources. Belgium was interested in financing and building a steel mill, and telecommunications operations, among other projects. West Germany offered 25 million to build a bridge in Lagos, a hospital, and to finance exports. Switzerland was interested in financing a power plant, and the Netherlands Development Bank was prepared to offer a small amount for export guarantees.[62]

The IMF insisted that Nigeria must pursue orthodox monetary and fiscal policies. Concerned that foreign debt could rise from 5.1 million pounds sterling in 1962 to 27.9 million in 1968, the IMF cautioned against short-term debt. The development plan assumed a current account deficit of just under half a billion pounds sterling, with the value of exports rising from 136 million in 1962 to 234 million in 1968. Caveats about balance-of-payments and budgetary deficits notwithstanding, the IMF approved Nigeria's fiscal and monetary policies and advised a liberal trade and exchange rate policy, while praising the government for not allowing wages to rise and discourage private investment.[63]

In June 1963 the consultative group discussed the World Bank mission's report and plans for the Niger Dam. Agreeing to contribute a 5 million pounds loan for the project, London insisted that was on the proviso of having British firms secure contracts for equal or higher amount of the loan. Canada agreed to a $15 million loan for Canadian contracts, while Holland agreed to $1 million to sell Dutch products and services. Germany proposed that the consortium members share the contracts. The intense competition among western countries to secure Nigerian contracts notwithstanding, the World Bank argued that the real problem was lack of technical experts and skilled workers. A month after the consultative group met, the Yaounde Convention formalized EEC integration with 18 African states, in effect making certain that the Organization of African States (OAS), established in May 1963, would remain under the patron-client model for the duration.[64]

By September 1963 all Commonwealth countries, except Ghana and Nigeria agreed that eventually they would become EEC associate members. Reluctant to have any Commonwealth member join the EEC, Great Britain was operating diametrically against de Gaulle whose government lobbied for African integration into the EEC. England, Nigeria, and other Anglo-phone African countries demanded that the EEC reduce tariffs, before considering integration. Nigeria, Kenya, Ghana, Uganda, Tanzania, and Sierra Leone were conducting more trade with the UK than the six EEC countries, but the rising economic and political power of the EEC could not be offset indefinitely by using the U.S. as a counterweight. The EEC had a dialogue with 18 African states to have them become associate members, but the greatest emphasis was on Nigeria. While Sierra Leone announced that it would join the EEC if the UK took the lead, Nigeria warned against such a move, largely on political grounds against the French.[65]

In December 1963, the EEC commission advised Lagos on trade, development, movement of capital, and institutional issues. Rejecting associate status with the EEC, partly on the advice of the Foreign Office, Nigeria was more comfortable with a bilateral arrangement similar to Iran's with the EEC. Refusing to reduce their tariffs for all EEC members equally, Nigerians argued that they preferred bilateral relations with each European country, and abhorred the concept of trading blocs or the European parliament concept. Because bilateral relations with 18 separate African countries was too cumbersome for Europe and GATT, the European commission argued that the UK remained the key obstacle to Africa's economic integration.[66]

Agreeing to lift tariffs equal to the value of Nigeria's exports to the EEC, Lagos proposed that the EEC accept duty free cocoa, vegetable oils, and plywood. In 1962 Nigeria's export to the EEC amounted to 35 million pounds, while Nigeria's imports from the EEC totaled 60 million pounds, or about one-third of all imports. London refused to intervene on behalf of the EEC to ask Nigeria to become an associate member. Nevertheless, Nigeria did not wish to appear opposing association with the EEC, especially after France had accused the British of obstructing Anglo-phone Africa from becoming integrated with the EEC. From behind the scenes, both London and Washington were reluctant to support Nigeria's association with the EEC for commercial and political considerations. In the absence of UK membership in the EEC, Nigeria and the Anglo-phone African countries were pressured to keep their Commonwealth solidarity.[67]

Given the lack of domestic capital formation, by 1966 80 percent of plant construction investment represented foreign-financed projects under lucrative terms for foreign contractors who bribed politicians. Concerned with rampant corruption involving government officials, foreign companies, the multilateral banks, and western governments, the Foreign Office noted that bribery had become a routine way of conducting business for domestic and foreign firms in Nigeria. The problem was especially egregious in the foreign ministry headed by chief Festus Okotie-Eboh who owned a number of companies. To secure contracts and to be able to conduct business, foreign firms bribed officials, adding to the cost of doing business and contributing to inefficient government and lower living standards. The most alarming aspect, according to the Foreign Office report, was that Nigeria financed its rampant corruption by borrowing from the IMF, Eximbank, Development Loan Fund, and foreign banks.[68]

The World Bank suggested that Lagos curtail high-interest, short-term loans to purchase machinery from the west, and focus instead on building the infrastructure and providing various incentives to encourage foreign capital. U.S.AID used the World

Bank's recommendations as a catalyst for U.S. companies interested in the Nigerian market, while the government in Washington exerted diplomatic influence in Lagos through the World Bank. Moreover, U.S.AID was working closely with the AFL-CIO, ICFTU, and U.S. representatives in Nigeria and throughout Africa to persuade trade unions to back the market system and western-style integration under the patron-client model.[69]

In October 1965 Gamal Abdel al-Nasser visited Kano, Nigeria before thousands of predominantly Muslim cheering crowds carrying signs against western imperialism. Describing Israel as the stooge of the U.S., Nasser called for African and non-aligned solidarity. Nigeria, however, was immersed in regional politics that eventually resulted in the Ibo-dominated Eastern Region's clash with the north and west. Lacking a strong national identity, people rallied behind their regional civilian and military leaders. Tribal conflict was increasingly exacerbated by the fact that economic growth and development was well below the Third World average, if the petroleum sector is excluded, or about average if included. The average annual per capita income was $100, and more than half of the babies born did not survive beyond five years.[70]

On 15 January 1966 an army faction staged a coup in which a number of ministers and premier Tafawa Balewa were killed. Suspecting that the civilian regime was unable to bridge the gap between the Hausa, Ibos, and Yaruba peoples that made up the three major groups, the military had been restless for months. After capturing the coup plotters, the military replaced the civilian regime with a military government. Headed by Major-General J. T. Aguiyi-Ironsi who claimed to clean corruption and engender regional harmony, the new regime enjoyed U.S. backing. Muslim Sudan and Egypt regarded the coup in Nigeria as a western imperialist plot designed to crush the Hausa northern Muslim minority. Egyptians and Sudanese, like most Arabs and Africans, suspected that the Johnson administration had a role in the Nigerian coup. The deaths of Muslims during the coup prompted the government in Khartoum to threaten severing ties with Lagos. That the new Nigerian dictatorship was seeking aid from Israel was all the confirmation Muslims needed of a U.S. role, further alienating those who mistrusted western intentions toward the Islamic world.[71]

At a consultative group meeting in Paris in February 1966, Bonn agreed to provide aid for Nigeria's air force, after the military coup. Both the aid recipient and the creditor nations understood that military aid was expected in connection with economic aid and market share and contracts given to the creditor. Recovering from a balance-of-payments deficit of 9 million pounds sterling in 1965, Nigeria enjoyed a 4 million pounds sterling surplus in 1966, largely because of higher oil revenues. Pleased that the military dictatorship and the Nigerian central bank adopted IMF-World Bank policy recommendations, the multilateral banks endorsed the regime's fiscal and monetary policies. The Johnson administration was equally pleased that the military dictatorship was receptive to U.S. foreign policy across the board.[72]

Because the dictatorship favored the Ibos, the military staged a second coup which the Ibos refused to accept and thus seceded calling their land Biafra. More than 30,000 Ibo people were killed and 700,000 to 2 million displaced in tribal clashes. Colonel Yakubu Gowon, army chief of staff and the most important northern officer staged a coup on 29 July 1966. Because the Biafran secession coincided with Israel's Six-Day War, and the escalation of the Vietnam War, the Johnson administration allowed London to take the lead on the matter once hostilities erupted, a policy that the Nixon administration continued, though the need to help alleviate starvation and disease was expressed as much in Washington as in continental Europe. Moreover, Nigeria was the tenth largest oil producer in the world, and oil played a role in Biafra.[73]

By the end of 1966 Nigeria opened its commerce more to the Soviet bloc, as a Hungarian trade exhibit signaled a more receptive policy to diversifying foreign trade. Enraged about Soviet involvement in Nigeria, the Johnson administration viewed Nigeria from a Cold War perspective. The civil war between Gowon's pro-British regime, and the secessionist and pro-French colonel Odemegwe Ojukwu as the head of Biafra on the other undercut U.S. hopes of using Nigeria as a frontline state in the East-West conflict and placing it under the patron-client transformation model. Despite an official neutral policy, U.S. interests rested with Gowon's regime which it backed throughout the war. Considering that France, China, and Portugal backed Biafra, the conflict was a reflection of rivalries among the great powers for regional influence.[74]

At the end of 1969, Gowon promulgated the Petroleum decree in an attempt to gain greater control of that commodity. British Petroleum and Shell produced 450,000 barrels daily, and both companies expected production to double by the end of 1970. Because 10 percent of British oil came from Nigeria, the Foreign Office was equally concerned that Franco-phone countries did not assume an advantage in the civil war which ended in January 1970 with a resounding victory for Gowon. Despite the sharp rise in oil production, Nigeria endured mass starvation and labor unrest. The Foreign Office blamed French policy, arguing that Nigerian businesses resented the French for their meddling in their country's domestic affairs. Because of the war, Gowon raised the size of the armed forces from 10,000 to 250,000, thus absorbing some of the surplus labor force.[75]

In October 1969 the State Department told the British government that the Nigerian civil war was far more disastrous than Vietnam, suffering more casualties from war and famine. Denying that Biafra was worse than Vietnam, the Foreign Office argued that only 100,000-180,000 people had died in Nigeria. Nevertheless, the UK acknowledged the gravity of Biafra for Africa, in addition to its impact on Anglo-EEC relations. An estimated 200,000 people died of famine and war during the Biafra affair, depending on the source. Starving babies captured by television cameras dramatized the tragedy throughout the world. Accusing France of backing Biafra to gain access to oil, London also argued that mass starvation and illnesses could have been avoided if Biafra rebels did not block foreign aid relief. Food shortages persisted through 1971. UNICEF, USAID, PL480, U.S., and European government and religious organizations provided aid.[76]

On 2 February 1970 the Nigerian government awarded U.S. firms a 2 million pounds sterling contract for satellite communications and air station. Japan and Italy sent economic missions to Lagos hoping to secure reconstruction contracts in the aftermath of the civil war. Owing to the sharp rise in oil revenues, Nigeria's credit improved, allowing advanced capitalist countries to seek lucrative contracts and market share under the new four-year development plan. The dictatorship invited more foreign capital, foreign advisers, and foreign technocrats at a time that it publicly proclaimed a desire toward economic nationalism. The press demanded that all key industries and key position be reserved for Nigerians, and that economic independence was essential. Gowon agreed that foreign advisers and technocrats must be kept in the background.[77]

On 11 November 1970 Gowon unveiled the second development plan, promising a strong economy, greater opportunities, democracy, and an egalitarian society. Affirming that he was committed to regional and continental integration, Gowon focused on reconstruction, infrastructure, and transportation. The plan called for a second oil refinery, salt refinery, passenger car assembly, chemical complex, fertilizer plant, liquified petroleum gas plant, pulp and paper plant, and fish and shrimp trawling, all to be financed with foreign loans. The government proposed 55 percent public ownership of iron and steel, petroleum, and building materials. The government proposed decentralizing the projects throughout all twelve states, rather than concentrating in Lagos. Having decided that Nigeria must be as reliable a "client" partner as Morocco, Nixon designated Nigeria as a regional communication center for which an Eximbank loan was approved to build a satellite station. U.S. geopolitical interest in Nigeria afforded Gowon leverage for economic aid to finance development.[78]

The second development plan (1970-1974) committed 1.6 billion Nigerian pounds of which 20 percent was initially proposed as foreign loans. Net public sector investment was 780 million, while 816 million would come from the private sector, of which 25 percent would be from the oil industry. The plan envisaged 215 million in loans, but that figure was very low. Hoping to be in control of their own economy by 1980, the new plan reflected the ambitions for greater self-sufficiency and frustrations with dependence and foreign exploitation. A state-owned company would be established to exploit off-shore oil reserves, and another to foster local ownership in strategic industries with fair compensation paid to foreign private owners. Retail and distributive industries would be reserved for Nigerians only, while other sectors remained open to foreigners. Despite such measures, UK-Nigerian and EEC-Nigerian trade was expected to rise sharply as the population and the economy grew. While the rhetoric was nationalistic, the laws protecting and welcoming foreign investment remained intact.[79]

Great Britain argued that Nigeria's post-Biafra political influence had actually grown to the degree that the west African country was ready to assume the economic and political leadership on the continent. Because Nigeria led the anti-French bloc in Anglo-phone Africa, the Foreign Office was seeking an advantage in the continental balance of power. Amid a global sluggish economy, the British and western Europeans looked to Nigeria's development plan as a means of securing a market share and securing contracts for businesses in their respective countries. Calling for a sharp rise in agricultural products and animal husbandry, the new plan offered opportunities to European and U.S. agro-exporters as well as contracts to develop power, water, sewage works, communications, health, and education.[80]

On 26 April 1971 Gowon announced the creation of the Nigerian National Oil Corporation which purchased SAFRAP, a subsidiary of French giant ELF oil. To placate Gowon, France sold 35 percent of SAFRAP to the government in Lagos. The agreement with ELF became the model for the rest of the oil companies until August 1973 when the government demanded majority control. Because oil prices were rising after 1971, Nigeria's balance of payments and the general economy was not as bad as the IMF and World Bank had feared. Oil contracts guaranteed Nigeria 300 million pounds sterling for the year, and 450 million by 1973-1974. The government granted new off-shore oil concessions to U.S., German, and Japanese companies. An OPEC member, Nigeria coordinated all aspects of the industry, partly to project the image of greater economic nationalism, and realize greater revenues.[81]

In 1971 Government workers received the first wage increase since 1964. Unemployment and underemployment was about one-third of the wage-earning population. Though there was some labor unrest and student protests, professional groups like lawyers, doctors, etc., limited their grievances to their particular interests, without becoming political. Trade unions generally avoided confrontation with the regime, partly because of minor economic improvements, but largely because some labor leaders were in prison and others feared that criticism entailed imprisonment. Moreover, the largest trade union United Labor Congress (ULC) was financed by the U.S., domestic and foreign companies, and the AFL-CIO's African American Labor Center which had close ties to the CIA. In the absence of political opposition, the press tried to play the advocate's role, especially in supporting economic nationalism. Faced with foreign exchange shortages, Gowon was content to borrow more from abroad on the advice of the consortium.[82]

An IMF mission to Lagos in June 1971 warned about the balance-of-payments deficits, a warning that coincided with a Business Decree designed to assume greater national control of the economy. Nigeria wanted the IMF to approve a loan that would assist with foreign exchange shortages, but the government was reluctant to go along with all of the Fund's policy recommendations. England agreed to approve loans to clear Nigeria's commercial arrears in return for contracts awarded to British firms. Nigerians felt that their country was overly dependent on the UK, at a time that Gowon was establishing a much closer relationship with the U.S. Nigeria criticized Britain's entry into the EEC as another nail in the Commonwealth coffin. The British & French Bank, a subsidiary of Banque Nationale de Paris, operated in Lagos and was lobbying to have Nigeria become an associate member of the EEC.[83]

Just before the UK joined the EEC, the French government, and European and British firms continued to urge the Foreign Office to influence the commonwealth's position regarding association with the EEC. London insisted that neither Nigeria nor Australia were likely to be persuaded, while New Zealand and other commonwealth countries were more open to integration. In January 1972 Nigeria announced that it would make a bid for EEC associate membership, as long as it could negotiate bilaterally with each member. Initially, neither Lagos nor London would acknowledge that Britain's membership would have any impact on the bilateral relationship between commonwealth countries and the UK. Interested in regional integration, the government in Lagos argued that French president Georges Pompidou was as predatory as de Gaulle in dividing Franco-phone and Anglo-phone Africa.[84]

Just as Europe was striving to have Africa associate with the EEC, the Nigerian government responded to a popular outcry for greater local control of the economy and less foreign dependence. Nigeria categorically rejected the socialist model, but was more receptive to a mixed economy in which national control could be exercised more readily. Whereas Nigerians feared that EEC integration entailed subjecting Africa's weak economies to European exploitation, Nigeria's neighbors viewed regional integration as a scheme for Nigeria to exert hegemony. Given mutual suspicions on all sides, the Gowon regime proposed the "Generalized Preference Scheme" in which the U.S. participated. The convergence of British and EEC interests, however, compelled London to lobby Nigeria to accept integration. Pressured by British Petroleum and Shell, the British government concurred with the French that Algeria's associate membership in the EEC was vital to offer some protection to the oil companies from possible nationalization.[85]

Africans resented the long-standing publicly-stated western assumption that Africa was incapable of self-rule or of solving its problems. There was also deep suspicion that western oil companies boosted production and were profiting amid Nigeria's political, economic, and social problems. Although oil revenue contributed to the economy, it made Nigerians increasingly aware that it was essential to have national control over that industry and to use it to achieve self-sufficiency. The Foreign Office was convinced that besides Nasser's radical influence, Algerian radicalism was a salient factor in influencing Africa. The most remarkable aspect of European and U.S. policy was that the west continued the 19th century notion of spheres of influence as relevant for geopolitical and economic interests.[86]

Though the Nixon administration sided with the Gowon regime during the civil war, Nigeria strongly protested the U.S. decision to allow the importation of Rhodesian chrome. Accusing Washington of hypocrisy and double-crossing Africans, Gowon had been pleading with the Nixon administration to support decolonization of southern Africa. In mid-February 1972 George H. W. Bush, U.S. permanent representative to the UN, told Gowon that Washington had no influence over Portugal. Acknowledging that Africa was the lowest continent in Washington's priority list, Bush argued that Rhodesian chrome was a national security issue. Because he needed U.S. aid, Gowon reassured Bush that Nigeria would continue to support U.S. Middle East policy, but hoped that Washington would make some gestures toward supporting decolonization.[87]

Multilateralization of foreign aid as a means of lessening dependence on any one country and achieving realignment of the patron-client model proved frustrating to Nigerians whose only option was to open the door to all potential foreign aid donors and either accept or reject their terms. With less than $100 annual per capita income as compared with $500 for Gabon, Nigeria had to raise living standards. Burdened with $350 million in short-term foreign debt, or equal to the foreign exchange receipts, oil revenue was not well utilized. As the population was rising rapidly, the majority was under 25 years of age amid grim prospects for employment. While the Nigerian consultative group insisted that the solution was foreign investment, the G-7 and IFIs demanded lucrative terms to which Gowon was reluctant to endorse initially, although he eventually supported. Influenced by western and Communist bloc intellectuals, many Nigerians warned that all aid was a mechanism of imperialist penetration responsible for Africa's endemic poverty.[88]

Toward the end of 1972, the U.S. and U.K. concurred with the EEC that it would be best for all parties concerned to foster regional integration in Africa and to open the markets to greater foreign investment. While the U.S. sought closer ties with Nigeria more than with any other sub-Saharan country other than South Africa, U.S. policy toward colonialism and the U.S. record toward the Third World was one that had many Nigerians wondering about the benefits of a patron-client relationship with a country that discriminated on the basis of race, class, and geography. For the sake of integration and the EEC, France was prepared to ameliorate relations between Anglo-phone and Franco-phone Africa. Because Nigeria was the most populous and wealthiest African country in resources, Franco-phone countries opposed its EEC accession as an associate member, fearing that Europe would divert funds from the rest of Africa.[89]

Dr. Okoi Arikpo, Nigerian Commissioner for Foreign Affairs, contended that Franco-phone countries adamantly opposed Nigeria's association with the EEC during Yaounde negotiations. Though Arikpo considered France a threat to Nigeria's security, the French government argued that the road from Lagos to Cotonou was a threat to

French influence in Dahomey. London and Lagos contended that Franco-phone countries were French puppets, while Paris leveled the same charge against the Anglo-phones. England wanted Nigeria to have commodity agreements with the EEC, especially in view of aggressive U.S. competition for markets, after Eximbank and commercial loans for the sale of two Boeing aircraft, machinery for the Aba Textile factory, and other Nigerian projects. Lagos insisted that it had no objection to bilateral trade agreements with EEC members, but opposed collective action by African states under Yaounde negotiations. The Nigerian road to EEC associate membership was a classic case of a struggle between western countries for dominant influence under the patron-client model.[90]

In January 1973 Arikpo repeated his claim that Nigeria's position on the EEC was the same, though it was obvious that England's membership in the community would have an impact on all 19 commonwealth partners. Favorably disposed to cooperating with the commonwealth, Nigeria preferred direct negotiations with the EEC regarding commodity agreements. London wanted to have a voice in shaping any type of agreement between commonwealth partners and the EEC, while the European governments reassured England that it would enjoy veto power as a full member of the community. Because Nigeria did not have any difficulties marketing its products in Europe, it had no incentive to join other than political, while recognizing that it would have to make tariff concessions in exchange for aid. After 1973, the pressure for Nigeria to join emanated from London, while Paris sided with its Franco-phone African allies opposed to Nigeria.[91]

Frustrated with the lack of economic and social progress, and continued press criticism of the military dictatorship and Nigeria's external dependence, general Hassan Katsina criticized Nigerians for lacking ambition and diligence to modernize the country, arguing that Nigeria was a sick country whose people needed to be whipped into discipline. Because oil as a percentage of GNP rose from 8.1 in 1970 to 31.9 percent in 1974, Nigeria enjoyed favorable terms of trade, just as Indonesia and other petroleum producers. Nevertheless, external dependence under the patron-client model entailed that the oil boom did not have a major impact on structural socioeconomic conditions.[92]

Between 1970 and 1973 annual per capita income rose from $343 to $517, although the majority of the population earned under $300. In early 1974 as prices of oil were heading higher, Nigeria nationalized the industry. Dependence on oil became more pronounced in the second half of the 1970s, starting with the Arab oil embargo after the Yom Kippur War. Earnings [from oil] rose from $1.7 billion in 1972 to $9.3 billion in 1974, dropped to $8.4 billion in 1975, and rebounded back to $9.7 billion in 1976. In 1976 oil accounted for 93 percent of Nigeria's exports, 87 percent of the government's revenues, and 45 percent of Nigeria's GDP. By the beginning of 1976 Nigeria had accumulated $5.8 billion in foreign exchange reserves, giving it an enviable position in the global economy.[93] Because of the oil revenues, there was an erroneous perception in the west that Nigerians were among the elite Third World countries like the Gulf states.

With the aid of the IFIs, EEC, and U.S., finance minister Alhaji Shehu Shagari established the Nigerian Bank for Commerce and Industry (NBCI) to operate on private bank principles, rather than issue politically-motivated loans. Ostensibly a measure toward lessening external dependence and fostering realignment of the patron-client model, NBCI was steeped in politics and it was a conduit of western capital in the domestic economy. Parallel to the economic dimension of the patron-client model, the labor dimension was as important, considering the ICFTU's and AFL-CIO's role in the Nigerian trade union central United Labor Congress (ULC). Resolving to continue funding ULC, the State Department was gratified that Nigerian labor, despite widespread discontent with the regime, was in no position to challenge either the government or foreign businesses. Confronting one of the weakest labor movements in the Third World, the government used emergency powers to imprison opposition labor leaders, or any one threatening a strike, slow-down, or work stoppage. Repressive measures toward urban labor were adopted while the government neglected the impoverished rural sector and invested in cities.[94]

A plan to build 18 airports at a cost of $300-$400 million gained European and U.S. backing because western companies would secure the contracts and banks would finance the projects. Though the Netherlands played a leading role, U.S. firms were positioned to receive lucrative contracts. Under U.S. and EEC influence and in desperate need of foreign loans, Gowon did not support the Arab oil embargo as a weapon against the west. U.S. oil imports from Nigeria rose from 459,000 barrels per day in 1973 to just over one billion in 1976, despite the fact that total output remained steady during the mid-1970s. The U.S. government encouraged direct foreign investment in oil-rich, market-friendly Nigeria, though U.S. companies had the more difficult task bribing Nigerian officials than their European counterparts which were relatively free of legal restrictions.[95]

On 29 July 1975 a group of officers led by Gowon's old enemy general Murtala Muhammad, seized power. Committed to solidarity with non-aligned countries and to black rule in sub-Sahara Africa, general Muhammad provided aid to the Angolan MPLA rebels that Cuba and the Kremlin supported against the Washington-backed FNLA. In January 1976 U.S.-Nigeria relations were at their nadir after a group of students stoned the U.S. embassy in Lagos, and the government and the press unleashed a public anti-American wave. In March 1977 General Muhammad was assassinated during a coup and general Olusegun Obasanjo took over. While he initially appeared anti-U.S. and rejected aid from the west, he accepted assistance once the popular outcry over Muhammad's assassination was over, leaving many to suspect U.S. involvement.[96]

Realizing that regional conflict in southern Africa could plunge the U.S. into a wider indirect conflict with the Soviet Union, in April 1976 Kissinger visited Africa and noted that majority rule in Rhodesia must take place, though he reiterated U.S. support for South Africa, condemning apartheid. Skeptical about Kissinger's policy, the Nigerian government expected Washington to match the rhetoric with deeds. When Jimmy Carter was elected, it appeared to some that U.S. policy toward Africa would change drastically. With Andrew Young as U.S. ambassador to the UN, and human rights as a component of foreign policy, the Carter administration became more involved in sub-Sahara Africa. In February 1977 Young convinced general Obasanjo that the Carter administration was serious about playing a constructive role in Nigeria, Rhodesia, and Southern Africa. Human rights was a hollow public relations mechanism to sustain the patron-client model by selectively castigating governments and movements that Washington opposed.[97]

At the end of March 1978 Carter visited Nigeria in a gesture that Washington recognized the western African nation as a major continental player, though many suspected that Carter's motive was rooted in America's appetite for oil. With the oil strike of Iranian workers in October 1978, a second oil crisis loomed on the horizon, especially after the Iranian Revolution in January 1979. Fearing an OPEC embargo, western countries purchased large stocks of crude, raising the price to $34 per barrel by June 1979. Nigeria's oil revenue jumped from $9.5 billion in 1978, to $20 billion in 1979, and $26 billion in 1980.

Despite rising oil revenues in the second half of the 1970s, real GNP was flat to declining. Besides world economic contraction in the late 1970s-early 1980s, Nigeria was caught off guard during the Iran-Iraq war which produced an oil glut instead of shortage. The Carter administration promoted more direct foreign investment and trade with Nigeria, but both trade and investment declined. In 1977 Britain had invested $2 billion, western Europe $1.4 billion, and the U.S. had $528 million mostly in Nigeria's oil industry. The combination of high oil prices and foreign investment notwithstanding, living standards remained among the lowest in the world and the country entered a long contracting cycle in the 1980s.[98]

The Reagan administration's policy toward Nigeria reflected a general policy toward the Third World. Reagan ideologues viewed the world through the prism of the Soviet-American conflict that could only be addressed by aggressive diplomacy and military solutions. Coinciding with the ideological decade of the Thatcher-Reagan decade, prices of raw materials plummeted, resulting in negative GNP growth and Third World debt crisis. Nigeria's oil revenues dropped from $26 billion in 1980 to $13 billion in 1982, precipitating a trade deficit of $400 million a month, and sending the value of the currency sharply lower.

Heavy dependence on oil impacted the entire economy, forcing president Alhaji Shehu Shagari to adopt a series of austerity measures that the IMF had been recommending to Third World countries facing similar problems. With three quarters of the people engaged in farming, but only 10 percent of GNP emanating from that neglected sector, Shagari adopted the World Bank's "Green Revolution" to make Nigeria less dependent on food imports and more dependent on western chemicals and technology. Though he had committed $13.5 billion to agriculture, mostly imports of agrochemicals, hybrid seeds, and machinery, production actually declined in the 1980s. As Nigeria's trade deficit with the U.S. rose from $4.3 billion in 1978, to $8.3 billion in 1979, and $10.3 billion in 1980, the balance-of-payments deficit and unemployment rose sharply, while living standards plummeted. Despite G-7 and IFI repeated promises of growth and development for Nigeria and Africa, if they agreed to greater global integration, average per capita income across the continent was lower in the 1980s than in the 1960s.[99]

When the World Bank issued its first major report on Africa in 1982, the focus was on regional integration as the catalyst to development, just as was the case with the Lagos Plan of Action, though there were differences in modalities. While regional integration was necessary, because it operates under a global economic system, Nigeria and the rest of Africa could not possibly make progress unless the modality of global integration was reconfigured to serve domestic needs instead of Europe and U.S. economies. Western corporations in collaboration with the local military, political, and small business elites perpetuated structural problems like monocultural dependence that precluded economic diversification. For example, Nigeria's oil constituted 93-96 percent of its GNP in the late 1970s and early 1980s, thereby the foreign-dominated oil industry determined the country's finances and economy.[100]

The sharp drop in oil revenue in 1982-1983 meant that Nigeria fell behind in debt payments by $5 billion, while foreign debt amounted to $12 billion. Because Shagari was reluctant to adopt IMF austerity, western banks refused to reschedule Nigeria's debt at a time that the country had a month's reserves to finance imports. Blaming Washington as the force behind the IMF, Lagos and the press faulted the U.S. for the global recession of the early 1980s. As unemployment and underemployment rose sharply in 1982, riots erupted in the northern region where many Muslims were killed fighting police.

Protesting against deplorable economic and social conditions, students lashed out against corrupt Nigerian officials, the U.S., Israel, and South Africa. Desperate to assuage the angry population, on 17 January 1983 the government announced that it was expelling all foreigners numbering between one and two million. Hundreds of thousands of people, mostly from Ghana, were forced to walk back home against the background of international condemnation for Nigeria's xenophobia. Despite dire economic and social conditions and debt restructuring, Shagari won the election only to be overthrown by the military on 31 December 1983.[101]

Denouncing the Shagari government as incompetent and corrupt, general

Muhammad Buhari, one of the most incompetent and tyrannical African leaders, promised to fix the economic and social problems. Because the Reagan administration viewed Buhari as a conservative pro-west leader, the State Department did not denounce the military coup that toppled a duly-elected regime. Against the background of U.S. covert operations to topple Nicaragua's elected government, and concerned about Iran's and Lybia's anti-west influences spreading in sub-Sahara Africa, the American media and government expected Lagos to cooperate with the State Department and IFIs on key policy issues. Unable to reverse the depressed economy, inflation, and unemployment after rescheduling foreign debt in 1983 and 1984, Buhari fell victim to a coup by general Ibrahim Babangida in August 1985.[102]

Between 1977 and 1986, per capita income dropped 35 percent, half of export revenues were devoted to serving the debt, and the prospects were not good either for export growth, or reversal of the manufacturing slump. Amid widespread popular perceptions that IMF austerity violated national sovereignty and only benefited foreign creditors without having long-term benefits for debtors, Babangida feared that the people would rebel if he went along with the IMF and the Paris Club. After the EEC, U.S., and commercial banks declared that there would be no debt rescheduling unless IMF austerity were implemented, Babangida capitulated. Under the IMF agreement, the naira's value dropped 75 percent and the cost of living rose sharply. A nation of more than 80 million, many of them starving to death, Nigeria was at the mercy of the Paris Club which agreed to reschedule the debt and began to provide meager aid. Despite anti-western and anti-U.S. rhetoric, especially regarding Israel and Southern Africa, Babangida remained committed to integration with the west under the traditional neo-classical model.[103]

Although Nigeria's average annual growth was negative -5.5 percent from 1981-86, in January 1987 Secretary of State George Schultz visited Lagos where he praised the IMF austerity. By the late 1980s U.S.-Nigeria economic and political relations reached their nadir. Most Nigerians were disgruntled with the IMF-imposed austerity program and U.S. foreign policy toward Southern Africa and Israel. Always last as a priority in U.S. foreign policy, sub-Sahara Africa, especially South Africa and Nigeria, was more significant in terms of trade than the Soviet Union.[104]

Reiterating the theme of regional integration as Africa's socioeconomic solution, in December 1993 UN secretary-general Boutros-Boutros Ghali urged greater efforts. However, as Robert J. Cummings points out in a justifiably pessimistic tone:

> From the 1950s to the present, more than 200 organizations have been founded on the continent of Africa for the purpose of fostering regional and sub-regional integration and economic cooperation ... . The performance record of these myriad organizations historically have not been particularly sterling. There have been many more difficulties and disappointments in the pursuit of their objectives than the modest successes that they achieved.[105]

The UN, World Bank, NGO's and African governments' efforts to forge regional integration and economic cooperation have not resulted in lifting the continent from endemic poverty and cyclical debt crises, largely because it has been operating under the patron-client model which is at the core of its neo-colonial dependence. Forging regional integration, therefore, was meaningless without addressing the terms of integration into the capitalist world system.

External dependence and the patron-client model have been perpetuated not only because of the world economic system, but because of Nigeria's political economy and social structure. That Shell Oil produces half of Nigeria's oil, that major business deals involve bribery, that the corrupt military has historically dominated the politically arena, that tribal rivalries have hampered reform, and that the interests of the political and business elites are inexorably linked to western corporations, are all salient factors which contribute to rebel activity, perpetual sociopolitical instability, and endemic poverty.

Dependence and Underdevelopment in Peru

Six times larger than Great Britain covering close to half-a-million square miles, Peru is rich in natural resources, though the majority of the population made up of Incas has always lived in poverty. Burdened with the legacy of Spanish colonialism, after independence Peru like its sister republics remained dependent on the primary sector and European capital. Composed of a landowning oligarchy and commercial-financial interests in Lima-Callao area, and backed by the military and the Catholic Church, traditional elites historically controlled the country's institutions, while the indigenous population residing mostly in the interior lived in abject poverty. The formation of the populist-reformist Alianza Popular Revolucionaria Americana (APRA) by Victor Raul Haya de la Torre in the 1920s endeavored to counterbalance the traditional elites by forging an alliance between labor, peasants, and the lower middle class. Suffering the economic dislocation of the Great Depression, Peru accepted reintegration under the aegis of the U.S. in the late 1930s.[106]

With more than half of the population, mostly Indian in the highlands, living outside the monetary system in the early 1960s, and 80 percent earning less than $53 annually, Peru had 40 families that controlled about 75 percent of the wealth. The white coastal elites whose fortunes were linked to the advanced capitalist countries, lived a world apart from the non-white peasants of the undeveloped interior where U.S.-owned mining companies produced one-third of the GNP. When the Alliance for Progress was promulgated, U.S. and Peruvian politicians promised to develop the interior. Ten years later, socioeconomic progress in Peru's rural sector was as absent in Peru as in the rest of Latin America.[107]

A State Department report analyzing the structure of Peru's economy acknowledged that lack of regional integration was part of its structural weakness along with concentration of wealth along the coastal region. The growth pattern depended on the "increase of economic dependence on foreign countries, conditioning the expansion of the system to variations in international crisis, and to a large degree, to the effects of the economy of the center on the configuration of the production structure of the modern segment of the economy."[108] External dependence based on the production of about half a dozen exports entailed financial dependence to cover balance-of-payments deficits, owing partly to deterioration in the terms of trade of the outward-oriented economy, and to the fact that the value of labor in Peru has been substantially lower than in the U.S. and Europe.

In 1948 General Manuel Odria seized power and remained dictator until 1956. For eight years he pursued export-led growth policies and went along with the U.S. and IFIs whose goal was integration under the patron-client model. Removing all trade controls, Peru allowed for a flood of U.S. imports and currency (sol) speculation that resulted in the depletion of foreign reserves during the early 1950s. Receiving World Bank and Eximbank loans, largely as rewards for adopting IMF stabilization and supporting U.S. foreign policy within the OAS, Odria passed laws favoring foreign investment especially in the lucrative mining and oil sectors. Because the oligarchy invested abroad and foreign companies' profits taken out of the economy far outweighed direct capital inflows, the government borrowed more money from abroad to finance imports and development. Consequently, Peru's foreign debt almost tripled from the end of the Korean War to the end of Odria's regime. Operating under the patron-client model, Peru was not much different than other Latin American dictatorships that had thrown themselves into the embrace of the U.S.-based international political economy and whose elites retained their privileges by supporting integration.[109]

After mass strikes and labor unrest in June 1956, accompanied by gross human rights violations amid financial problems and economic contraction, Odria lost the confidence of some leading capitalists, the military, and the lower middle class. A product of the 40 oligarch families, Manuel Prado y Ugarteche won after receiving APRA's backing and promising reforms. Though Prado pledged political realignment that included a course toward economic nationalism, the IMF, World Bank, U.S., and the oligarchs in Lima convinced the president to adopt an austerity program at a time that a number of other Latin American republics had implemented stabilization and devalued their currencies. To qualify for $40 million in World Bank loans and $7 million from Eximbank, Prado went along with Washington and the IFI policy recommendations.[110]

Suffering higher U.S. tariffs on Peruvian zinc and lead, the Prado regime was rebuffed when the U.S. refused to sell commercial vessels. The strongest and almost universal denunciations by all sectors of society were reserved for the International Petroleum Corporation, (IPC), a subsidiary of Standard Oil of New Jersey that exploited the country's petroleum and natural gas reserves. Though the U.S. constantly pressured Lima to accept IFI policy recommendations and to provide lucrative terms for the multinationals, anti-Americanism found expression in the streets of Lima during vice president Richard Nixon's visit in May 1958. The global recession coinciding with the IMF-imposed stabilization plan sunk Peru deeper into debt and dependency, thereby precipitating greater social unrest and popular animosity toward the domestic elites, U.S. companies, and Washington. A very similar situation existed in most of Latin America which had high hopes for industrial-technological development after the war, but found itself more dependent as a result of the modality of its integration under the patron-client model.[111]

Frustrated with the lack of economic progress, president Prado appointed Pedro Beltran as finance minister and premier. Arguably the most influential oligarch, Beltran enjoyed the support of the domestic elites, U.S., IFIs, and Wall Street. His plan was national integration of the economy under a World Bank plan of fostering commercial agriculture that only strengthened the large farmers and U.S. exporters of farm machinery and agrochemicals. Securing a $53 million loan from Eximbank and Development Loan Fund in July 1960, the Peruvian government claimed that it would become self-sufficient.

Because of the Cuban Revolution, the U.S. promulgated the Dillon Act of 1960 which committed $500 million to raise living standards in Latin America. Initiated by the Kennedy administration in March 1961, the Alliance for Progress provided support for both the Latin American Free Trade Association (LAFTA) and Central American Common Market (CACM) operating under GATT rules. A continuation of the Eisenhower administration's efforts to make certain that the patron-client model remained intact against the background of rising revolutionary threats and anti-Americanism, the Alliance for Progress was both an instrument of containment and economic integration.[112]

Joining LAFTA, which was established in February 1960 after the signing of the Treaty of Montevideo, Peru tried to broaden its integration within the regional bloc and globally. In 1961 the U.S. became concerned that western Europe and Japan were competing aggressively in Peru and Latin America for market share in trade and loans. The Prado regime, like most of Latin America, was actively multilateralizing the country's economic relations, but it was merely an attempt to gain leverage with the U.S. for better terms on loans, investment, and trade. U.S. ambassador J. I. Loeb wrote to president Kennedy that U.S. aid had no effect on the average Peruvian, but U.S. corporations exerted preponderate political and economic influence through the Comite Norte-Americano Pro-Peru.[113]

Like the other Latin American republics, Peru tried to use the Alliance for Progress to secure foreign aid without pursuing agrarian reform. Although 2 percent of the people owned 90 percent of the land, the politically-entrenched oligarchy resisted reform, and Washington did not press the issue. A mechanism of containment designed to strengthen the patron-client model against the background of radicalism in Latin America, the Alliance for Progress served as a tool for capital accumulation at a time that the republics were multilateralizing commercial and financial relations. In the election of 1962 Haya de la Torre promised sweeping reforms, but after informing the U.S., general Ricardo Perez Godoy staged a military coup on 18 July and set up a junta.[114]

Within two months after the coup, an IMF mission met with the Junta to discuss policy. Despite widespread popular opposition and human rights violations, the Kennedy administration normalized relations. IMF policies in Peru and a number of Latin American republics resulted in greater labor and middle class opposition to pro-U.S. regimes, which prompted more CIA and other U.S. covert operations involving labor, the armed forces, the police, and various social and business groups. A year after the coup, Fernando Belaunde Terry won on a reformist platform which he never kept. To supervise $100 million of foreign loans absorbed by hiring foreign contractors for projects along the coastal Lima-Callao region, U.S.-IFI experts promised to restore external equilibrium, stimulate economic growth, and generate jobs. Unable to forge a governing coalition to satisfy all constituencies, Belaunde Terry promised favorable treatment of foreign capital to receive IFI loans.[115]

During the Alliance for Progress, ostensibly designed to foster social and economic reforms, direct U.S. investment rose from $500 million to $600 million, and half of Peru's exports were produced by U.S. companies. If capital and profits were reinvested in the domestic economy to create jobs and improve living standards, as was the case in western Europe, Japan, Canada, and Australia, Peru would have benefited. However, between 1950 and 1967 $605 million in foreign investment produced $712 million in profits of which $628 million was repatriated. The nature of foreign capital's dominance entailed that Peru, like the rest of Latin America, was a commercial satellite for the U.S., perpetually under an outward-oriented economy geared to serve the advanced capitalist countries instead of the domestic market.[116]

On 3 October 1968 general Juan Velasco Alvarado overthrew the government and established a reformist agenda that included expropriating the assets of a number of U.S. companies, including W. R. Grace and IPC's assets, prompting the U.S. to threaten sanctions. Salient causes of the coup included the IMF austerity program of 1967, which included devaluing the sol from 27 to 44 to the dollar, and incentives to foreign capital amid widespread disillusionment about economic progress. Though the government defended its actions as part of a larger reform movement, the U.S. and IFIs castigated Peru for violating international law and discouraging free enterprise and foreign capital. Nor was the U.S. enthralled that Peru opened commercial relations with the Communist bloc and bought French Mirage aircraft, instead of ordering from U.S. companies. Washington warned that aid would not be restored until Lima stopped raising taxes.[117]

After the U.S. threatened economic sanctions against Peru over the IPC case, OAS secretary-general Galo Plaza noted that the OAS charter prohibited sanctions, and appealed to Washington to abandon coercive maneuvers. Enjoying majority popular support, the Velasco government accused the previous regime of corruption, arguing that it had defrauded the people of funds derived from USAID and World Bank loans, in addition to bribes paid by companies like IPC. Contending that Peruvian workers earned 10-15 times less than U.S. workers, the Velasco government noted that Latin Americans struggled so that their North American counterparts could enjoy high living standards.

Because Lima demanded that IPC deposit $690 million in debt it owed to Peru before winning the right to appeal its case in court, Nixon sent secretary William Rogers to mediate, thus inviting Latin American criticism that the State Department was a tool of Wall Street. It should be stressed, however, that the egregious IPC case notwithstanding, Peru, like other Latin American governments, used Yankee imperialism as a pretext to deflect attention from the corruption, incompetence, wasteful spending, exorbitant defense allocations, and refusal to carry out social and institutional reforms.[118]

Between 1960 and 1972 food production dropped while imports rose, affecting mostly children and the rural poor. Lima looked to USAID and other IFIs for assistance. At $340 annual per capita income, Peru was well below the Latin American average. In 1969 the State Department correctly predicted that grossly uneven income distribution amid a rapid population growth would spell serious sociopolitical problems in the last quarter of the century. Against the background of a U.S. fishing boats violating Peru's territorial waters, Nixon sent Nelson Rockefeller to discuss bilateral and multilateral issues. This was a sensitive issue because U.S. companies had $63 million invested in Peru's fishmeal industry at a time that Velasco promised that U.S. companies would not be above the law or take advantage of Peru.[119]

In October 1969 Lima bought 69 percent of ITT's holdings in Compania Peruana de Telefonos for $16.4 million. ITT agreed to build a Sheraton Hotel and a telephone assembly plant. The government had a minority stake in both, which began operations in 1972. Despite Velasco's cordial relations with foreign capital, Nixon cut the USAID mission in half and delayed all loans until the IPC case was settled. Kissinger was concerned that Velasco's leftist advisors opposed U.S. multinational corporations. Trying to secure new loans, Lima was negotiating with the IMF and World Bank on the existing foreign debt.[120]

In the aftermath of the earthquake, Lima requested $250 million in foreign aid for reconstruction. Washington and the IFIs argued against such a large amount, while

U.S.AID was willing to contribute up to $10 million for earthquake relief, and more after the IPC and W. R. Grace cases were settled. After consulting with IPC executives and other U.S. businessmen in Lima, the NSC concluded that the Peruvian government had every right to expropriate IPC assets. Marcona Corporation, which operated the largest iron mine and pelletizing mill in Peru, maintained that the Velasco government was not against foreign capital, and that it had in fact observed the law in the procedure against IPC.[121]

A congressional memo to Kissinger in February 1969 indicated that the expropriation of IPC and W. R. Grace was popular not just among Peruvians, but Latin Americans and Europeans.

> If the U.S. Government, in its foreign policy and foreign aid, is influenced by such situations as in Peru, then foreign investment ought to be closely regulated by the U.S. Government in a way which would help improve relations with foreign countries. You have here a case of the U.S. Government coming to the rescue of private investment which it doesn't control adequately. Too many countries see this as an extension of colonialism. It is time to make some changes and put a better face on American foreign policy and on private investment abroad.[122]

The decision was to have major media publications extol the virtues of U.S. foreign investment to other countries. That assumed the problem of U.S. investments could be solved by launching a public relations campaign rather than analyzing the underlying causes of poverty. Some congressmen wanted the U.S. to punish Peru by cutting off all aid, recalling all U.S. vessels on loan to Peru's navy, and asking the OAS to support punitive measures against Lima. Because of the foreign policy imperative of hemispheric solidarity dating to the war years, the measures the U.S. used to enforce the patron-client model in Latin America were invariably harsher than those used in southern Europe.[123]

At a January 1970 meeting between IMF, World Bank, IDB, Treasury and State department officials the decision was made to coordinate foreign economic policy toward Peru while keeping with Kissinger's policy guidelines of non-overt economic pressure. Requesting if the U.S. wanted the IMF mission to Lima to delay or inhibit negotiations for a standby agreement, the State Department reminded Fund officials that Velasco had fostered an unfriendly business climate and spent too much on defense for French-made planes. Given that the economy and finances actually improved since the coup, the World Bank noted that there were U.S. and European business pressures to make loans to Peru. Comparing Peru-U.S. bilateral problems with Nasser's Egypt, the World Bank reassured the State Department that it would use loans in both countries as leverage to induce conformity with U.S. policy.[124]

In its pursuit to rationalize the economy and lessen foreign companies' influence, in August 1970, a year after confiscating the sugar plantations, the government bought U.S. investor interests in Banco Continental and Banco Internacional, while pressuring the U.S.-owned mining companies to delineate a schedule of future financing. Though Toyota, Datsun, Volkswagen, Chrysler, and American Motors won the right to continue assembly operations, Ford and GM were forced to shut down. Besides problems with foreign capital during the same year that Chile held the controversial election in which Socialist presidential candidate Salvador Allende came to power, Peru was also facing problems raising loans. The Velasco government reminded the Nixon administration that Peru needed at least $250 million for earthquake reconstruction, but it had received a tiny percentage of that amount from abroad.[125]

Because of the devastating earthquake in 1970, and chronic balance-of-payments deficits, Velasco sought to refinance the public foreign debt of $830 million, amid a drop in exports, deteriorating terms of trade, higher inflation, and low-growth prospects. In May 1971 Lima asked the World Bank that Europe and Japan reconstitute Peru's consortium to negotiate immediate debt relief for $183 million. Though U.S. and Canadian commercial banks had already rescheduled half of Peru's debt, it was insufficient. After consulting the State Department, the Velasco government hoped that G-7 governments would favor debt rescheduling by European and New York banks. Projecting $800 million in balance-of-payments deficit in the first half of the decade, Peru requested $700 million in new loans to finance the 1971-1975 development plan, one third of which would be in mining. The IMF was prepared to provide $14.5 million which of course carried the usual austerity strings.[126]

Under international pressure to assist Peruvian earthquake victims, Eximbank approved $11.3 million which went to Lockheed for the sale of cargo aircraft to Peru. In addition, the U.S. agreed to guarantee $28 million in private bank loans paid to U.S. construction companies building homes in Peru's earthquake areas. To punish Velasco for his treatment of IPC and other U.S. companies, Eximbank and the World Bank, under NSC and State Department pressure, used loans as leverage to exact policy concessions. Southern Peru Copper company (SPCC), partially owned by Dodge Phelps, Newmont Mining, and Cerro de Pasco, applied for $275 million in direct credits and guarantees, Root & Brown and Belco Petroleum requested $5.6 million to start offshore drilling, and other companies followed suit. Under agreement with Lima, SPCC was obligated to invest $515 million by 1976. The company argued that Peru's Cuajone region contained the world's most valuable unexplored copper deposits that could be produced at the lowest labor cost in the world.[127]

Turning to European and Japanese investors, SPCC tried to secure $230 million in the Euro-dollar market, $150 million in European supplier credits, and an additional $135 million from British, Belgian, and Japanese investors. Though the U.S. remained the dominant force in Peru as in the rest of the hemisphere, in the late 1960s-early 1970s the combination of a declining dollar, rising European-Japanese competition, and intransigence on the part of U.S.-based multinationals were salient factors in the multilateralization of commercial and financial relations, as the case of Peru under the Velasco regime illustrates.[128]

When the government promulgated the national development plan (1971-1975), the emphasis was clearly on a labor-intensive self-sufficient modernized economy that elevated all Peruvians to higher living standards. In an attempt to ease U.S. concerns about Peru's political and orientation that seemed leftist to Washington and Wall Street, finance minister Francisco Morales Bermudez told U.S. officials that the government opposed Communism, but it also opposed extreme right wing elements responsible for polarization in the past. Contending that Peru was rich in natural resources but suffered endemic poverty, general Morales Bermudez noted that the Velasco regime was pursuing a third way. Such economic nationalist arguments were an anathema to U.S. officials and businessmen, especially at a time when Kissinger and the CIA were covertly undermining the Allende regime.[129]

To increase foreign exchange reserves, the government made it more difficult for companies to repatriate profits and dividends. Though such policy was no different than what some European countries had been practicing, the U.S. expected its client states to allow free movement of capital regardless of the consequences to the national economy. This became especially significant after Allende adopted a Socialist-nationalist course designed to break away from the patron-client model of dependency. It was of grave concern to the U.S. that Peru contracted a Yugoslav scholar to draft an economic plan based on a stronger public sector and a stronger national private sector. In October 1971 the government announced that the private sector had failed to make the investments to move the economy forward, or to help alleviate poverty. Consequently, Peru accepted the concept of a self-managed economy. The Nixon administration was concerned that it was losing a traditional client to neutralism, and argued that quasi-statist policies resulted in higher budgetary deficits.[130]

Peru's debt service of $216 million was due in 1972, but a consortium of European banks provided refinancing loans, mostly for the state-owned agency CORMAN that was in charge of the Mantaro hydroelectric project. Because of the loan gap from U.S. public and private sources for Peru, private banking capital from German, French, and Italian sources penetrated many sectors. Historically closer to Peru than any other Latin American republic, Tokyo provided financing for Japanese firms to build electricity transmission lines, a microwave system, and a fertilizer plant. After the World Bank had refused to fund a major energy project, Peru signed an $80 million contract with Yugoslavia's Export Expansion Fund, which in turn secured an $8 million loan from Eximbank for the Peruvian irrigation project. The U.S. rushed to be a part of the Yugoslav loan project, only after Velasco's decision to move rapidly toward multilateralizing financial and trade relations in the same manner as other client states.[131]

In May 1972 the Nixon administration again reminded Peruvian officials that the IPC controversy precluded IFI and U.S. bilateral loans, except for disaster relief associated with earthquake reconstruction. Accusing the Nixon administration of pressuring the World Bank not to make loans to Lima, foreign minister Pablo de la Flor noted that Peru was in compliance with the reformist spirit of the Alliance for Progress, a policy that was abandoned since the Johnson administration. Kissinger blamed Allende's policies for angering the U.S. congress in adopting punitive measures against the Velasco government. In response to U.S. criticism of Peru's multilateral foreign economic policy, de la Flor noted that though Peru paid higher prices for U.S. products, if other countries offered credits and markets, Lima would accept.

> It was fortunate for Peru – and for factories in such countries – that export-promotion organizations of British, French, Italians, Germans, Japanese, not to mention Socialist countries, did not suffer from the same self-defeating policies as Ex-Im Bank.[132]

Proud that financial institutions were strengthened significantly, debt refinancing was successful in reducing debt service ratio from 18.1 percent in 1968 to 14 percent in 1972, and the Consultative group provided development loans, in August 1972 Morales Bermudez announced that Peruvians had more economic control over their destiny than ever. A member of the Andean Pact, Peru suffered a technology deficit and lacked capital formation to raise living standards. Though Morales Bermudez decried both Communism and capitalism, de la Flor asked the State Department to allow IFI loans for Peru as a good faith gesture before Velasco took any steps to resolve outstanding grievances with IPC.[133]

In June 1973 the State Department informed Velasco that the U.S. would support World Bank loans to Peru, after the latter submitted the legal dispute with IPC to international arbitration. Failure of mediation, however, would result in U.S. refusal to provide any type of aid. The U.S. drafted a statement for Velasco to read to the press, pledging good faith negotiations to resolve all foreign investment issues and to enhance bilateral relations. Under domestic business and military pressure amid global economic contraction and stagflation, and considering the CIA-backed coup of Allende in 1973, Velasco reconsidered his earlier position of tinkering with the traditional patron-client model and angering Washington.[134]

In January 1974 the Peruvian government agreed to settle with U.S. companies for $76 million. The companies compensated included Cargill, H. B. Zachary, and International Pretein. On 19 February 1974 Velasco signed a settlement agreement to resolve the dispute with the U.S. over IPC, thereby giving the opportunity of other U.S. firms to settle as well. In May during the Watergate hearings, Kissinger arranged a meeting between Nixon and Velasco, after considerable criticism in Latin America and throughout the world that the U.S. was responsible for overthrowing Allende and installing a military dictatorship in September 1973.[135]

Like many Third World countries in the late 1960s, Peru borrowed increasingly from commercial banks at higher interest rates. By the mid-1970s almost half of the foreign loans came from commercial banks. As public debt rose from one billion dollars in 1970 to $8.5 billion in 1981, at 77 percent Peru had the third largest percentage of debt to GNP ratio. Though neo-classical economists and other scholars view each debt occurrence separately from a historical pattern, the fact is that Peru's like Latin America's debt crises have been cyclical since the war of independence in the early 19th century. And because neo-classical scholars make the same assumptions about the fundamental causes about balance-of-payments and debt crises, they invariably offer solutions that perpetuate the patron-client model and account for the cyclical nature of crises.[136]

In 1980 Fernando Belaunde Terry was elected after the military regime had failed to deliver on the promise of economic and social progress. From 1974 to 1982 capital outflow amounted to $3.1 billion, affecting a 17 percent drop in capital formation and sharp decrease in living standards. Unable to deal with the debt crisis and its consequences on the majority of the population, in 1981 Belaunde Terry adopted a law that made it easy to detain political opponents as terrorism suspects amid the rising popularity of Sendero Luminoso founded by professor Abimael Guzman in the late 1960s.[137]

In an apparent attempt to break the cycle of debt and dependence, in July 1985 APRA's reformist-populist president Alan Garcia promised to keep debt-service ratio at 10 percent of export receipts. Garcia was merely interested in strengthening national capitalism and readjusting the patron-client model so that foreign corporations, especially the U.S., would not exert such inordinate influence. A centrist with backing from reformists that included many Catholics, Garcia was viewed by the Reagan administration, the IFIs, and multinationals as moving too far to the left. In comparison with right-wing dictatorships that the U.S. historically supported in Latin America, Garcia was indeed too far to the left. But his policies, which ultimately failed, were merely designed to strengthen national capitalism and address social problems.[138]

The combination of widespread poverty, public and business corruption, foreign dependence, exclusion of the Indian and mestizo population from the institutional mainstream, and repeated failures of reform accounted for a thoroughly alienated and disillusioned population, a segment of which turned to revolutionary opposition, others to religion, and most to resignation with the status quo. A large segment of the population was part of the informal economy, some of whom grew coca leaves refined into cocaine. Another segment of mostly young idealists inspired by Maoism joined the guerrilla movement Sendero Luminoso, just as other Latin Americans backed indigenous rebels against the domestic elites and foreign interests that the majority believed were responsible for the exploitation of the masses.

In 1990 the right-wing populist Alberto Fujimori won the election promising to end corruption and strengthen the economy. Following the IFI's-U.S. advice, Fujimore invited foreign investment under favorable terms. He deregulated the economy, eased import restrictions, curbed subsidies to public companies and sold some assets to private investors. Had these measures yielded higher living standards for the majority as its advocates claimed, Fujimore's dictatorship would have enjoyed popular backing. Though inflation was stabilized at around 140 percent a year after Fujimori took office, workers and peasants paid the price of further income redistribution toward the upper income groups.

Once the army captured Guzman in 1992, Fujimore and the military installed a brutal dictatorship backed by the U.S. and the domestic business community. Structural problems ranging from unemployment and underemployment to economic underdevelopment worsened during the 1990s, as living standards declined amid a thriving drug trade and rise in guerrilla activity from Sendero Luminoso and Tupac Amaru. Containing radicalism and perpetuating the patron-client model via a military solution only invited more political violence without addressing the root causes of guerrilla movements and popular opposition to a decadent U.S.-backed government.[139]

Dependent development under the patron-client model in Peru has not worked in the same manner as in Brazil which is a very large country and has recently developed the ability to forge mutually beneficially economic relationships with China, India, and other large countries, thereby modifying dependence on the U.S. Because of geography and history, the U.S.-led patron-client model in Peru and the rest of Latin America is much more firmly entrenched than in other parts of the world. Nor can ephemeral bursts of economic growth be confused with any meaningful readjustment in the neo-classical integration model. Whether in Indonesia and its sister "Asian tigers" undergoing a reality check in the financial crisis of the late 1990s, Nigeria during the spikes in oil prices, or Mexico's and Argentina's euphoria with liberalization in the 1990s, behind such cyclical phenomena rests the perdurable patron-client integration model which results in capital accumulation and benefits the indigenous elites and the core during the expansionary and contracting cycles.[140] Indonesia, Nigeria, and Peru have not undergone the bourgeois transformation phase comparable to southern Europe in the mid-1990s, nor have they been successful in forging an inter-dependent integration relationship.

Notes

1.   L. H. Palmier, *Indonesia and the Dutch* (London, 1962), pp. 2-6, 10-6, 46-96; Anne Booth et al. (eds), *Indonesian Economic History in the Dutch Colonial Era* (New Haven, 1990);

Bernard Dahm, *Sukarno and the Struggle for Indonesian Independence* (Ithaca, NY, 1969); Ruth Sheldon Knowles, *Indonesia Today* (Los Angeles, CA, 1973), pp. 55; N. Keyfitz, "Indonesian Population and The European Industrial Revolution," *Asian Survey* 10 (1965): 503-14.

2. FCO 15/198, EAP 308/85/01, 7 February 1967; Hal Hill, *The Indonesian Economy since 1966* (Cambridge, 1996), 11; Cindy Adams, *Sukarno: An Autobiography* (New York, 1965), pp. 221-74.

3. F. B. Weinstein, *Indonesian Foreign Policy and the Dilemma of Dependence* (Ithaca, NY, 1976), p. 161; F.O. 371/99041, No. 87, 9 August 1952; Ibid., No. 98, 18 August 1952.

4. F.O. 371112/112162, No. 136, 20 September 1954; F.O. 371/112162, No. H 1102/7, 28 October 1954; Ibid., N. H1102/2, 23 October 1954.

5. F.O. 371/175099, No. 138, 7 October 1954; F.O. 371/112162, No. 1102/23/54, 4 November 1954; Knowles, *Indonesia*, 60-1.

6. Weinstein, *Indonesian Foreign Policy*, pp. 164-65; F.O. 371/170771, No. FJ 113162/2, 8 November 1963.

7. D. E. Weatherbeee, *Ideology in Indonesia: Sukarno's Indonesian Revolution* (New Haven, CT, 1966); F.O. 371/150966, No. 66E, 27 August 1960; Weinstein, *Indonesian Foreign Policy*, pp. 165-66.

8. F.O. 371/156593, 9 May 1961; F.O. 371/158511, 26 June 1961; F.O. 371/169944, No. 249, 1 June 1963; J. V. Kofas, "The Politics of Austerity: The IMF and U.S. Foreign Policy in Bolivia, 1956-1964," *The Journal of Developing Areas* 29/2 (1995): 227-29; F.O. 371/169944, No. 192, 12 March 1963; F.O. 371/169939, No. JH 1461/2, 26 February 1963; Ibid., No. 707, 18 December 1963.

9. F.O. 371/172369, 8 March 1963; Payer, *Debt Trap*, p. 77; F.O. 371/172369, 28 February 1963.

10. F.O. 371/172479, No. 262, 3 April 1963; F.O. 371/172369, No. 153, 12 July 1963; Ibid., No. 180, 25 July 1963.

11. *Financial Times*, 24 June 1963; Ibid., 17 July 1963; F.O. 371/169944, No. 151, 25 July 1963; Ibid., 181, 26 September 1963; Ibid., No. 197, 1 October 1963.

12. F.O. 371/170771, No. FJ 113162/1, 10 September 1963; Ibid., No. FJ 11316212, 8 November 1963; Weinstein, *Indonesian Foreign Policy*, p. 169.

13. SDNA LAB 13 INDO, No. A-855,13 March 1964; Ibid., No. A-147, 24 August 1964.

14. FN 17 INDO, No. A-953, 8 April 1964; Ibid., No. A-244, 25 September 1964; F.O. 371/176026, No. 172, 9 April 1964; SDNA UN 6-2 INDO, No. 1271,14 January 1965; FN 9-3 INDO, No., A-871, 18 March 1964; F.O. 371/176026, No. 316, 9 June 1964; Ibid., No. 11942, 15 June 1964.

15. SDNA UN 6-2 INDO, No. 343, 29 January 1965; F.O. 371/175099, No. D113123/1, 25 June 1964; F.O. 371/176026, No. 382, 2 July 1964; Ibid., 11231/4/64, 11 August 1964; Weinstein, *Indonesian Foreign Policy*, pp. 166-67; Hill, *The Indonesian Economy*, p. 3.

16. FN 9 INDO No. 114, 16 August 1965; Donald Hindley, *Communist Party of Indonesia*.

(Berkeley, CA, 1964); Kofas, *Sword of Damocles*, pp. 66, 137, 161.

17. Payer, *Debt Trap*, pp. 75-6; Hill, *Indonesian Economy*, pp. 1-2; Stevens, *Mystical World*, p. 254; K. Conboy and J. Morrison, *Feet to the Fire: CIA Operations in Indonesia* (Washington, D.C., 1999); SDNA POL 15-1 INDO, No. A-61, 5 August 1967.

18. P. D. Scott, "The United States and the Overthrow of Sukarno, 1965-1967," *Pacific Affairs* 58 (1985): 239-64; FN 9 INDO, 16 March 1965; Vadney, *The World since 1945*, pp. 376-78; Knowles, *Indonesia*, pp. 71-5.

19. FCO 24/24/1117, 7 July 1971; F.O. 371/188758, No. 10711/18/8, 18 August 1966.

20. SDNA FN 4 INDO, No. A-156, 13 September 1966; Ibid., SDNA, FN 9 INDO-US, No. A-143, 21 September 1966; Ibid., 14 September 1966; Vadney, *The World since 1945*, p. 379; Weinstein, *Indonesia's Foreign Policy*, pp. 170-71.

21. FCO, 15/200, No. DH6/4, 19 July 1968; Ibid., 12 July 1968; FCO 15/197, 5 January 1967; FCO 15/198, No. 565, 11 January 1967.

22. FN 10 IMF, No. A-854, 23 November 1966; FCO 15/198, EAP 308/85/01, 7 February 1967; FCO 5/197, 5 January 1967; Stevens, *World of Indonesia*, pp. 256-57; FCO 5/197, 6 January 1967; Ibid., 13 January 1967; Financial Times, 21 December 1966.

23. FCO 24/246, No. 263, 18 March 1967; Ibid., No. 249, 15 March 1967.

24. SDNA LAB 3-2 INDO, No. A-286, 28 December 1966; Ibid., No. A-331, 10 November 1966; FCO 24/246, 3 April 1967; Ibid., No. 57, 2 June 1967; Ibid., 14 July 1967.

25. FCO 15/197, No. 565, 18 January 1967; Ibid., No. 11413/1/67, 20 January 1967; Payer, *Debt Trap*, p. 82; FCO 24/246, No. DH620, 13 March 1967.

26. SDNA POL-13, INDO, No. 162, 20 September 1967; Ibid., No. 802, 9 October 1967; Ibid., 9 September 1967; SDNA POL 15-1 INDO, No. A-100, 23 August 1967; FCO 24/246, No. DH620, 13 March 1967; FCO 24/246, DH6/20, 1 March 1967; FCO 15/198, No. 257, 10 April 1967; Ibid., DH 614, 25 May 1967.

27. SDNA POL 15-1 INDO, 2 October 1967; Ibid., No. A-100, 23 August 1967; FCO 24/246, No. HK6/1, 14 July 1967; Ibid., No. 22 November 1967; SDNA POL 29 INDO, No. 302, 20 June 1969; FCO 15/200, No. 249, 3 April 1968.

28. SDNA LAB 3-2 INDO, No. A-23, 2 February 1970; Ibid., No. A-51, 5 March 1970; FCO 24/246, No. 249, 24 April 1968; Ibid., No. 21, 11 January 1968; Ibid., No. HK6/1, 19 August 1968.

29. SDNA POL 12 INDO, No. A-27, 18 September 1969; OD 39/103, 12 September 1969.

30. FCO 24/1117, 21 May 1971; 3 June 1971.

31. FN 9 INDO-US, No. A-199, 12 June 1970; FCO 24/1117, 8 June 1971; Payer, *Debt Trap*, pp. 83-4; FN 9-INDO-US, 20 March 1973.

32. SDNA LAB 2 INDO, No. A-122, 27 April 1970; SDNA, LAB 3-2 INDO, No. A-84, 20 March 1970; Ibid., 12 September 1970; Ibid., No. A-167, 11 June 1971; Ibid, No. A-033, 10 February 1972.

33. Brian Pinto, "Nigeria During and After the Oil Boom: A Policy Comparison with Indonesia," *The World Bank Economic Review* 1/3 (1987): 420-22; Knowles, *Indonesia*, p. 163.

34. FN 6-1 INDO, No. A-174, 18 June 1971; FCO 24/1117, 7 July 1971; FCO 24/1111, No. FW 01/18, 31 August 1971.

35. SDNA AID 9 INDO, 24 November 1971; Ibid., 30 November 1971; FCO 24/1111, No. FWD 1/8, 13 September 1971; Ibid., 13 October 1971.

36. FN 9 INDO, No. A-109, 14 May 1973; FCO 24/1398, 30 August 1972.

37. FCO 24/1398, 7 January 1972; Ibid., 4 January 1972; Ibid., 27 June 1972.

38. FCO 24/1395, 22 August 1972.

39. Ibid., 30 August 1972; Nixon Project, WHCF, Box 755, Kissinger to the President, 20 January 1972; Ibid., Nixon to Suharto, 21 January 1972.

40. Nixon Project, WHCF, Box 755, J. H. Holdridge to Kissinger, 8 December 1971; Ibid., George Schultz to the President, 8 December 1971; FCO 24/1395, 21 December 1972; Ibid., 27 October 1972; Ibid., 6 November 1972; FCO 24/1398, 2 January 1973.

41. FN 9 INDO-JAPAN, No. A-041, 18 February 1972; Ibid., 5 March 1973; FN 6 INDO-US, No. A-115, 18 March 1973.

42. SDNA POL 15-4 INDO, 16 December 1972; SDNA AID 9 INDO, 18 December 1972; Ibid., No. A-100, 16 May 1973; SDNA FN 16 INDO, No. A-175, 20 July 1973; SDDNA FN 10 IMF, No. 1404, 3 February 1973; SDNA FN 6-1 INDO, No. 1-161, 9 July 1973; Ibid., No. A-18, 22 January 1973.

43. Little, *Crisis and Adjustment*, pp. 38-9, 42-3; Vadney, *The World since 1945*, p. 379.

44. Vadney, *The World since 1945*, p. 379; Hill, *Indonesian Economy*, pp. 11, 16-17.

45. Hill, *Indonesian Economy*, 248-49; Erik Thorbecke, "Adjustment, Growth and Income Distribution in Indonesia," *World Development* 19/11 (1991): 1595-1641; Hill, *Indonesian Economy,* pp. 16-7.

46. Little, *Debt and Adjustment*, pp. 113-14; Hill, *Indonesian Economy*, p. 17.

47. Clare Fermont, "Indonesia: the Inferno of Revolution," *International Socialism* 80 (1998); M. R. J. Vatikiotis, *Indonesian Politics under Suahrto* (London, 1999); Stefan Eklof, *Indonesian Politics in Crisis: The Long Fall of Suharto* (Copenhagen, 1999).

48. Samir Amin, *Neo-Colonialism in West Africa* (New York, 1973), pp. vi-xviii, 3-40; A. G. Hopkins, *An Economic History of Nigeria* (New York, 1973), pp. 124-235.

49. John Smith Ikpuk, *Militarisation of Politics and neo-colonialism: The Nigerian Experience, 1966-1990* (London, 1995); M. L. Martin, *La militarization des systemes politiques africains, 1960-1972* (Sherbooke, 1976).

50. Fantu Cheru, *The Silent Revolution in Africa* (London, 1989), pp. 1-8.

51. Barbara Callaway, "The Political Economy of Nigeria," in R. Harris (ed), *The Political Economy of Africa* (New York, 1975), p. 102.

52. F.O. 371/172384, No. ECA 124/12/1, 29 January 1963.

53. F.O. T 312/2031, 16 April 1960; Ibid., 26 April 1960; Ibid., 20 June 1960; Ibid., No. 89, 27 May 1960; No. 92, 31 May 1960; Ibid., 1 October 1960; Ibid., 30 March 1961; F.O. 371/161374, No. J345/19, 29 June 1962; Shepard, *Nigeria*, 21-3.

54. F.O. 371/156471, No. 323, 16 May 1961; Ibid., No. AU 1163/9, 17 July 1961; F.O.

371/156471, No. 481, 7 July 1961.

55. F.O. 371/156471, No. 103/2/1, 31 August 1961; Ibid., No. Nig. A/57B, 21 August 1961.

56. F.O. 371/156471, No. 198, 9 September 1961; Ibid., No. 3373, 12 December 1961.

57. F.O. 371/183087, No. 31, 7 February 1962; F.O. 371/164456, No. 31, 7 February 1962; Ibid., No. 39, 9 March 1962.

58. F.O. 371/164456, No. 264, 14 April 1962.

59. F.O. 371/183087, 14 April 1962; Ibid., No. 465, 29 July 1962.

60. F.O. 371/17145, No. BF/622/42, 3 September 1962; Ibid., No. 180, 19 September 1962; Ibid., No. 217, 29 November 1962; Ibid., UEE 10356/6, 28 September 1962 F.O. 371/172384, No. ECA 124/12/1, 29 January 1963.

61. F.O. 371/164456, 9 August 1962; Ibid., No. 180, 20 September 1962; Ibid., No. BF/62/42, 3 September 1962; Ibid., No. , 29 November 1962; Ibid., 28 December 1962.

62. F.O. 371/172384, No. 30, 21 February 1963.

63. F.O. 371/172384, No. 40, 11 April 1963; Ibid., No. 60, 21 April 1963.

64. F.O. 371/172384, No. 73, 9 May 1963, Ibid., No. 74, 9 May 1963; I. W. Zartman, "The Future of Europe and Africa," in T. M. Shaw (ed), *Alternative Futures for Africa* (Boulder, 1982), p. 263; J. Isawa Elaigwu "Toward Continental Integration," in Ibid., pp. 136-37; F.O. 371/172384, No. 122, 30 June 1963; Ibid., 30 June 1963.

65. F.O. 371/171459, No. M10917/8, 24 September 1963; Ibid., No. 297, 20 September 1963; Ibid. No. 244, 23 September 1963; *Financial Times*, 18 September 1963.

66. F.O. 371/172384, No. 283, 30 November 1963; Ibid. No. 187, 18 September 1963; Ibid., No. 147 (s), 3 December 1963.

67. F.O. 371/171459. No. Pol 14/29/4, 28 December 1962; Ibid., No. 1164/63, 3 January 1962; Ibid., No. M10917/1, 10 January 1963; F.O. 371/177384, No. 4, 7 January 1963; Ibid., No. 25, 30 January 1964; Ibid., No. 84 5 February 1964; Ibid., No. M10917/111, 20 August 1964.

68. Callaway, "The Political Economy of Nigeria," 104-105; F.O. 371/183087, RG 113215/1, 29 October 1965; U.S. Embassy, Lagos, Nigeria, Charles W. Corey, "Past Corruption is Nigeria's Single Biggest Problem," 26 May 2000.

69. SDNA E 5-Nigeria, No. A-39, 24 November 1965; SDNA AID-IBRD 9, Nigeria, No. A-2, 3 July 1965; SDNA LAB-3-2 Nigeria, No. A-320, 13 November 1964; Ibid., No. A-353, 4 December 1964; Ibid., No. A-152, 21 July 1965

70. F.O. 371/183903, 30 November 1965; Shepard, *Nigeria*, 28-9.

71. Ben Gbulie, *Nigeria's Five Majors: coup d'etat of 15 January 1966* (Onitsha, Nigeria, 1981); Shepard, *Nigeria*, 30-1; F.O. 371/190426, No. 803215/1, 7 February 1966; Ibid., No. 589, 10 February 1966; Ibid., No. 48, 12 February 1966.

72. F.O. 371/187893, No. 10519, 1 February 1966; Ibid., No. 356, 18 March 1966; F.O. 371/187891, No. 56, 21 July 1966; Ibid., No. 202, 10 August 1966; SDNA AID (US) 9, Nigeria, 6 July 1966.

73. A. Obiora, Uzokwe, *Surviving Biafra: The Story of the Nigerian Civil War* (Lincoln, NE,

2003); Shepard, *Nigeria*, pp. 34-5; Callaway, "Nigeria," pp. 118-19.

74. F.O. 371/188725, 10 December 1966; Shepard, *Nigeria*, 37-41; T 312/2031, No. 9, 1 January 1968; Nixon Project, WHCF Box 56, CO-113, 27 January 1969; Okere Steve Nwosu, "The National Question: issues and Lessons of Boundary Adjustment in Nigeria," *Journal of Third World Studies* 15/2 (1998): 86-7.

75. FCO 65/742, No. 205/70, 11 March 1970; Callaway, "Nigeria," 124.

76. FCO 65/742, 10 October 1969; FCO 51/212, 24 February 1972; Ibid., 2 April 1972; Ibid., 22 September 1972; FCO 6/1011, 5 August 1971; Ibid., 2 July 1971; Ibid., 31 May 1971; Ibid., 29 April 1971.

77. Shepard, *Nigeria*, p. 48; FCO 65/999, No. 86/71, 14 January 1971.

78. FCO 65/999, No. 86/71, 14 January 1971; Shepard, *Nigeria*, p. 52.

79. FCO 65/999, No. 86/71, 14 January 1971; OD 30/358, No. 1062, 11 November 1970; Nixon Project, WHCF, CO-113-Nigeria, Box, 55, 28 November 1970; Ibid., 23 November 1970; Ibid., 20 November 1970; SDNA EN-Nigeria, 19 August 1970. OD 30/358, No. 570/70, 23 December 1970.

80. OD 30/358, 16 November 1970; Ibid., 7 December 1970; Ibid., No. CA/5/016, 11 December 1970; Ibid., 10 December 1970; FCO 65/999, 22 January 1971; OD 30/358, 18 March 1971; Ibid., 23 March 1971.

81. SDNA FN-9 Nigeria, No. A-138, 22 April 1971; Callaway, *Nigeria*, p. 130; Shepard, *Nigeria*, pp. 57-9.

82. FCO 65/1192, No. 126/72, 15 January 1972; SDNA LAB 2-Nigeria, No. A-229, 25 June 1970; J. V. Kofas, *The Struggle for Legitimacy* (Tempe, AR, 1992), pp. 370-71; Carl Gershman, *The Foreign Policy of American Labor* (Beverly Hills, CA, 1975), pp. 55-62.

83. SDNA AID-US-Nigeria, No. A-262, 23 September 1972; FCO 30/892, 24 June 1971; Ibid., 26 June 1971; Ibid,, No. 6/310/1, 9 October 1971; Ibid., 11 January 1972; Ibid., No. 6/310/1, 6 July 1971; Nixon Project, WHCF, CO-113-Nigeria, Box, 55, 3 March 1971.

84. FCO 30/892, 24 January 1972; Ibid., 26 January 1972; FCO 65/1200, 6/310/1, 11 January 1972; Ibid., 27 September 1971; FCO 30/892, 24 February 1972.

85. Ibid., 31 January 1972; Ibid., 16 March 1972; Ibid., 6 April 1972; Ibid., 5 May 1972.

86. FCO 65/1194, 30 June 1972.

87. FCO 65/1194, 20 October 1972 ; FCO 30/1362, 7 November 1972; Ibid., 8 November 1972.

88. SDNA AID U.S.-Nigeria, No. A-307, 31 July 1971; Ibid., No. A-106, 10 December 1971.

89. Ibid., 29 November 1972; FCO 65/1200, No. JWN/3/304/1, 13 December 1972; FCO 30/892, 13 December 1972 Nixon Project, WHCF, CO-113-Nigeria, Box, 55, 31 July 1972; FCO 30/1362, 5 December 1972.

90. Ibid., No. 6/310/1, 1 December 1972; Ibid., 6 December 1972; FCO 65/1200, 3/310/1, 11 December 1972; SDNA FN 6-1 Nigeria, 24 February 1972; Ibid., 18 February 1972; Ibid., 10 February 1972.

91. FCO 30/1362, No. 3/310/1, 15 January 1973.

92. FCO 65/1194, 30 December 1972; Brian Pinto, "Nigeria during and after the Oil Boom: A Policy Comparison with Indonesia," *The World Bank Economic Review* 1/3 (1987): 419-21; Callaway, *Nigeria*, p. 126.

93. Sayre Schatz, *Nigerian Capitalism* (Berkeley, CA, 1977), pp. 32-5.

94. Shepard, *Nigeria*, pp. 86-93; Little, *Crisis and Adjustment*, p. 39; World Bank, *Adjustment in Africa*, p. 32.

95. SDNA, AV-14 Nigeria, No. A-259, 15 September 1972; Ibid., No. A-267, 29 November 1973.

96. SDNA FN 6-Nigeria, No. A-229, 11 October 1973; SDNA, LAB 2-Nigeria, No. A-64, 5 April 1973; Ibid., No. A-42, 12 February 1972.

97. Shepard, *Nigeria*, pp. 95-7, 103-06; H. E. E. Newsum and O. Abegunrin, *United States Foreign Policy toward Southern Africa: Andrew Young and Beyond* (New York, 1987).

98. Little, *Crisis and Adjustment*, pp. 93-5; World Bank, *Adjustment in Africa*, 32; Shepard, *Nigeria*, pp. 109, 118-21.

99. A. A. N. Orizu, *Insight into Nigeria: the Shehu Shagari era* (Ibadan, Nigeria, 1983); Shepard, *Nigeria*, 129-133, 147; Carol Lancaster, "Africa's Economic Crisis," *Foreign Policy* 52 (1983):152-53.

100. R. S. Browne and R. J. Cummings, *The Lagos Plan of Action vs. The Berg Report* (New Brunswick: Brunswick Publishing, 1985); Little, *Boom, Crisis, and Adjustment*, 95.

101. Lancaster, "Africa's Economic Crisis," pp. 150-51; Shepard, *Nigeria*, pp. 134-37; J. G. Liebenow, *African Politics*. (Bloomington, IN, 1986), p. 251.

102. Cheru, *Silent Revolution in Africa*, pp. 38-9; Shepard, *Nigeria*, pp. 137, 144-49.

103. Ibid., pp. 149-53.

104. World Bank, *Adjustment in Africa* (Oxford, 1994), p. 249; Shepard, *Nigeria*, pp. 155-57; Christopher Landsberg, "The United States and Africa: Malign Neglect," in *Unilateralism and U.S. Foreign Policy*, op. cit., pp. 352-53, 362.

105. R. J. Cummings "Africa's Case for Economic Integration: Arguing for an Institute of African Regional Integration," <www.HUArchives.net>

106. Yepes, *La Modernizacion en el Peru*, pp. 61-3; Olivier Dolfuss, *Le Perou: Introduction Geographiques a l'Etude de Development* (Paris, 1968), pp. 110-20, 200-34, 335-45; D. P. Werlich, *Peru: A Short History* (Carbondale, IL, 1978); R. J. Alexander, *Aprismo: The Ideas and Doctrines of Victor Raul Haya de la Torre* (Kent, 1973), pp. 4-35.

107. John Gerassi, *The Great Fear in Latin America* (New York, 1973), pp. 19-20; D. P. Kilty, *Planning for Development in Peru* (New York, 1967), pp. 50-2.

108. SDNA POL, Peru-U.S., No. A-127, 24 March 1969.

109. Humala Tasso, *Subdesarrollo en el Peru*, pp. 66-8; J. M. Ramirez Gaston, *Medio siglo de la politica economica y finaciera del Peru* (Lima, 1964), pp. 228-29.

110. J. M. Ramirez y Gaston, *Politica Economica y Financiera: Manuel Prado* (Lima, 1969), pp. 104-06; Jorge Melgar, *A Belaunde lo que es de Belaunde* (Lima, 1973), pp. 39-48; IMF C/Peru/1760, Standby Arrangement, 1952-1957, 31 October 1956; SDNA 823.10/6-

457, Memo; F.O. 371126342, AF 1104, No. 61E, 31 May 1957.

111. Kofas, *Foreign Debt and Underdevelopment*, pp. 161-76; Virgilio Roel Pineda, *Problemas de la economia Peruana.* (Lima, 1959), pp. 30-103.

112. Rosemary Thorp and Geoffrey Bertram, *Peru, 1890-1977* (New York, 1978), pp. 264-66; Miguel Teubal, "The Failure of Latin America's Economic Integration," in J. Petras and M. Zeitlin (eds), *Latin America: Reform or Revolution?* (New York, 1968), pp. 122-40; Jerome Levinson and Juan de Onis, *The Alliance that Lost its Way* (Chicago, 1970), pp. 5-60.

113. G. Pope Atkins, *Latin America in the International Political System* (New York, 1977), pp. 290-93; C. H. Gardiner, *The Japanese and Peru* (Albuquerque, NM, 1975), pp. 110-20; Humala Taso, *Subdesarrollo*, 73-5; Kofas, *Foreign Debt and Underdevelopment*, pp. 191-92.

114. Paul Sigmund, *Multinationals in Latin America* (Madison, WI, 1980), pp. 180-82; Arnold Payne, *The Peruvian Coup d'Etat of 1962* (Washington, D.C., 1968); Werlich, *Peru*, pp. 265-75.

115. Melgar, *A Belaunde lo que es de Belaunde*, 45-60; Anibal Quijano Obregon, "El Peru en la crisis de los anos treinta," in Luis Antezana E. et al. (eds), *America Latina en los anos treinta* (Mexico City, 1977), pp. 118-22; Thomas Skidmore, "The Politics of Economic Stabilization in Postwar Latin America," in James Malloy (ed), *Authoritarianism and Corporatism in Latin America* (Pittsburgh, 1977), pp. 149-83.

116. Santiago Segura et al. "Tecnologia y desarrollo de la dependencia," in H. Espinosa Uriarte (ed), *Dependencia economica y tecnologica: caso Peruano* (Lima:, 1971), pp. 35-40; Hector Bejar, *Peru 1965* (New York, 1969), pp. 20-26.

117. Dirk Kruijt, *Revolution by Decree: Peru 1968-1975* (Amsterdam, 1994); Carlos Franco, *El Peru de Valasco* (Lima, 1983); SDNA POL, Peru-U.S., 12 September 1969; Ibid., No. A-283, 23 July 1969; Ibid., No. A-15, Enclosure 2, 12 February 1969.

118. SDNA POL 12 DOM-REP, 22 April 1969; SDNA POL, Peru-U.S., No. A-148, 9 April 1969.

119. Nixon Project, WHCF, Box 60, CO-119-Peru, AID 15-8-Peru, No 67, 4 April 1972; SDNA POL, Peru-U.S., No. A-127, 24 March 1969; SDNA FN 9, Peru, No. A-166, 22 May 1972; Ibid. No. A-157, 12 June 1971.

120. Nixon Project, WHCF, Box 60, CO-119-Peru, 23 May 1969; SDNA, POL, Peru-U.S., 23 June 1969; Ibid., No. A-56, 18 April 1969.

121. SDNA Nixon Project, WHCF, Box 60, CO-119-Peru, 8 June 1970; Ibid., AID-IDB 9-Peru, 12 June 1970; Ibid., 5 August 1970; Nixon Project, WHCF Box 60 CO-119, Peru, 10 February 1970.

122. Nixon Project, WHCF Box 60 CO-119, Peru, 13 February 1969.

123. Nixon Project, WHCF Box 60 CO-119, Peru, 27 February 1969.

124. SDNA FN AID-U.S.-PERU, 19 January 1970.

125. SDNA FN 9 Peru, No. A-287, 3 September 1970; SDNA POL7 Peru, 26 June 1970.

126. SDNA FN 14 Peru, 6 July 1970; Ibid., No. A-224 9 July 1970; Ibid., No. A-148,28 May 1971; Ibid., No. 576, 18 May 1971.

127. SDNA FN 6-1 Peru, 21 September 1971; SDNA AID (US) 9 Peru, 11 December 1970; SDNA FN 6-1 Peru, 3 February 1971; SDNA FN 9 Peru, 7 August 1970.

128. Nixon Project, WHCF, Box 60, CO-119-Peru, 17 November 1972.

129. SDNA FN 6-1 Peru, 21 June 1971; SDNA E-5 Peru, No. A-193, 2 July 1971; James Petras and Robert La Porte, "U.S. Response to Economic Nationalism in Chile," in James Petras (ed), *From Dependence to Revolution* (New York, 1973).

130. SDNA, FN 10 Peru, A-329, 16 October 1970; Ibid., No. A-397, 29 December 1971; SDNA E-5, Peru No. A-352, 26 September 1972; Kofas, *Sword of Damocles*, 172-73.

131. SDNA FN 6-1 Peru, No. A-351, 27 September 1972; Ibid., No. A-349, 25 September 1972; Ibid., 12 July 1971; SDNA FN 2, Peru, No. A-363, 6 December 1971.

132. SDNA FN 1 Peru, No. 2841, 13 May 1972.

133. SDNA FN 2 Peru, No. A-301, 16 August 1972.

134. Osvaldo Silva Galdames, *Breve Historia Contemporanea de Chile* (Mexico City, 1995), pp. 310-15; SDNA FN 2 Peru, 30 June 1973.

135. Nixon Project, WHCF, Box 60, CO-119-Peru, 16 January 1974; Ibid., 24 January 1974; 22 January 1974; Ibid., 27 May 1974; Cingranelli, *American Foreign Policy*, p. 167.

136. Stallings, *Banker to the Third World*, pp. 310-20; Molineu, *Latin America*, pp. 105-07.

137. Jonathan Eaton, "Public Debt Guarantees and Private Capital Flight," *The World Bank Economic Review* 1/3 (1987): 378; S. J. Stern, *Shining and Other Paths* (Durham, NC, 1998); Cynthia Brown, *With Friends Like These* (New York, 1985), pp. 208-09.

138. John Crabtree, *Peru under Garcia* (Pittsburgh, 1992); J. D. Rudolph, *Peru: The Evolution of a Crisis* (Westport, CT, 1992); Little, *Crisis and Adjustment*, p. 171.

139. H. Pease Garcia, *La autocracia Fujimorista: del estado intervencionista al estado mafioso* (Lima, 2003).

140. Fischer, *The United States and the European Union*, 183-86; Hill, *Indonesian Economy*, pp. 81-92.

Conclusions

The Promise of Global Integration: Apocalypse or Inequality?

A fundamental question in the world development debate is whether the neoclassical or patron-client integration model has served to promote or retard economic and social justice, democracy, sovereignty, and human rights in the past six decades. Has integration lifted underdeveloped countries from the depths of poverty and inequality, or sunk them even deeper into poverty and external dependence. A comparative analysis of postwar history between the advanced capitalist countries, on the one hand, and the semi-developed and underdeveloped, on the other, demonstrates that exogenous dynamics in southern Europe were significant in accounting for broad progress in the region after the end of authoritarianism, though each country's unique domestic dynamics cannot be underestimated.

Southern Europe's full membership in the EEC entailed that integration necessitated a political, economic, financial, and social system comparable to northwest Europe's, although convergence did not extend to the political realm identically for each country. Comparable progress did not take place in Indonesia, Nigeria, and Peru which remained under the patron-client model along with the rest of the Third World. Though social inequality was as much a reality after southern Europe's full EEC membership as before, and the new proletariat included immigrants from Eurasia, Africa, Asia, and Eastern Europe, socioeconomic and political conditions were far better than in most of the Third World.

Superimposed patron-client integration that promotes inequality while proclaiming to alleviate it, contributes to chronic social problems that lead to political instability. Because expectations are raised for democracy and upward social mobility that rarely materialize, people in underdeveloped countries become cynical and nihilistic. Radical groups actively oppose the political-military establishments that sustain international capitalism and the hierarchical world-system hiding behind the veneer of democratic rhetoric. Rather than addressing the structural causes of inequality, lack of social justice, and exploitation associated with globalization, western politicians, businessmen, journalists, and academics wonder why there are so many people in the Third World who reject the linear Hegelian assumptions of progress under globalization which has been synonymous with Americanization.[1]

Americanization apologists justify hegemony by using arguments ranging from messianic ideologies about disseminating freedom and democracy to industrial-technological diffusion that presumably best serves less developed countries. But does the rest of the world agree? In 1997 Samuel Huntington noted that at a Harvard University conference on "Conflict or Convergence: Global Perspectives on War, Peace, and International Order," participants from all over the world reported that:

> ...the leaders of countries with at least two-thirds of the world's people - Chinese, Russians, Indians, Arabs, Muslims, Africans, - see the United States as the single greatest external threat to their societies. They do not see America as a military threat; they see it as a threat to their integrity, autonomy, prosperity, and freedom of action to pursue their interests as they see fit. They see the United States as intrusive, interventionist, exploitative, unilateralist, hegemonic, hypocritical, applying double standards, engaging in what they label "financial imperialism" and "intellectual colonialism" ...[2]

Seven years after Harvard's international conference, world public opinion polls indicated that perceptions of the U.S. policies were sharply critical. Are the people and their leaders around the world justified fearing that U.S. foreign policy and superimposed globalization poses a threat to their autonomy and sovereignty, or are the advocates of Pax Americana and globalization offering the only practical solution?

Some cultures, most notably those under Islam and Confucian ideologies, may not be as receptive to individualism and pluralism as westerners. Before even delving into the nature of cultural traits, there is the question of how westerners, and especially U.S. scholars, journalists, and politicians define democracy as a system based solely on promoting the free enterprise system and its integration into the world economy. Such a narrow definition of democracy assumes a direct correlation between capitalism and western bourgeois institutions that have evolved in the past four hundred years, and are now the standard by which the G-7 view the rest of the world's institutions. Since the end of WWII, the historical record demonstrates that economic integration under the patron-client model actually undermines democracy, western-style, Scandinavian, or any other type, by widening the gap between rich and poor and allowing for political conditions ripe for authoritarianism. This was certainly the case in southern Europe and many Third World countries during the Cold War.[3]

Of course there is no doubt that cultural proclivities toward a more communitarian value system and way of life are much stronger in traditional societies where John Locke's, Adam Smith's, and John Stuart Mill's secular ideologies are irrelevant. Because poverty is widespread and material culture is not at the core of traditional societies as in the west, exporting western bourgeois institutions has been a far greater challenge than exporting products. Global integration has been perceived as a threat to a communitarian way of life and values, largely because only the comprador bourgeoisie benefit from integration while the vast majority witnesses the withering of traditional culture with consumerism and foreign dependence that only exacerbates social inequality. Under such conditions, not only are revolutions inevitable even in

Catholic Central America as Walter Lafeber observed during the Reagan era, but sociopolitical instability, guerrilla movements, and political violence of all types are inevitable throughout the Third World against western interests and their local collaborators.[4]

The IFIs, multinational corporations, and western governments led by the U.S. have promised people around the world deliverance from material privation, sustainable development, and environmental and social justice. Far from the dream of social and economic panacea, integration based on the patron-client model and IMF monetarist policies perpetuate inequality by transferring income from hundreds of millions of workers to the metropolis. By contrast, the EU integration model allows for convergence between "democracy" and economic interdependence. Theoretically and in reality, it provides legitimacy for integration, but also poses a challenge to the patron-client model from which the EU benefits.[5]

By accepting the assumptions of neoclassical trade theory that consumer welfare is raised as a result of a larger market where output increases, one must also assume that the market system is predicated on social welfare, rather than the profit motive. Does price convergence, which the neoclassical model assumes, necessarily entail per capita convergence under globalization, or is the real world different? Certainly there are studies on the EU model that suggest some validity to the theory, though the reality of price and labor value convergence by no means corresponds to neoclassical theory.[6]

Contrary to euphoric claims, especially during the 1990s, that globalization can lead to democracy on a world scale, social justice, and improve welfare for the world's masses, the tragic reality, as this book demonstrates, is that global poverty along with ·Third World debt have been rising since 1970, as has political instability. Though the EU model holds greater promise for social and geographic fairness than the patron-client model, its significance in not so much that it is as symmetrical as its proponents contend, but it has become a friendly counterweight to Pax Americana after the collapse of the Communist bloc.[7]

There is no doubt that new EU applicants will benefit by having imposed upon them social justice criteria which are no different than for Western Europe, and that working conditions and living standards will improve primarily for their skilled workers. The same claim, however, cannot be made as a result of the U.S. patron-client model in Mexico, Central America, Caribbean, or South America. Martin Hopenhayn's *No Apocalypse, No Integration: Modernism and Postmodernism* in Latin American notes that globalization has only intensified the north-south conflict, but the same conclusion can be arrived at by examining foreign debt-to-GDP ratios, wage scales, the welfare system, and poverty, among other economic and social indicators.[8] Just as significant, Vito Tanzi's observations that globalization precludes the state's ability to provide a safety net for the poor necessarily spells trouble for the future.

Today, however, the growing integration of economies and the free movement of capital across borders threaten to undermine the effectiveness of these [minimum wage laws, rent controls, subsidized student loans, and reduced rates on public utilities] policy tools. Even as the forces of globalization boost the demand for strong social safety nets to protect the poor, these forces also erode the ability of governments to finance and implement large-scale social welfare policies.[9]

It is true that economic and cultural nationalism throughout history has contributed to demise of civilizations while cultural diffusion has led to progress. Social justice, however, does not trickle down under the patron-client model any more than income distribution under supply-side economics. While the advanced capitalist countries operating under the interdependent model manage the expanding-contracting cycles through fiscal and monetary policy, for semi-developed and underdeveloped countries IMF stabilization programs invariably accompany and exacerbate contracting cycles. The results are lower living standards, and underdeveloped and semi-developed nations falling deeper into debt, thus remaining prisoners to the patron-client integration system.[10]

Besides the fact that it perpetuates polarization, the problem with the neo-classical integration theory, which as an integral part of the Cold War, is that it is anachronistic in the post-Cold War era. Because Communism has obviated traditional international relationships, regional blocs have lost as raison d'etre the traditional foreign policy categorical imperative and can only stand primarily on an economic imperative. To justify perpetuating Americentric globalization in the post-Cold War era, the U.S. relies not just on traditional instruments like the IFIs, WTO, Paris Club, and other multilateral instruments, but also on coercive diplomacy, military intervention in pursuit of new enemies, and public relations delivered by the mass media.

Using all means necessary to perpetuate the patron-client model in the absence of a menacing Communist bloc also serves the goal of deflecting from the internal inter-class differences on to the national struggle against external forces endeavoring to obstruct Pax Americana. Since the Reagan administration some neo-conservatives invoked various ideologies based on everything from Manifest Destiny to Wilson's "moral imperialism" as a means of justifying imperial policies.

And there are scholars who contend that the U.S. has been an imperial power serving not only its own but the world's best interests. A 21st century version of Kipling's *White Man's Burden*, not only has this naive ethnocentric assumption been proved wrong throughout history, but it is dangerous because the underlying doctrine of unilateralism and disregard for internationally-sectioned procedural legitimacy is obvious to the rest of the world. Arnold J. Toynbee's observation in the early 1960s, that three-fourths of the world's population hitherto suppressed have awakened to demand a better future, still holds true to this day.[11]

Half a century after the Bretton Woods system gave birth to IFIs operating under the aegis of the U.S., the world economy is more integrated, wealth is more concentrated with the top one hundred multinational corporations having larger market capitalizations than most countries. About a dozen or so countries and the multinational corporations representing a tiny percentage of the world's population enjoy preponderate influence than ever over the planet's fate, and the world is more vulnerable to the trends at the metropolis than at any period in history. On 14 April 2004 IMF chief economist Raghuram Rajan noted that U.S. deficits would shave off 4.2 percent of global economic output from 2005 to 2020. The IMF report pointed to increased U.S. borrowing owing to rising budgetary and trade deficits. Linked to defense spending at a time that huge tax reductions were approved for the top five percent of the population, the U.S. determined the fate not only of its own economy, but of the world's for the next 15 years.[12]

Though the historical record demonstrates that a panacea has yet to be unveiled, there is no shortage of solutions to global inequality. Possible solutions within the existing capitalist world system include forgiving foreign public debt of the poorest nations, improved terms of trade to be negotiated between the advanced capitalist countries and the rest of the world through the officers of the WTO, empowering local communities and fostering grass-roots organizing toward sustainable development with UN and NGOs. More radical solutions include abolishing the IMF, World Bank, and Paris Club for their raison d'etre is to serve as a front for finance capital. Armed struggle at the grass-roots level to eradicate all forms of exploitation is yet another solution that exists in various countries.[13]

Inequality on a global scale, though much more prevalent in the southern hemisphere than in the northern, exists to maintain a world-system of capital concentration that serves a social pyramid trying to preserve itself while warring against itself. A reflection of an international division of labor, a global social order, a global system, it is also a manifestation of the irrational proclivities in human nature, of the greed, egoism, hedonism, and transparent attempt to transcend temporal existence by accumulating surplus capital to the detriment of the many. Capitalism has remained a strong system after six centuries of evolution from its mercantile phase to its current structure of neo-mercantilism as the new mode of empire as James Petras correctly observed. The question is whether the future rests with this mode of empire or global realignment that starts at the grass roots level.[14]

As a pluralistic society, the U.S. has many noble qualities that extend from personable accountability and merit-based opportunities to a generous spirit of philanthropy. But should it export its institutions to the rest of the world under a superimposed transformation policy for its own benefit to the detriment of the other? The U.S. has high violent crime rates and imposes the death penalty that the EU has abolished. Barely 4 percent of the world's population, the U.S. has 2.2 million prisoners, or 20 percent of the world's prisoners, 80 percent of which are minorities. And despite the fact that the U.S. share of $38 trillion annual world economy was $11 trillion in 2003, more than 35 million people live below the poverty line and about 44 million have no health insurance.

Twenty percent enjoy the American dream, with the top 5 percent owning more than two thirds of the wealth, while the bottom 80 percent struggle to make the dream come to reality. The corporate media has made the CEO, whether he goes to prison for fraud or retires with hundreds of millions in stock options, into a modern-day deity, while the worker who lost his job to outsourcing is castigated as lacking positive character traits. The patron-client model, which operates globally, runs deep inside American society and to a degree also in the EU and Japan, although the Europeans and Japanese are more communitarian-oriented and their value system remains distinct from the U.S. Only when there is a grass-roots revolt against domestic social inequality in the G-7 will the global system evolve toward a less polarizing social and geographic world system.[15]

Considering that the EU has the largest GNP in the world, the largest trade, most of the largest corporations, and it is the largest humanitarian aid donor places a special burden on its role in the realignment of the patron-client model. Through their membership in the EU, Spain, Portugal, and Greece modestly raised their living standards, improved the social security system, health, and education, abided by more rigorous laws governing everything from the environment to human rights and the gender relations. By surrendering certain aspects of their sovereignty, they actually strengthened it, though this remains a hotly contested issue with the European Parliament. The EU can be an integration model for the Third World and the former Soviet republics. The combination of technology transfers and subsidies from the advanced countries to the underdeveloped and quasi-statist policies by the client state are among some of the key measures that can lead toward an interdependent model.

The Scandinavian countries present an even better model, though extraordinarily difficult to replicate. Ultimately, solutions must come from the grass roots at the core, semi-periphery, and periphery, because macroeconomic models always reflect what happens at the microeconomic level. Far from a panacea, integration models' influence on national and local institutions is limited. Eradicating tribal and religious conflict in the Sudan, ending India's caste system, or stopping subjugation of the Mayans by a white oligarchy are primarily but not exclusively local problems requiring local democratic-communitarian solutions.

Acknowledging that U.S. global leadership is temporary, Zbigniew Brzezinski correctly concluded that:

> Transitional responsibility carries with it the obligation to prepare an institutionally sound basis for the development of our current preponderance ... . Similarly we must be fully aware, if it is to be successful, must offer a form of capitalism with a human face. In a world

that is increasingly impatient with social inequality, economic development and reform must ultimately be driven by a sense of social responsibility. [16]

A profound philosophical question since the 17th century, scholars have pondered whether mankind is best served in a world modeled after Thomas Hobbes' *Leviathan* where life is short and brutish, where atomistic proclivities prevail and an authoritarian state is necessary to prevent chaos and impose order where elitism is inevitable. To some the Leviathan engenders conflict and chaos as it endeavors to contain innate destructive tendencies of the oppressed, while to others it fosters social order although the benefits accrue mostly to the elites. Can society transcend the Leviathan's ubiquitous reach by fostering enlightened institutions for the sake of harmony and the welfare of all?[17]

Notes

1. Jean-Marie Guehenno, "Globalization and Fragmentation," in *Globalization, Power, and Democracy*, op cit., pp. 14-7; Robert Gilpin, *The Challenge of Global Capitalism: The World Economy in the 21ˢᵗ Century* (Princeton, NJ, 2000) pp. 170-293.

2. Samuel P. Huntington, "Culture, Power, and Democracy," in *Globalization, Power, and Democracy*, op cit. pp. 7-8.

3. Joshua Muravchik, *Exporting Democracy: Fulfilling America's Destiny* (Washington, D.C., 1992), pp. 182-88; Noreena Hertz, *Global Capitalism and the Death of Democracy* (New York, 2003).

4. Walter Lafeber, *Inevitable Revolutions* (New York, 1984); Alberto Alesina and Roberto Perotti, "Income Distribution, Political Instability, and Investment," *European Economic Review* 40 (June 1996): 1203-28.

5. M. F. Plattner and Smolar, eds. *Globalization, Power, and Democracy* (Baltimore, 2000), pp. ix-x.

6. Paul J. J. Welfens, "Enlargement - Conflicts and Policy Options," in J. M. van Brabant (ed), *Remaking Europe: The European Union and the Transition Economies* (Lanham: MD, 1990), pp. 171-74.

7. J. D. Sachs and Andrew Warner, *Economic Reform and the Process of Global Integration* (Washington, D.C., 1995), pp. 62-5; Gavin Kitching, *Seeking Social Justice through Globalization* (College Park, PA, 2001); Roberto Barro, "Democracy and Growth," *Journal of Economic Growth* 1 (March 1996): 1-27; E. B. Kapstein and Dimitri Landa, "The Pluses and Minuses of Globalization," in *Globalization, Power, and Democracy*, pp. 133-46.

8. Martin Hopenhayn, *No Apocalypse, No Integration: Modernism and Postmodernism in Latin American.* Translated by C. M. Tompkins and E. R. Horan (Durham, 2001).

9. Vito Tanzi, "Globalization Without a Net," *Foreign Policy* (July-August 2001): 68-70.

10. E. S. Rosenberg, "Revisiting Dollar Diplomacy: Narratives of Money and Manliness," *Diplomatic History* 22 (1998): 160-171; Arghiri Emmanuel, *Unequal Exchange: A Study of the Imperialism of Trade* (New York, 1972), pp. 80-90.

11. Walter Russell Mead, *Special Providence: American Foreign Policy and How it Changed the World* (New York, 2001). Toyoo Gyohten, "The United States and the Global Financial Arena," in D. M. Malone and Yuen Foong Khong (eds), *Unilateralism and U.S. Foreign Policy* (Boulder, 2003), pp. 286-87; Gelson Fonseca, Jr., "The United States and Latin America: Multilateralism and International Legitimacy," in ibid., pp. 336-37; Arnold J. Toynbee, *America and the World Revolution* (Oxford, 1962).

12. International Monetary Fund, "World Economic Outlook," 14 April 2004,<www.imf.org>.

13. H. K. Jacobson et al., *The Anatomy of Influence: Decision-Making in International Organizations* (New Haven, CT, 1973).

14. James Petras, *The New Development Politics* (London, 2003).

15. Stavrianos, *Global Rift*, pp. 25-6; R. Perrucci and Earl Wysong, *New Class Society* (Lanham, MD, 2002); Jeremy Rifkin, *The European Dream* (New York, 2004).

16. Brzezinski, "Democracy's Uncertain Triumph," p. 154.

17. Thomas Hobbes, *Leviathan* (New York, 1977).

Bibliography

Archival Sources

Ann Arbor, MI: Gerald Ford Library.
Athens, Les Archives Historique des Affairs Etrangeres de Grece.
Atlanta, Carter Presidential Papers.
College Park, MD, Nixon Presidential Materials Papers, National Security Council.
College Park, Maryland, State Department, National Archives, Record Group 59.
College Park, Maryland, Central Intelligence Agency, Record Group 263.
College Park, Maryland, National Security Council, Record Group 273.
Kew Gardens, UK, Public Records Office, FO & FCO records.
Simi Valley, CA: Ronald Reagan Library.
Washington, D.C., International Monetary Fund Archives.
Washington, D.C., World Bank Archives.

Published Official Documents

Franco, Francisco, *Discursos y mensajes del Jefe del Estado, 1960-1963* (Madrid: Direccion General de Informacion, 1964).
International Bank for Reconstruction and Development, *The Economic Development of Spain* (Baltimore: The Johns Hopkins University Press, 1963).
International Monetary Fund, *Articles of Agreement of the International Monetary Fund* (Washington, D.C.: IMF, 1973).
Karamanlis, Konstantinos, *Archeio Gegonota kai Keimena* [Archives: Facts and Documents] (Athens: Karamanlis Foundation, 1993-98).
Ministerio de la Presidencia y Secreteria General de Portavoz del Gobierno, *Espana en la Union Europea* (Madrid: Imprenta Nacional del Boletin Oficial del Estado, 1995).
OECD, *Recent Public Management Initiatives in Greece* (Paris: OECD, 2001).
OECD, *Financial Action Task Force on Money Laundering. Annual Report, 1993-1994* (Paris: OECD, 1994).
OECD, *Economic Survey of Greece, December 1998* (Paris: OECD, 1998).
United States, Department of State, *Spain* (Washington, D.C.: U.S. Government Printing Office, 1973).
World Bank, *Adjustment in Africa* (New York: Oxford University Press, 1994).
— , *OECD Countries and Transition Economies* (Washington, D.C.: The World Bank, 1999).

Books, Articles, Dissertations

Abad de Santillan, Diego, *Contribucion a la historia del movimiento obrero espanol* (Mexico City: Ediciones Cajica, 1971).

Adams, Cindy, *Sukarno: An Autobiography* (New York: Bobbs-Merril, 1965).

Alam, M. Shalid, *Poverty and the Wealth of Nations: Integration and Polarization in the Global Economy since 1760* (New York: Palgrave-Macmillan, 2000).

Alesina, Alberto and Roberto Perotti, "Income Distribution, Political Instability, and Investment," *European Economic Review*, 40 (1996): 1203-28.

Amin, Samir, "On the Origins of the Economic Catastrophe in Africa," in S. C. Chew and R. A. Denemark (eds), *The Underdevelopment of Development* (London: Sage, 1996).

—— , *L'echange inegal et la loi de valeur* (Paris: Economica, 1988).

Anderson, James, *The History of Portugal* (Westport, CT: Greenwood, 2000).

Armero, Jose Mario, *La Politica Exterior de Franco* (Barcelona: Editorial Planeta, 1978).

Arrighi, Giovanni, "Fascism to Democratic Socialism: Logic and Limits of a Transition," in Giovanni Arrighi (ed), *Semiperipheral Development: The Politics of Southern Europe in the Twentieth Century* (Beverly Hills: Sage, 1985).

Aseniero, George, "Asia and the World System," in S. C. Chew and R. A. Denemark (eds), *The Underdevelopment of Development* (London: Sage, 1996).

Axt, Jurgen-Heinz and Heinz Kramer, *Entspannug im Agaisonflikt? Griechiesch-turkische Bezeihungennach Davos* (Baden-Baden: Nomosd, 1990).

Barro, Roberto, "Democracy and Growth," *Journal of Economic Growth*, 1 (1996): 1-27.

Beaud, Michel et al. (eds), *Mondialisation: Les mots et les choses* (Paris, Karthala, 1999).

Beddoes, Z. M., "From EMU to AMU," *Foreign Affairs*, 78(4) (1999): 8-13.

Bejar, Hector, *Peru 1965* (New York: Monthly Review Press, 1969).

Birdsall, Nancy, "Population Growth and Poverty in the Developing World," *Population Bulletin*, 35(5) (1980): 3-45.

Blank, Stephen, "American Grand Strategy and the Transcaspian Region," *World Affairs*, 163(2) (2000): 65-79.

Booth, Anne, et al. (eds), *Indonesian Economic History in the Dutch Colonial Era* (New Haven, CT: Yale University Press, 1990).

Boutillier, Sophie and Dimitri Uzundis, *La Grece Face a L'Europe: Dependance et industrialization truquee* (Paris: Editions Harmattan, 1991).

Bret, E. A., *The World Economy since the War* (New York: Praeger, 1985).

Brogan, Patrick, *The Fighting Never Stopped: A Comprehensive Guide to World Conflict since 1945* (New York Vintage, 1990).

Browne, R. S. and R. J. Cummings, *The Lagos Plan of Action vs. The Berg Report* (New Brunswick: Brunswick Publishing, 1985).

Buira, Ariel, "La promocion financiera y la condicionalidad del FMI," *El Trimestre Economico*, 50(197) (1983): 117-49.

Callaway, Barbara, "The Political Economy of Nigeria," in *The Political Economy of Africa*, edited by R. Harris (New York: John Wiley and Sons, 1975).

Catsiapis, Jean, *La Grece: dixieme membre des Communautes europeennes* (Paris: Documentation Francais, 1980).

Ching-yuan Lin, *Latin America vs East Asia: A Comparative Development Perspective* (Armonk, NY: M. E. Sharpe, 1989).

Chomsky, Noam, *Hegemony or Survival: American's Quest for Global Dominance* (New York: Henry Holt, 2003).

Cingranelli, D. L., *Ethics, American Foreign Policy, and the Third World* (New York: St. Martin's, 1993).

Crabtree, John, *Peru under Garcia* (Pittsburgh: University of Pittsburgh, 1992).

Cravinho, Joao, "The Portugese Economy: Constraints and Opportunities," in K. Maxwell (ed), *Portugal in the 1980s* (Westport, CT: Greenwood, 1986).

Craxi, Bettino, *Il Progresso Italiano* (Milano: Sugar, 1985-1989).

Curry, Jr., R. L., "Challenges of Asymmetry Associated with ASEAN's Evolution to a Larger-sized Group," *Journal of Third World Studies*, 14(1) (1997): 13-36.

D'Assac, J. Plonchard, *Dictionario Politico de Salazar* (Lisbon: SNI, 1964).

Dahm, Bernard, *Sukarno and the Struggle for Indonesian Independence* (Ithaca, NY: Cornell University Press, 1969).

de Areilza Carvajal, J. M. et al., *Espana y las transformaciones de la Union Europa* (Madrid: Fundacion para el Analiis y los Estudios Sociales, 1999).

de Carmoy, Guy, *The Foreign Policies of France, 1948-1968* (Chicago: University of Chicago, 1970).

Dolfuss, Olivier, *Le Perou: Introduction Geographiques a l'Etude de Development* (Paris: Institute des hautes etudes de l'Amerique latine, 1968).

Dos Santos, Theotonio, "Latin American Development: Past, Present, and Future," in S. C. Chew and R. A. Denemark (eds), *The Underdevelopment of Development* (London: Sage, 1996).

Dowd, Douglas. *Capitalism and its Economics* (London: Pluto Press, 2000).

Duarte, A. G., *Resistencia em Portugal* (Sao Paolo: Editora Felman-Rego, 1962).

Eaton, Jonathan. "Public Debt Guarantees and Private Capital Flight," *The World Bank Economic Review*, 1(3) (1987).

Ellwood, Sheelagh, *Franco* (London: Longman, 1994).

Elsenhans, Hartmut, *La guerre d'Algerie, 1954-1962* (Paris: Publisud, 1999).

Emmanuel, Arghiri, *Unequal Exchange: A Study of the Imperialism of Trade* (New York: Monthly Review, 1972).

Evans, Peter, "Shoes, OPIC, and the Unquestioning Persuasion: Multinational Corporations and U.S.-Brazilian Relations," in R. R. Fagen (ed), *Capitalism and the State in Latin America* (Stanford: Stanford University Press, 1979).

Fanon, Franz, *The Wretched of the Earth* (New York: Grove, 1976).

Feinberg, R. E., "Reaganomics and the Third World," in *Eagle Defiant* edited by K. A. Oye et al. (Boston: Little Brown, 1983).

Fernandes, H. Blasco, *Portugal atraves de algunas numeros* (Lisbon: Prelo, 1976).

Flynn, S. E., "Beyond Border Control," *Foreign Affairs*, 79(6) (2000): 57-68.

Franco, Carlos, *El Peru de Velasco* (Lima: Centro de Estudios para el Desarrollo y la Participacion, 1983).

Frank, Andre Gunder, "The Underdevelopment of Development," in S. C. Chew and R. A. Denemark (eds), *The Underdevelopment of Development* (Beverly Hills: Sage, 1996).

Frigerio, Rogelio, *La Integracion Regional Instrumento del Monopolio* (Buenos Aires: Editorial Hernandez, 1968).

Furtado, Celso, *Les Etas-Unis et les sous-developpement de L'Amerique Latine* (Paris: Calman-Levy, 1970).

Galeano, Eduardo, *Las Venas obrietas de America Latina* (Madrid: Siglo XXI Editores, 1993).

Garcia Herras, Raul. "La Argentina y los organismos financiera internacionales," *El Trimestre Economico*, 67(268) (2000): 523-56.

Gardiner, C. H., *The Japanese and Peru* (Albuquerque: University of New Mexico Press, 1975).

Gomiz Diaz, P. L., "Las Nuevas Politicas de empleo y de asuntos sociales en el Tratado de Amsterdam," in Ministerio de Asunto Exteriores de Espana (eds), *Espana y la negociacion del Tratado de Amsterdam* (Madrid: Biblioteca Nueva, 1998).

Gregoroyiannis, A., *To Xeno Kefalaio stin Ellada* [Foreign Capital in Greece] (Athens: Asteri, 1980).

Guehenno, Jean-Marie, "Globalization and Fragmentation," in M. F. Plattner and A. Smolar (eds), *Globalization, Power, and Democracy* (Baltimore: Johns Hopkins University Press, 2000).

Guerra, Alfonso, *Felipe Gonzalez: de Suresnes a la Moncloa/recuerdos e impresiones de Alfonso Guerra* (Madrid: Novatex, 1984).

Hansen, S. G., *Economic Development in Latin America* (Westport, CT: Greenwood Press, 1974).

Heisbourg, Francois, "American Hegemony? Perceptions of the U.S. Abroad," *Survival* (Winter 1999-2000): 5-19.

Herman, E. S. and R. W. McChesney, *The Global Media: The New Missionaries of Global Capitalism* (London: Cassell, 1997).

Hertz, Noreena, *Global Capitalism and the Death of Democracy* (New York: Harper Collins, 2003).

Hill, Hal, *The Indonesian Economy since 1966* (Cambridge: Cambridge University Press, 1996).

Hopkins, A. G., *Economic History of West Africa* (New York: Columbia University Press, 1973).

Humala Tasso, Ulises, *Subdesarrollo o Camino al Colapso: Desarrollo del Subdesarrollo en el Peru* (Lima: Graphos 100 Editors, 1987).

Iriye, Akira, *Cambridge History of American Foreign Relations: The Globalizing of America, 1913-1945* (New York: Cambridge University Press, 1995).

Jimeno, Juan F. et al., "Integration and Inequality: Lessons from the Accession of Portugal and Spain in the EU," in The World Bank (ed), *Making Transition Work for Everyone: Poverty and Inequality in Europe and Central Asia* (Washington D.C.: The World Bank, 2000).

Kagan, Robert, "The Benevolent Empire," *Foreign Policy*, 111 (1998): 24-35.

Keyfitz, N., "Indonesian Population and The European Industrial Revolution," *Asian Survey*, 10 (1965): 503-14.

Kilty, D. P., *Planning for Development in Peru* (New York: Praeger, 1967).

Kitching, Gavin, *Seeking Social Justice through Globalization* (College Park, PA: Penn State Press, 2001).

Kofas, J. V., *The Sword of Damocles: U.S. Financial Hegemony in Chile and Colombia* (Westport: CT: Praeger, 2002).

—, *Under the Eagle's Claw: Exceptionalism in Postwar U.S.-Greek Relations* (Westport, CT: Praeger, 2003).

Kolko, Gabriel, *Confronting the Third World: United States Foreign Policy, 1945-1980* (New York: Knopf, 1988).

Kritsantonis, Nicos D., "Greece: From State Authoritarianism to Modernization," in Anthony Richard (ed), *Industrial Relations in the New Europe* (Cambridge: Blackwell, 1992).

Krueger, Anne O., "Origins of the Developing Countries' Debt Crisis, 1970-1982," *Journal of Development Economics*, 27/1 (1987): 165-86.

Kruijt, Dirk, *Revolution by Decree: Peru 1968-1975* (Amsterdam: Thela Publishers, 1994).

Lacouture, Jean, *Mitterand: Une histoire de Francais* (Paris: Editions du Seuil, 1998).

Lancaster, Carol, "Africa's Economic Crisis," *Foreign Polic*, 52 (1983): 149-66.

Landsberg, C., "The United States and Africa: Malign Neglect," in D. M. Malone and Yuen Foong Khong (eds), *Unilateralism and U.S. Foreign Policy* (Boulder: Lynne Rienner, 2003).

Lehmkuhl, Ursula, *Pax Anglo-Americana. Machtstrukturelle Grundlagen anglo-amerikanischer Asien-und Fernostpolitik in den 1950er Jahren* (Muchen: Oldenberg, 1999).

Liebenow, J. G., *African Politics* (Bloomington, IN: Indiana University Press, 1986).

Lipski Seth and Raphael Pura, "Indonesia: Testing Time for the New Order," *Foreign Affairs*, 57/1 (1978): 186-202.

Little, I. M. D. et al., *Boom, Crisis, and Adjustment* (New York: Oxford University Press, 1993).

Macheras, Dimitrios, *Die Mitgliedschaft Griechenlands in den Europaischen Gemeinschaften* (Frankfurt am Main: Peter Lang, 1988).

Madeiros, F., *A Sociodade e a economia portugesas nas origems do salarismo* (Lisbon: A Regra do Jogo, 1978).

Makin, J. H., *The Global Debt Crisis: America's Growing Involvement* (New York: Basic, 1984).

Mandel, Ernst, *Europe vs. America* (New York: Monthly Review Press, 1970).

Marini, Ruy Mauro, *Dialectica de la Dependencia* (Buenos Aires: CLASCO, 2000).

Marques, Antonio and Mario Bairrada, "As Classes sociais na populacao ativa portugesa," *Analise Social* 17, nos. 72-74 (1982): 1279-97.

Marques, Silva J. A., *Relatorios da clandestinidade: O PCP Visto por dentro* (Lisbon: Edicoes Jornal Expresso, 1977).

Martin, M. L., *La militarization des systemes politiques africains, 1960-1972* (Sherbooke: Naaman, 1976).

Melgar, Jorge, *A Belaunde lo que es de Belaunde* (Lima: 1973).

Melo, Joao de, *Os Anos da guerra, 1961-1975: os portugeuses em Africa* (Lisbon: Dom Quixote, 1988).

Merkl, Wolfgang, *Systemtransformation. Eine Einfuhrung in die Theorie und Empire der Transformationsforschung* (Opladen: Leske & Budrich, 1999).

Micklethwait J., and A. Woodbridge, *A Future Perfect: The Challenge and Hidden Promise of Globalization* (New York: Crown Business, 2000).

Milward, Alan et al., *The European Rescue of the Nation-State* (London: Routledge, 1992).

Minter, William, *Portuguese Africa and the West* (New York: Monthly Review Press, 1972).

Moncada Sanchez, Jose, *Economia y globalizacion* (Quito: Abya-Yala, 2001).

Monti, Luciano, *I Fondi Strutturali per la coesione Europea* (Roma: Edizione SEAM, 1996).

Morata, Francesc, *La Union Europea: Procesos, actores y politicas* (Barcelona: Ariel, 1998).

Morcillo, Almendros Fernando, et al., *El Sindicalismo de clase en Espana, 1939-1977* (Barcelona: Ediciones Peninsula, 1978).

Mundo, Equipo, *Los 90 ministros de Franco* (Barcelona: Dopesa, 1970).

Nunes, A. Sedas, *Sociologia e ideologia do desenvolvimento* (Lisbon: Marais Editora, 1969).

Okita, Saburo, "Japan, China, and the United States," *Foreign Affairs*, 57/5 (1979): 1090-1110.

—— , "Japan's Role in Asia-Pacific Cooperation," *Annals AAPSS*, 513 (1991): 25-37.

Orizu, A.A.N., *Insight into Nigeria: the Shehu Shagari era* (Ibadan, Nigeria: Evan Brothers, 1983).

Palmier, L. H., *Indonesia and the Dutch* (London: Oxford University Press, 1962).

Payer, Cheryl, *The Debt Trap* (New York: Monthly Review Press, 1974).

Pease Garcia, H., *La autocracia Fujimorista: del estado intervencionista al estado mafioso* (Lima: Universidad Catolica del Peru, 2003).

Petras, James and Robert La Porte, "U.S. Response to Economic Nationalism in Chile," in James Petras (ed), *From Dependence to Revolution* (New York: John Wiley, 1973).

Pimlot, Ben. "Were the Soldiers Revolutionary? The Armed Forces Movement in Portugal," *Iberian Studies*, 7(1) (1978): 13-22.

Pinto, Brian, "Nigeria During and After the Oil boom: A Policy Comparison with Indonesia," *The World World Bank Economic Review*, 1(3) (1987): 420-22.

Pitcher, M. Anne, *Politics in the Portuguese Empire* (New York: Oxford University Press, 1993).

Poulantzas, Nicos, *The Crisis of Dictatorships* (Atlantic Highlands: Humanities Press, 1976).

Prebisch, Raul, "Commercial Policy in Underdeveloped Countries," *American Economic Review*, 49 (1959): 251-61.

Puga, E, Alvarez. *Matesa. Mas alla del escandalo*. Barcelona: Dopesa, 1974.

Quijano Obregon, Anibal, "El Peru en la Crisis de los Anos Treinta," in Luis Antezana E. et al. (eds), *America Latina en los Anos Trienta* (Mexico: Universidad Nacional Autonoma de Mexico, 1977).

Raby, Dawn Linda, "Portugal," in J. P. Campbell (ed), *European Labor Unions* (Westport, CT: Greenwood, 1992).

Ramirez Gaston, J. M., *Medio siglo de la politica economica y finaciera del Peru* (Lima: La Confianza, 1964).

Reiser, Pedro, *L'Organisation Regionale Inteameriaine des Travaileurs de la Confederation Internationale de Syndicats Libres de 1951 a 1961* (Paris: Libraire Minard, 1962).

Robles, A. C., *The Political Economy of Inter-Regional Relations: ASEAN & the EU* (Aldershot: Ashgate, 2004).

Roel Pineda, Virgilio, *Problemas de la economia Peruana* (Lima: Grafica Popular, 1959).

Romero, Emilio, *Historia Economica del Peru* (Lima: Editorial Universo, 1968).

—— , *Proceso y Crisis de las Economias Peruanas* (Lima: Editorial el Alba, 1984).

Romero, Federico, *GLI Stati Uniti e il sindicalismo europeo, 1944-1951* (Rome: Edicione Lavoro, 1989).

Roy, Joaquin and Aimee Kanner, "Spain and Portugal: Betting on Europe," in E. E. Zeff and E. B. Pirro (eds), *The European Union and the Member States* (Boulder: Lynne Rienner, 2001).

Rubio, Jose Luis, *Dependencia y liberacion en el sindicalismo iberoamericano* (Madrid: Salc, 1977).

Rudolph, J. D., *Peru: The Evolution of a Crisis* (Westport, CT: Greenwood, 1992).

Salmon, Keith, *The Modern Spanish Economy: Transformation and Integration into Europe* (London: Pinter, 1995).

Schaeffer, R. K., *Understanding Globalization* (Lanham, MD: Rowman Littlefield, 2003).

Schatz, Sayre, *Nigerian Capitalism* (Berkeley, CA: University of California Press, 1977).

Schittek, Carsten, *Ordnungsstrukuren im Europaischen Intehrationsprozess: ihre Entwicklung bis zum Vertag vo Maastricht* (Stuttgart: Lucius and Lucius, 1999).

Schmitter, Philippe C., "La Democratie dans l'Europe politique naissaante," in Mario Tello and Paul Magnette (eds), *Repenser l'Europe* (Brussels: Editions de l' Universite de Bruxelles, 1996).

Segura, Santiago et al., "Tecnologia y desarrollo de la dependencia," in H. Espinosa Uriarte (ed), *Dependencia economica y tecnologica: caso Peruano* (Lima: Universidad Nacional, 1971).

Shepard, R. B., *Nigeria, Africa, and the United States* (Bloomington, IN: Indiana University Press, 1991).

Sinova, J. (ed), *Historia del Franquismo* (Madrid: Dario, 1985).

Siotis, J., "La situation internationale de la Grece et la demande hellenique d' adhesion aux Communautes," in Institut d'Etudes Europeennes, *La Grece et la Communaute* (Buxelles: Universitaires de Bruxelles, 1978).

Smith Ikpuk, John, *Militarisation of Politics and neo-colonialism: The Nigerian Experience, 1966-1990* (London: Janus, 1995).

Spinola, Antonio de, *Portugal e o futuro* (Lisbon: Arcadia, 1974).

Stremlau, John, "Clinton's Dollar Diplomacy," *Foreign Policy*, 97 (1994): 18-35.

Su, Tieting, "World Trade Networks from 1928 to 1938," *Journal of World Systems Research*, 7(1) (2001), 32-50.

Suarez Fernandez, L., *Francisco Franco y su Tiempo* (Madrid: Ediciones Azor, 1984).

Thorbecke, Erik, "Adjustment, Growth and Income Distribution in Indonesia," *World Development*, 19(11) (1991): 1595-1641.

Tnazi, Vito, "Globalization Without a Net" *Foreign Policy* (July-August 2001): 78-80.

Turone, Sergio, *Storia del Sindicato in Italia, 1943-1969* (Bari: Laterza, 1974).

Urriola, Rafel, *Crisis: FMI y neo-liberalismo* (Quito, Ecuador: Centro de Planificacion y Estudios Sociales, 1985).

Valinakis, Yiannis, *Eisagoge stin Ellinike Exoterike Politike*, 1949-1988 [Introduction to Greek Foreign Policy, 1949-1988] (Thessalonike: Paratiritis, 1989).

Vedrine, Hubert, *Face a l'hyperpuissance: textes et discours, 1995-2003* (Paris: Fayad, 2003).

Wall, Irving, *L'Influence americaine sur la politique francais, 1945-1954* (Paris, Balland, 1989).

Weinstein, F. B., *Indonesian Foreign Policy and the Dilemma of Dependence* (Ithaca: Cornell University Press, 1976).

Wionczek, M. S., "Integration and Development," *International Journal*, 24(3) (1969): 449-62.

Yepes, Ernesto, *La Modernizacion en el Peru del siglo XX* (Lima: Mosca Asul Editores, 1992).

Index